# HIGH IMPACT
## Reading Instruction
### and Intervention in the Primary Years

## FROM THEORY
## TO PRACTICE

## Julie Scali

# Praise for *High Impact Reading Instruction and Intervention in the Primary Years*

Knowing Julie professionally as I do, I sense her teacher voice in the words of this book, and the passion for her subject shines through on each page. She marries practice with pedagogy with ease, drawing upon her years of experience and of reflection of what works well in the classroom. I have seen Julie putting these words into action in the years before she put them into print.

*Zoe Sharman, retired Headteacher, London*

This book is essential reading for all passionate teachers. It is beneficial for both experienced teachers in providing up-to-date best practice recommendations and for new teachers, to guide them through a seemingly complicated process in a gentle, manageable way. Julie clearly explains all elements of teaching reading, supported by relevant international research, in a friendly, approachable manner.

*Diane Pursell, Teacher, WA*

This easy-to-read, yet thoroughly comprehensive and informative, book academically outlines through the eyes of a mum, educator and literacy consultant the many areas of classroom practice and interventions that will 'shift' your students. Julie dives deep into the science of reading and other research-backed practices to provide educators with a useable handbook to drive learning. Implementing the approaches outlined in this book will result in a significant improvement in reading achievement. For schools like ours that are prioritising the provision of research-based high-quality reading instruction and intervention across all grades, it is a must-read.

*Donna Reeves, Principal, Tumut Public School, NSW*

It was such a pleasurable experience reading this book. It was well written with warmth (the same way Julie presents) shining through. Although it was absolutely packed with information, it was not dry like some academic texts. This is a text that will clearly help teachers to build their capacity around high impact reading instruction.

*Tamara Johansen, Literacy Leader, Humpty Doo Primary School, NT*

Published in 2023 by Amba Press, Melbourne, Australia
www.ambapress.com.au

© Julie-Ann Scali 2023

Cover design: Tess McCabe
Internal design: Amba Press
Editor: Rica Dearman

ISBN: 9781922607744 (pbk)
ISBN: 9781922607751 (ebk)

A catalogue record for this book is available from the National Library of Australia.

# CONTENTS

# INTRODUCTION

For as long as I remember, I wanted to be a teacher. Fortunately, my parents made it easy for me to practise being one at a young age, by bearing me with three younger sisters for which I could 'play schools'. I don't know what the appeal was for me, but perhaps it had something to do with my love of books and imparting knowledge to others – but the appeal always stuck.

Although I didn't know it at the time (as the resident six-year-old teacher of the family), I was one of the lucky ones. I had always been surrounded with a plethora of books in the home and I found the process of learning to read to be highly uneventful. I don't remember how I learnt, but for me, I don't recall it being difficult. But as an adult as a 'real teacher', I quickly learnt that this isn't the case for a vast number of students.

Enter my second year of teaching. I was a graduate, teaching Year 4, and on my first day of the school year, I vividly remember the excitement, anticipation and, dare I say it, confidence, I felt on that initial day as the students entered the room. I also remember having the wind blown out of my sails when I discovered a new student to the school, who I will name Jacob, could not read. Although perplexing and of huge concern to me, the bit that got me was that when I delved into my mental toolkit on how to help him, I came up short. I realised that after completing a full undergraduate degree, I had no idea how to teach a student how to read.

Probably naively, I had made a promise to Jacob that by the end of that year, he was going to be reading, yet I had no idea where to start to make that happen. I hadn't been taught this at university, knew nothing about the alphabetic code or phonemic awareness, explicit teaching of phonics or vocabulary, or structured literacy, as I had been taught the now debunked 'whole language' approach.

I spent that year reading every bit of research I could get my hands on, attended every professional learning event I could during my holidays, and each school day I spent every spare moment with Jacob doing what I now know as 'intervention' to try and catch him up. I am not saying for a moment I did this well and the more you know, the better you become, but I do know that by the end of that year, Jacob was reading Goosebumps books, which was his goal for the year.

By the end of that year, he was a different child to the one that first walked through the door. He wasn't reading with amazing fluency, but he was cracking the code and he was comprehending what he was reading. As a side note, his behaviour also changed – he was happier, and the challenging behaviours exhibited from the start of the year had all but vanished. For him, yes somehow, I haphazardly taught him to read, but for me, I was the one that benefitted the most; as unbeknown to Jacob, he paved the way for my career to not only upskill myself in what is evidence-based practice and the science of reading, but also to advocate for every Jacob of the world. And that brings me to this book.

I have written this book for every passionate teacher, education assistant, principal or deputy principal that has a deep desire to maximise the literacy progress and achievement of their students. Through this book, I aim to take the research of what makes the greatest impact in reading instruction and translate it into accessible, practical knowledge and routines for the primary classroom. My hope is that this book supports you in knowing that your teaching is aligned with scientifically based research to ensure literacy success is experienced by every student. To support you on your way, you will find a QR code and URL link to the templates throughout the book for use in your context.

The book is broken into two parts, the first being the fundamentals of high-impact instruction and the second specifically targeting the reading science.

In Part 1 we will discuss the fundamentals of high impact literacy instruction and intervention – practices that are going to take your classroom teaching to the next level. In this section, we will delve into data-informed practice, the importance of high expectations, explicit instruction, daily review and response to intervention.

In Part 2 we will explore the science of reading. I will walk you through the underpinnings of the reading science, of how children best learn to read, while connecting the research to practical examples on how to implement structured literacy in the classroom. This section concludes with a chapter on how to pull it all together into a literacy block within a knowledge-rich curriculum.

Like our physical health, wellness is an ongoing journey of work. Adopting a structured literacy approach is similar. I like to use a flying analogy. You might be on the runway, taking off or already in flight. You may even be in the departure lounge! However, depending on how far along you are, we still have students that we see face to face each day and any tweaks are being made along the way in flight. Some of these changes will be quick and others will take time, but when we are clear about our why for change, then it is all worthwhile.

In the words of Laura Fontina, "Literacy is the jump-off point for which all of life's success take flight", and my vision is this for every student. If you are reading this book, then I know you are with me, too.

Let's get our students flying.

Access resources and templates from the book here:

# Part 1

# THE FOUNDATIONS OF HIGH IMPACT INSTRUCTION

"Literacy is the jump-off point for which
all of life's success take flight"
~ Laura Fontina

## Chapter 1

# HIGH EXPECTATIONS AND STUDENT ASPIRATIONS

"High achievement always takes place in the framework of high expectations"

~ Charles Kettering

### Chapter overview

- Self-reflection
- The 'why' behind high expectations and student aspirations
- High expectations – more than what we believe and say
- What do teachers with high expectations do?
- Differentiation and ability grouping in a high-expectations classroom
- The link between student voice, aspirations and motivation
- Summary
- Professional discussion
- Interest Inventory: Tell me all about you!

## Self-reflection

| Self-reflection | Give yourself a rating out of 5 |
|---|---|
| In my classroom, I cultivate a culture of high expectations for *every* student | |
| I explicitly teach year level appropriate content for *every* student in literacy *every* day | |
| I embed well-established, tight routines and procedures in my classroom | |
| I establish a culture of visible learning and goal setting in my classroom | |
| I actively establish a positive culture and tone in my classroom | |
| I plan for and engage in high-level questioning in my classroom | |
| I use evidence-based, quality data to inform teaching and learning, such as standardised one-minute timed fluency, decoding and phonemic awareness assessments | |
| I provide prompt, specific and effective feedback to my students during lessons | |
| I provide opportunities for students to work with a variety of peers in literacy and not just students of similar ability | |
| I explicitly teach social-emotional wellbeing programs as a priority for building student self-belief | |

## The 'why' behind high expectations and student aspirations

When we have high expectations of our students, there is a 0.43 effect size on student learning (Hattie & Zierer, 2017*). Considering anything above 0.4 is considered a positive effect, this is good news – and when coupled with evidence-based practice, the possibilities for students are very promising.

The New South Wales Government conducts an annual study called Tell Them from Me (TTFM), based on student voice (CESE, 2020). This survey provides a range of information from students, including whether they believe their teachers have high expectations of them. The TTFM research found that students who experience high expectations have improved learning outcomes, are more likely to have increased interest and motivation, higher attendance, more positive school behaviours and a higher likelihood of completing school.

## High expectations – more than what we believe and say

So, what do we mean by having 'high expectations' for students? I pose this question because the term gets thrown about a lot and I believe it is often misunderstood. Having high expectations for students is not only about telling our students we think they can do something and that we believe in them, but it is also about what *we do* that counts. It is about how *we show* students we have high expectations, the level of challenge in the *content* we teach them and the quality of *feedback* we provide.

A pertinent research study conducted in the United States delved into this notion of how we *show* students we hold high expectations. Referred to as The Opportunity Myth (TNPT, 2018), the large study found that, despite 94% of students having big dreams to attend college and half of the students being awarded As and Bs, the students spent more than 500 hours per school year being taught content below their appropriate year level. This equated to six months of wasted learning in each core subject, meaning that, despite the surveyed teachers' best intentions, tireless efforts and dedication, consciously or not, the vast number of teachers were providing a substandard level of academic opportunities, with expectations set at a low bar, with only 17% of students actually achieving grade level proficiency.

On the contrary, when students worked on year level appropriate content, they gained nearly two months of learning time compared to their peers. Likewise, with classrooms that provided year level content and assignments, students gained more than four months of learning. Even more significantly, when students who were a year behind their peers in terms of ability were provided with grade level content and assignments, the learning growth for these students increased by 7.9 months.

There are two phenomenon at play here. The first phenomenon – the Pygmalion Effect – is when teachers have high expectations for students, they are more likely to rise to these expectations and achieve higher academic outcomes. The second and countering phenomenon, the Golem Effect, is where an educator places low expectations on a student and, as a result, that student's performance drops (Williams, n.d.). Self-fulfilling prophecies are inadvertently created.

## What do teachers with high expectations do?

In a quest for schools to deepen their inclusive practices, it is essential that teachers cultivate a culture of high expectations for every student. Teachers with high expectations demonstrate the following:

**Know and provide 'year level' content for all students:** As identified in the study above, teachers must be very clear on the year level content, benchmarks and end-of-year expectations for the students they teach. Student learning gains are greater when they are provided with content that pushes them in terms of lesson content and assignments. The first consideration of differentiation should not be by complexity of content.

**Embed well-established routines and procedures:** Students are taught to be independent in how they manage themselves with routines and procedures. Teacher talk is directed at gaining attention to what children are learning rather than students' activities and behaviours. When classroom routines and procedures are clearly established at the start of the year, it frees up the majority of teacher talk for student learning.

**Establish a culture of visible learning and goal setting:** Learning intentions and success criteria are clearly explained to students. Specific goals are set with individual students that are regularly reviewed and used for teaching and learning. Achievement is linked to effort, growth and motivation, rather than ability.

**Establish a positive classroom culture and tone:** Teachers with high expectations manage behaviour positively and proactively. The tone of teacher statements throughout the day is positive.

**Engage in high-level questioning:** Teachers with high expectations ask open questions to enhance thinking and extend student learning. Higher-level open questions are not only reserved for higher-ability students.

**Use quality data to inform teaching and learning:** Teachers with high expectations know where their students are at in terms of student strengths, growth areas and where to go next. They use a range of effective assessment tools to provide data that directs planning and where to provide support where appropriate. They frequently ask themselves, 'What is the *impact* of my teaching?' to ensure every child is making maximum progress.

**Provide effective feedback:** Teachers with high expectations provide ongoing and prompt, specific feedback to students in relation to student goals and learning growth. Feedback in relation to process-orientated goals is prioritised over those that are outcome-oriented; therefore, directing students how to move forward. For example, if a child spells *walked* as *walkt*, effective feedback would be to praise the child for hearing all the sounds accurately and for spelling the correct grapheme for w, a, l, k; but then explain that when 'walk' changes to 'walked', it means it has happened in the past, and for past tense, we always write 'ed'.

**Provide opportunities for students to work with a variety of peers:** Teachers work with a range of students in many different contexts, rather than a focus on ability groupings. Teachers use a high level of formative assessment and progress monitoring to allow flexibility in teacher instruction and responsiveness to student need and support.

**Explicitly teach social-emotional wellbeing programs as a priority for building self-belief:** When students have high expectations of themselves, there is an effect size of 1.44 (Hattie & Zierer, 2017*), which is four times the effect size of teachers having high expectations for their students. The link between literacy and social emotional wellbeing is crucial here.

## Differentiation and ability grouping in a high-expectations classroom

Where does differentiation fit in a high-expectations classroom? While differentiation is an essential aspect of inclusive education, in my experience as a classroom teacher and school leader, more often than not, I have noticed two extremes of differentiation: either non-existent, or too much – but rarely hitting the sweet spot of 'low' differentiation.

In the case of too much differentiation, quite often, despite teachers' tireless efforts and well-meaning planning, students are frequently grouped by ability for large portions of instructional time, with little flexibility in movement. In this scenario, the lowest-ability group is often provided with significantly lower content or activities than the rest of the class, leaving them little room to grow and mix with other peers. The issue here is twofold. Firstly, the students are inadvertently singled out as the 'low achievers' with a low expectation placed upon them, and the second aspect is that they have almost no chance of catching up to their peers because they are missing the current year level instruction. That is not to say that, at times, it is not highly appropriate to take a small group to the side to specifically reteach or focus on a gap that has been identified; and in fact, this is effective, quality Tier 1 differentiated instruction. But the point here is that there is a specific focus of support, for a specific focus of instructional time, to meet a specific goal, rather than being grouped by ability for an extended period of time.

On the other extreme, with classrooms that have virtually no differentiation, it leaves students struggling throughout the year in terms of either being too difficult or not challenging enough, often leading to disengagement and behavioural issues.

Grouping students by ability has little benefit for students. It is also associated with negative effects on self-esteem for both high and low achievers.

The ideal scenario is to provide *low* differentiation where there is a high level of whole-class instruction and challenge, with high-quality, high expectations for every student. Coupled with frequent formative assessment and progress monitoring, this approach equips teachers to be able to flexibly adjust their instruction and level of support to meet student needs. When low-achieving students are provided with challenging instruction in a warm and supportive class environment, the achievement gap can be narrowed. The Education Hub, NZ (2018) cites:

> *"Research demonstrates that low-achieving students are able to narrow the achievement gap when they are provided with challenging instruction in a warm and supportive class environment. Studies show few positive benefits for ability grouping. When teachers differentiate, they tend to form low expectations for students in the lower groups, and potentially limit their learning activity to review and repetition within a slower and heavily structured instructional pace. Differentiation is also associated with negative effects on self-esteem for both high and low achievers."*

Teaching year level content in a classroom with a range of learning needs, however, is a complex skill to master. The answer here is scaffolding and differentiation by support and outcome, rather than significantly varied content. Of course, however, there are times when differentiation by content is highly appropriate, for example, content for independent reading, such as a child reading a decodable reader based on their stage of decoding proficiency.

One effective way to provide scaffolding in the classroom is to establish mixed-ability pairs. Pairing in this way is an effective way to provide support on a larger scale across the classroom. This approach is particularly supportive for students with English as an Additional Language (EALD).

## The link between student voice, aspirations and motivation

I think it is well known by teachers that creating authentic student-teacher relationships can have positive impacts on academic achievement, social-emotional growth and the classroom climate. It is essential to know our students well and engage with them in a personal and group setting. In addition, when teachers engage with students on a personal and learning level – and know a child's future dreams and aspirations – students feel valued, which has a significant impact on self-esteem and motivation for learning. This link to motivation may be somewhat underrated, as Dr Russell Quaglia (2015) cites:

> *"When we know our students' hopes and dreams, they are 18 times more likely to be motivated to learn."*

One of the ways that we can build strong teacher-student relationships at the start of the school year is through a simple Interest Inventory, where we can find out about our students on a personal level, their interests and goals for the future. In the table at the end of this chapter, you will see an Interest Inventory that you may like to use in your class context. This is a simple way to get to know our students at the start of the year, and for our students to see that we are invested in them from the outset.

## Summary

- High expectations are critical in the classroom, as when we place high expectations for students, they are not only more likely to achieve them, but it also has a significant impact on self-esteem, behaviour, attendance and likelihood of completing school.
- Teachers with high expectations provide year level content for all students, establish routines, set challenging goals for all students, engage in high-level questioning, use effective data to inform teaching and learning, establish positive classroom culture and tone, provide many opportunities to work with students of mixed ability and explicitly teach social and emotional wellbeing curriculum.

- There is little benefit in ability grouping for students, and there is evidence of negative effects on self-esteem for low- and high-ability students.
- While differentiation is essential in an inclusive classroom, the ideal scenario is low differentiation, where differentiation is predominantly based on outcome and support, rather than vastly different content.
- Taking a small group for a specific focus, goal and instructional purpose, such as additional support to practise decoding in a small group, in a choral reading approach is effective high-quality differentiated Tier 1 instruction, but the key is that it is for a specific time and purpose, not ability grouping per se.
- Students are 18 times more likely to be motivated to learn when we know their hopes and dreams. A simple way to get to know our students at the start of the year is through an Interest Inventory.

## Professional discussion

- How do you and your colleagues demonstrate high expectations for your students in terms of what you personally believe, say, plan and teach?
- To what extent do you/your team set year level content for your students? Based on the research from The Opportunity Myth, are there adjustments you may make to your teaching and learning?
- Are there any unconscious biases you may not have considered that may be reducing your level of expectations for students? If so, what small or large tweaks will you make to adjust this?

*Hattie & Zierer (2017) references included in Hattie & Zierer (2018).*

# Interest inventory: Tell me all about you!

**Name:**          **Date:**

My favourite things in the world are:

The thing I like most about school is:

My favourite school subjects are:

When I am older I want to:

My best friends are:

My favourite song is:

My favourite hobbies are:

My favourite place is:

My favourite thing to do at home is:

I dream that one day:

My superpower is:

## Chapter 2

# DAILY REVIEW AND COGNITIVE LOAD THEORY

*"The aim of all instruction is to add knowledge and skills to long-term memory. If nothing has been added to long-term memory, nothing has been learned"*

~ Clark, Kirschner & Sweller (2012)

## Chapter overview

- Anticipation Guide
- The case for daily review
- Cognitive load theory and working memory
- The Forgetting Curve
- Spaced learning
- How does daily review look in a literacy block?
    - Practical implications for the classroom: Foundation to Year 2
    - Practical implications for the classroom: Years 3–6
- Tips for successful daily review
- Example of daily review schedule: Literacy Foundation to Year 2
- Example of daily review schedule: Literacy Years 3–6
- Summary
- Professional discussion
- Anticipation Guide answers

## Anticipation Guide

| Anticipation Guide | True/False |
|---|---|
| The biggest drop in memory retention occurs soon after the initial learning | |
| A review session soon after initial learning can improve our retention | |
| Overlearning concepts are not essential for improving retention | |
| Working memory has a large capacity for information | |
| Daily or regular review helps to reinforce learning recall and automaticity of concepts and skills | |
| The brain has a limited capacity for long-term memory retention | |
| Stress and sleep do not play a significant part in how well we retain information | |

## The case for daily review

Barak Rosenshine (2012) identified daily review as one of the 10 essential components of effective instruction. Based on cognitive science, research on master teachers and research on cognitive supports, beginning a new lesson with a review of previous knowledge, skills and concepts taught has been identified as a recommended instructional approach. Students who engaged in just eight minutes of daily review at the start of each maths lesson significantly outperformed their peers in an elementary study in the United States.

The review of previous learning activates prior knowledge, strengthens previous learning and promotes fluent recall. When students have regular opportunities to review previous learning, it helps them to recall vocabulary, concepts and procedures with ease, making it readily accessible when required for new learning; therefore, freeing up valuable working memory space. A lesson without a review of previously learnt material means that students are required to work hard to recall previous learning, while learning the new material or solving a problem – thus, creating excessive cognitive load.

## Cognitive load theory and working memory

To fully comprehend the rationale for daily review, it is important to have insight into how the brain learns and stores information. This is known as cognitive load theory, of which there are two key components: long-term memory and working memory. To use a visual analogy, long-term memory is like a huge *mental warehouse* stored with things we know – words, people and skills like driving or playing the piano. Working memory, on the other hand, is like a *mental work bench* – it is where we think and where cognitive processing occurs. Where our long-term memory has an infinite capacity, our working memory is limited and can only hold five to seven pieces of information at any one time. If the working memory is overloaded and not able to actively retrieve previously learnt information effortlessly – particularly when learning new material – then students will reach cognitive load. The challenge for us as teachers is to help students transfer knowledge into long-term memory. Daily review is one way to support students to do this – by activating prior knowledge for effortless recall, overlearning essential knowledge and concepts, and integrating new connections and material being taught.

When students have daily – or even weekly – review, this allows them to build well-connected networks of ideas (schemas) in their long-term memory. When knowledge on a topic is organised and well connected, it is easier to learn new information and makes prior knowledge more accessible. When children have strong vocabulary and understandings of the meanings of these words, it also frees up the mental space for higher-level skills, such as reading comprehension and written composition.

## The Forgetting Curve

In 1880, a German psychologist by the name of Hermann Ebbinghaus discovered a memory model called the Forgetting Curve to explain how memories are lost over time. This research was more recently replicated and reverified in 2015 by Jaap and Dros.

Ebbinghaus found that soon after learning new information, our memory fades, and this memory decline continues over time. Ebbinghaus identified five key things about memory:

1. Memories weaken over time.
2. The biggest drop in retention happens soon after initial learning.
3. It's easier to remember things that have meaning.

4. The way something is presented affects learning, such as engaging content that is well structured and lacking distraction.
5. How you feel affects how well you remember, with sleep and stress having a significant effect on memory retention.

## Spaced learning

According to the research of Ebbinghaus, the Forgetting Curve shown below depicted how quickly memory fades after initial learning. However, when there was a review session soon after the original learning, it reduced the amount and rate of memory loss. Ebbinghaus referred to this review process as 'spaced learning'. He found that regular review freshens the memories and could halt the Forgetting Curve. After several reviews, the memory loss slows, and with each subsequent review, the curve becomes less shallow. The spacing between reviews can be stretched out over time and the key information is retained.

This image shows the rapid and significant drop in memories after initial learning.

### Ebbinghaus's Forgetting Curve

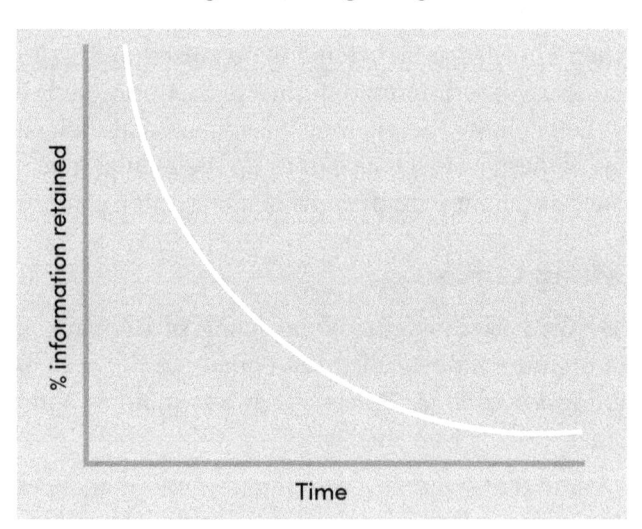

This visual shows the impact of each review (spaced learning) and how memory retention improved over time with subsequent reviews. It also shows that after the second and third reviews, the amount of memory loss is reduced and the curve is less shallow, hence halting the Forgetting Curve.

## Impact of spaced learning on memory retention

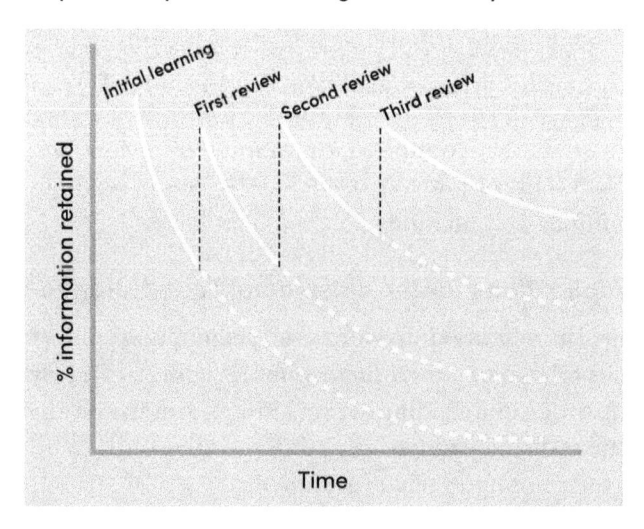

This image shows how Jaap and Dros replicated the same results of the Forgetting Curve some 135 years after it was initially discovered by Ebbinghaus.

## Forgetting Curve examples

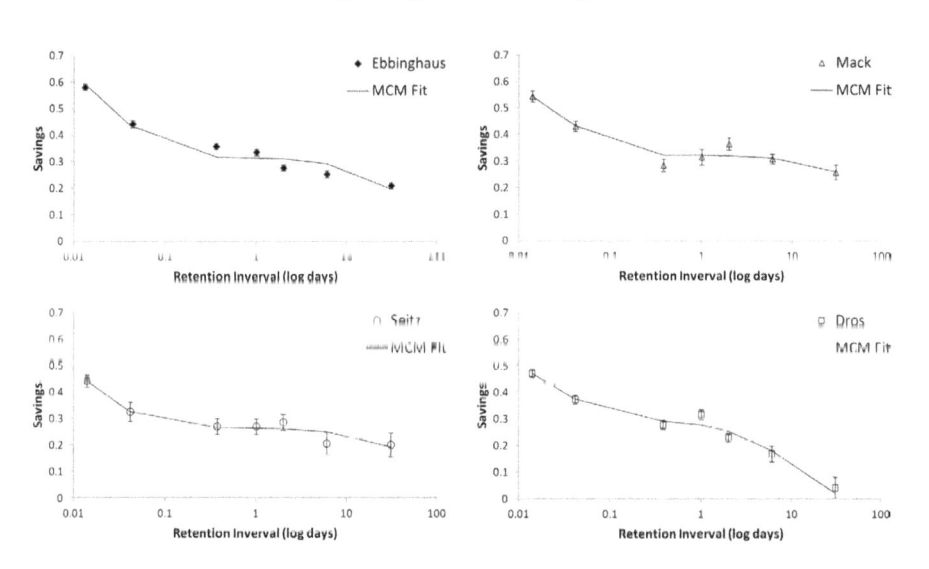

Replication and analysis of Ebbinghaus's Forgetting Curve, reproduced with kind permission of Jaap and Dros, 2015.

## How does daily review look in a literacy block?

When planning for daily review, teachers need to consider what concepts and skills are required to be automatic, and what skills or concepts require multiple reviews, such as vocabulary and their meanings. As per Rosenshine's study, I recommend 10 minutes of review per day. In the literacy block, it is important to consider all aspects of reading, writing and spelling. Examples may include:

### Practical implications for the classroom: Foundation to Year 2

- Blending of graphemes into words and segmenting words into phonemes related to the synthetic phonics code previously taught
- Explicit practice in decoding of previously learnt words aligned with alphabetic code knowledge
- Tapping out phonemes of words shown
- Phoneme manipulation practice, using mini whiteboards to write words, changing one phoneme each time
- Review of previously learnt graphemes, and graphemes with alternate pronunciations (such as 'ow' – as in crow and cow)
- Review of previously learnt morphemes and their meanings, such as '-un'
- Previously learnt high-frequency words
- Review of previously learnt vocabulary and applying these through instructional routines, such as: word association, word relationships, sentence stems, examples and non-examples
- Spelling of previously learnt words and their meanings
- Grammar concepts linked to writing, such as: common verbs, adjectives, adverbs and propositions
- Sentence-level writing based on previously taught syntax concepts
- Sub-lexical and lexical fluency practice, such as: grapheme-phoneme correspondences (GPCs), consonant vowel consonant (CVC), consonant consonant vowel consonant (CCVC) words and sentences
- Repeated reading of small decodable passages to build fluency
- Common errors needing reteaching

### Practical implications for the classroom: Years 3–6

- Breaking multisyllabic words into their morphemes and identifying individual meanings and etymology
- Review of complex spelling rules or generalisations

- Morphology review – using Word Matrices, Word Sums and Word Webs
- Whole-class dictation incorporating previously taught vocabulary and morphology
- Choral reading of previously learnt morphographs and homonyms
- Previously taught sentence level grammar, sentence doctor activities
- Sentence and paragraph level writing based on previously learnt content knowledge
- Fluency practice at connected text level and sub-lexical level, such as: morphemes, phrases and complex sentences, paragraphs and chapters
- Whole-class reading of connected text and inferring or summarising key concepts
- Previously learnt Tier 2 and Tier 3 vocabulary and applying these words through instructional routines, such as: word association, word relationships, sentence stems, examples and non-examples
- Frequent errors requiring reteaching

## Tips for successful daily review

1. **Use of PowerPoint slides** – this helps systematise daily review and reduce teacher load. The use of slides is also helpful as they can be hidden for spaced review and then accessed again easily.

2. **Use of mini whiteboards** – develop a routine for each day where students are very clear on the process of having their mini whiteboard, marker pen and eraser ready.

3. **Use of engagement norms** – having clear and explicit guidelines for daily review provides consistency, a streamlined approach and effective classroom management. For example, using terms such as: 'hover it' for when they are ready to show you their board, 'chin it' to show the teacher their board, 'bin it' to clean it and 'park it' to place it down on the floor/desk. Spending some time investing in the high expectations of these routines will be worth it and the automaticity of the actions will free up cognitive load for focusing on the task at hand.

4. **Fast-paced** – this is a fun, engaging, interactive aspect of the school day.

An example of a daily review schedule is included on the next pages as a guide.

## Example of daily review schedule: Literacy Foundation to Year 2

| | Four-year-old | Foundation | Year 1 | Year 2 |
|---|---|---|---|---|
| **Oral language** | **Grammar:**<br>Common verbs, prepositions (in, on, under, behind, in front of), pronouns (I, me, he, she we, him, her, they), adverbs (luckily, unfortunately, fortunately)<br><br>Retell simple five-part story with five-finger story prompts or Story Mountain | **Grammar:**<br>Common verbs, prepositions (in, on, under, behind, in front of), pronouns (I, me, she we, him, her, her, they), adverbs (luckily, unfortunately, fortunately)<br><br>Retell simple five-part story with five-finger story prompts or Story Mountain | **Grammar:**<br>Common verbs, prepositions (inside, outside, towards, across, under), pronouns (I, me, he, she we, him, her, they), conjunctions (but, because, so, then), adverbs (luckily, unfortunately, fortunately)<br><br>Determiners (the, a, my, your, an, this, that, his, her, their, some, all, lots, of, many, more, those, these) | **Grammar:**<br>Prepositions (behind, above, along, before, between, after)<br>Adverbs for description (for example, Snow fell gently and covered the cottage in the wood)<br><br>Upgraded simple sentences orally using:<br>Adjectives – The girls peeped inside the dark tree stump.<br>Adverbs – Sam ran quickly down the hill. |
| **Phonological awareness** | **Syllable level:**<br>Clap out the syllables in multisyllabic words, segment, blend, manipulate<br><br>**Phoneme level:**<br>Identify initial, middle, final sounds using graphemes in CV and CVC words (Term 4), segment CV and CVC words with graphemes | **Phoneme level:**<br>Identify initial, final and middle sound of CVC words with graphemes<br><br>Blend, segment and manipulate phonemes in CV, CVC, CVCC, CCVCC words, with graphemes<br><br>Sound swapping – phoneme manipulation – deletion, substitution, addition using previously learnt graphemes and phonemes | **Phoneme level:**<br>Blending and segmenting of polysyllabic words with graphemes<br><br>Sound swapping – phoneme manipulation – deletion, substitution, addition using previously learnt graphemes and phonemes | **Phoneme level:**<br>Sound swapping – phoneme manipulation – deletion, substitution, addition using previously used graphemes and phonemes |

| | Four-year-old | Foundation | Year 1 | Year 2 |
|---|---|---|---|---|
| **Phonics, spelling and morphology** | **Letter identification:**<br><br>Names with graphemes as prompts<br><br>Alphabet songs<br><br>Alphabet rainbows – putting the alphabet in order in a rainbow shape | **Decoding and encoding:**<br><br>Following schoolwide Scope and Sequence of Grapheme-Phoneme correspondences, Phonics and Morphology<br><br>Whole-class daily dictation of previously taught code | **Decoding and encoding:**<br><br>Following schoolwide Scope and Sequence of Grapheme-Phoneme correspondences, Phonics and Morphology<br><br>Whole-class daily dictation of previously taught code | **Decoding and encoding:**<br><br>Following schoolwide Scope and Sequence of Grapheme-Phoneme correspondences, Phonics and Morphology<br><br>Whole-class daily dictation of previously taught code |
| **Fluency** | | **Previously taught graphemes:**<br><br>For example, 'ar' as in 'car'<br><br>High-frequency words – following schoolwide Scope and Sequence of Grapheme-Phoneme correspondences, Phonics and Morphology<br><br>Read short decodable passages<br><br>Repeated choral reading of sub-lexical (single sounds) and lexical (CVC, CVCC CCVC and CCVCC words) fluency practice and decodable passages (one per week) | **Previously taught graphemes:**<br><br>For example, 'ar' as in 'car'<br><br>High-frequency words – following schoolwide Scope and Sequence of Grapheme-Phoneme correspondences, Phonics and Morphology<br><br>Read short decodable passages<br><br>Repeated choral reading of sub-lexical (single sounds) and lexical (CVC, CVCC CCVC and CCVCC words) fluency practice and decodable passages (one per week to build fluency and confidence) | **Previously taught alternate graphemes:**<br><br>For example, a/a-e/ay/eigh/ey<br><br>High-frequency words – following schoolwide Scope and Sequence of Grapheme-Phoneme correspondences, Phonics and Morphology<br><br>Read short decodable passages<br><br>Repeated choral reading of decodable passages (one per week to build fluency and confidence) |
| **Vocabulary** | Tier 2 and Tier 3 words revised from rich text units | Tier 2 and Tier 3 words revised from rich text units | Tier 2 and Tier 3 words revised from rich text units<br><br>Homonyms review | Tier 2 and Tier 3 words revised from rich text units<br><br>Homonyms review |

## Example of daily review schedule: Literacy
## Years 3–6

| | Year 3 | Year 4 | Year 5 | Year 6 |
|---|---|---|---|---|
| **Phonics, spelling and morphology** | **Decoding and encoding:** Following schoolwide Scope and Sequence of Grapheme–Phoneme correspondences, Phonics and Morphology<br><br>**Spelling rules and morphology:** Review following schoolwide grammar and syntax sequence<br><br>Whole-class daily dictation of previously taught code | **Decoding and encoding:** Following schoolwide Scope and Sequence of Grapheme–Phoneme correspondences, Phonics and Morphology<br><br>**Spelling rules and morphology:** Review following schoolwide grammar and syntax sequence<br><br>Whole-class daily dictation of previously taught code | **Decoding and encoding:** Following schoolwide Scope and Sequence of Grapheme–Phoneme correspondences, Phonics and Morphology<br><br>**Spelling rules and morphology:** Review following schoolwide grammar and syntax sequence<br><br>Whole-class daily dictation of previously taught code | **Decoding and encoding:** Following schoolwide Scope and Sequence of Grapheme–Phoneme correspondences, Phonics and Morphology<br><br>**Spelling rules and morphology:** Review following schoolwide grammar and syntax sequence<br><br>Whole-class daily dictation of previously taught code |
| **Fluency** | Choral reading of previously learnt morphographs<br><br>Choral, repeated reading of decodable, fiction and non-fiction texts/passages at year level | Choral reading of previously learnt morphographs<br><br>Choral, repeated reading of fiction and non-fiction texts/passages at year level | Choral, repeated reading of fiction and non-fiction texts/passages at year level | Choral, repeated reading of fiction and non-fiction texts/passages at year level |
| **Vocabulary** | Tier 2 and Tier 3 words revised from rich text units<br><br>Homonyms review | Tier 2 and Tier 3 words revised from rich text units<br><br>Homonyms review | Tier 2 and Tier 3 words revised from rich text units<br><br>Homonyms review | Tier 2 and Tier 3 words revised from rich text units<br><br>Homonyms review |

## Summary

- Daily review is identified as one of the 10 essential components of effective instruction (Rosenshine, 2012).
- Eight minutes of daily review has been proven to significantly impact upon maths achievement.
- The review of previous learning activates prior knowledge, strengthens previous learning and promotes fluent recall.
- Long-term memory is like a huge mental 'warehouse' stored with things we know – such as words, people and skills like driving or playing the piano. Working memory, on the other hand, is like a mental 'work bench' – it is where cognitive processing occurs.
- Long-term memory has an infinite capacity, however, working memory is limited and can only hold five to seven pieces of information at any one time.
- If the working memory is overloaded and not able to actively retrieve previously learnt information effortlessly – particularly when learning new material – then students will reach cognitive load.
- When planning for daily review, teachers need to consider what concepts and skills are required to be automatic, and what skills or concepts require multiple reviews, such as vocabulary and their meanings.
- In 1880, Hermann Ebbinghaus discovered a memory model called the Forgetting Curve to explain how memories are lost over time. This research was replicated and reverified in 2015 by Jaap and Dros. This is an essential underpinning of the need for daily review.
- When our long-term memory is well organised, it frees up space in our working memory, reducing cognitive load. When children have strong vocabulary and understandings of the meanings of these words, it also frees up the mental space for higher-level skills, such as comprehension.
- Tips for daily review include using mini whiteboards, PowerPoint slides and engagement norms.

## Professional discussion

- The work of Rosenshine, as well as Clark, Kirschner and Sweller, are excellent papers for whole-school professional learning and discussions. How might you use their research to fine-tune instructional processes in your classroom, or school as a whole?
- How might daily review look in your classroom and school context?
- Considering the impact of low variance in high-performing schools, how might a whole-school approach to daily review look?

*"The best way to become an expert is through practice – thousands of hours of practice. The more practice, the better the performance"*
~ Rosenshine (2012)

## Anticipation Guide answers

| Anticipation Guide | True/False |
|---|---|
| The biggest drop in memory retention occurs soon after the initial learning | True |
| A review session soon after initial learning can improve our retention | True |
| Overlearning concepts are not essential for improving retention | True |
| Working memory (WM) has a large capacity for information | False, WM can only hold five to seven pieces of information at any one time |
| Daily or regular review helps to reinforce learning recall and automaticity of concepts and skills | True |
| The brain has a limited capacity for long-term memory retention | False. It is large and unlimited |
| Stress and sleep do not play a significant part in how well we retain information | False. Stress and sleep play a significant part in how well we retain information |

## Chapter 3

# EXPLICIT INSTRUCTION AND VISIBLE LEARNING

"When teaching new content and skills to novices, teachers are more effective when they provide explicit guidance accompanied by practice and feedback, not when they require students to discover many aspects of what they must learn"

~ Clark, Kirschner & Sweller (2012)

## Chapter overview

- Self-reflection
- Introduction
- Why explicit instruction in teaching literacy?
- Where does 'visible learning' fit in?
- The key components of visible learning
- My visible learning journey
- A visible learning lesson
- Models of explicit instruction
- The importance of worked examples
- Worked example in action
- Supporting cognitive load and working memory in reading
- Support for students with working memory difficulties
- Practical considerations for the classroom for explicit instruction
- Summary

- Professional discussion
- Visible learning self-reflection tool

## Self-reflection

| Self-reflection | Give yourself a rating out of 5 |
|---|---|
| I have a very thorough understanding of why explicit instruction is so crucial for teaching essential skills | |
| My goal is always to present new material in small steps with student practice, after each step | |
| While demonstrating new material or concepts, my goal is always to model, think aloud and show worked examples, so students have a clear guide of what they are striving towards | |
| At the start of each lesson, my goal is to clearly explain learning intentions and success criteria for new learning or multistep instructions, which students can refer to as needed | |
| I am aware there will likely be students with working memory difficulties, and I anticipate and plan adjustments for these | |
| I believe every child can make progress when new learning is taught explicitly, including high rigour, low differentiation and high impact approaches | |
| My goal is always to provide opportunities for students to reflect on and self-assess against learning goals | |

## Introduction

Successful student outcomes in literacy require teachers to be highly skilled in not just the content of reading science (the what), but also the pedagogical practices that make the greatest impact on student learning (the how). Neither one is sufficient alone. We may know the framework of explicit teaching, but if we are lacking the content knowledge, then student outcomes will be hindered. Conversely, if we know the content of reading science but do not teach it in a structured, systematic, explicit approach, then student outcomes will also be affected. The key is for teachers to be skilled in both. Dr Shayne Piasta (2022) refers to this as 'pedagogical content knowledge' – bringing content and pedagogy together.

Much of what I've covered up until this point in terms of the fundamentals of high impact instruction, is culminated in what is explicit teaching. For example, explicit teaching is about having high expectations for our students. It's about ensuring there is a daily review component to activate prior knowledge and consolidate learning for fluent recall. It's about ensuring that the start of every lesson has very clear learning intentions. All these aspects are included in an explicit teaching approach.

## Why explicit instruction in teaching literacy?

As children, acquiring spoken language is a natural skill. Our brains are wired to learn spoken language. However, the architecture of the human brain is not wired to read, spell or write. These academic skills are not 'natural' or easily learned, and for most of us, need to be explicitly taught (Clark, Kirschner & Sweller, 2012; Dehaene, 2010).

Since 2000, the research has been clear that explicit teaching in literacy is the most effective way for students to learn how to read, write and spell. Approaches that do not teach students explicitly – with modelling, guidance, practice and feedback – puts novice readers at risk from the start. However, that's not to say that explicit teaching needs to be happening all day, every day. Small group or independent projects can be effective, but as a means of practising skills already learnt, not when learning new material.

## Where does 'visible learning' fit in?

*"When teaching and learning are visible there is a greater likelihood of students reaching higher levels of achievement"*

~ John Hattie (2012)

Explicit instruction and visible learning are mutually supportive of one another. Visible learning is based on the work of Dr John Hattie and his 20-plus years of research. Using a simple analogy, visible learning could be compared to a basketball game. In basketball, everyone on the court is clear about the end goal – to get the ball in the hoop as many times as possible and score more points than the opposition. If we translate this to the classroom, then visible learning means that every student is made aware of the learning intentions – what we are trying to achieve.

Another analogy is a road trip. On a long road trip, most times we have a destination in mind with planned pitstops. If we apply this to the classroom context, the destination, and the learning steps/success criteria (pitstops), are made clear to students with a clear path to the learning destination.

## The key components of visible learning

These are as follows:

- Teaching and learning are made *visible to the student*. Teachers use explicit and succinct learning success criteria and provide helpful feedback with next steps.
- Teachers hold high expectations for every child. They know students well and where to take them next. Teachers also teach students to reflect on their learning and progress.
- Learning is *visible to the teacher*. Students are aware of the steps to achieve the goal(s), making it easier for students and teachers to see and discuss progress.
- Teaching is considered primarily in terms of its impact on student learning. Teachers are evaluators of their own practice utilising the mindset 'What is the impact of my teaching?'
- Evaluation is at the centre of teaching – not the teaching methods themselves.

## My visible learning journey

Five years into my teaching career, needing a new adventure, I moved to Belfast and then London. My plan to do relief teaching for six months turned into an unexpected stint of five years. In 2003, my second year of being away, I accepted a teaching and special education needs coordinator role in a South East London school and it was there that I really honed my teaching craft.

I quickly learnt that visible learning (I didn't know it was called this at the time), was an expectation in every lesson. The expectation was that in every lesson, the teacher had to clearly state the learning intention and the success steps/criteria, so the students had a very clear understanding of what they were learning, why they were learning it and how to get to their end goal. This was recorded on the board and in student workbooks. This was foreign to me, as it is certainly not how I had been taught, and the concept of a success criteria was new, but it made so much sense.

At the end of every lesson, students had to self-assess against the learning intention and indicate in their workbooks using a traffic light system – using green, orange or red pencils – the extent to which they thought they had achieved the goal.

This approach was mandated across the school. In addition, every six weeks, student workbooks were collected. Books from a variety of student abilities – two top children, two middle and two lower – were collected to check that every lesson had these elements present. In addition was the regular observations and detailed weekly planning for both literacy and numeracy, and non-core subjects, with differentiation clearly indicated, key focus questions and vocabulary to be explicitly taught. This planning was handed into my wonderful Head Teacher, Zoe, every Monday morning for review. Although very different to my previous experiences in Australia, I soon learnt to love this approach, as the high-rigour planning helped to 'up my game' as a teacher.

Similar to a sprint approach, each term, we had schoolwide layered targets for each year level that every teacher was required to work towards. Based on the focus of the strategic plan, we were required to anticipate what targets each child would achieve by the end of each half term. One term, I vividly recall a syntax improvement focus. Three times per week we would explicitly teach a 15-minute syntax warm-up related to our reading and writing focus with the aim of achieving the targets by the end of the six-week cycle. We would then meet with the leadership team each half term to discuss student progress and achievement towards goals set.

Now, I am not going to lie – this was tricky to begin with, as it was like learning a whole new way of doing things, but it didn't take long to get the hang of it, and the quality of my teaching and the level of achievement of my students just blew me away. I am just so thankful for that experience for many reasons, but mainly for helping me to become a high-quality practitioner and visible learning convert.

## A visible learning lesson

So, how does a visible learning lesson look?

**Before learning, teachers:**

- Know where students are at before teaching, as they use assessment *for* learning and not just assessment *of* learning.
- Have a deep understanding of what students already know and what they can do.
- Set high expectations for *every* child (Teacher expectations have a 0.43 effect size on student learning (Hattie & Zierer, 2017*).

**At the start of lessons, teachers:**

- Are crystal clear about what is to be learnt and share the learning intentions with the class. Learning intentions are clear, measurable and in student-friendly language.
- Clearly explain the steps for students to know how to get to the learning intention so that they can refer to these steps and know if they are on the right track. This teaches children how to be meta-cognitive about their learning.

**During each lesson, teachers:**

- Demonstrate high encouragement of student strengths, encourage confidence and self-belief/self-concept (0.47 effect size on student learning, Hattie & Zierer, 2017*). Students' personal expectations of themselves was identified as having a significant effect size of 1.44 (Hattie, 2012 in Fisher, Frey & Hattie, 2017).
- Limit teacher talk, to reduce cognitive overload for students.
- Are responsive and agile. Teachers demonstrate a high level of flexibility within a lesson, so they know when to intervene to advance the learning, reteach or extend, with a high level of formative assessment.
- Provide prompt and explicit feedback, helping students answer three questions: *Where am I going? How am I going there? And where do I go next?*
- Utilise a range of high impact teaching strategies are in place and may include – but are not limited to – explicit instruction, self-monitoring skills (effect size 0.69, Hattie & Zierer, 2017*), planning and organising before writing (effect size 0.85) and peer tutoring (effect size 0.55, Hattie & Zierer, 2017*).

**At the conclusion of each lesson, teachers provide opportunities for:**

- Students to self-assess against the learning intention. This may include a traffic light system, score out of five with their fingers on one hand, or simple thumbs-up, side or down.

**After each lesson, teachers:**

- Examine the impact of the learning. Teachers ask themselves: What was the impact of my teaching? (Hattie & Zierer, 2018)
- Examine the effectiveness of the learning intention and success criteria are also reviewed.

## Models of explicit instruction

Anita Archer – voted one of the top 30 best educators of the world – identifies explicit teaching as consisting of six key steps:

1. **Review**
   a. Review homework and relevant previous learning.
   b. Review prerequisite skills and knowledge.

2. **Presentation**
   a. State lesson goals.
   b. Present new material in small steps.
   c. Model procedures.
   d. Provide examples and non-examples.
   e. Use clear language.
   f. Avoid digressions.

3. **Guided practice**
   a. Expect a high frequency of responses.
   b. Ensure high rates of success.
   c. Provide timely feedback, clues and prompts.
   d. Have students continue practise until they are fluent.

4. **Corrections and feedback**
   a. Reteach when necessary – be responsive.

5. **Independent practice**
   a. Monitor initial practise attempts.
   b. Students continue practise until skills are automatic.

6. **Weekly and monthly reviews**

## I Do, We Do, You Do approach

A model you may be more familiar with is the I Do, We Do, You Do model, which entails the following:

- A brief review of previous prerequisite knowledge – children need to activate prior knowledge to process new information.

- Teacher states the learning intention.

- **I Do:** In this teacher-led phase, the new material is presented in small steps with student practice after each step – with modelling, think alouds and worked examples. There are clear and detailed explanations and examples provided with frequent checks for understanding.

- **We Do:** In the guided practice stage, teachers may incorporate cooperative learning activities, including but not limited to: Think, Pair, Share, mixed-ability paired practice; all scaffolded by the teacher who provides guidance and feedback.
- Teachers provide a high level of practice for all students, with frequent checks for understanding. The use of pop sticks (with every child's name on one) is great, as it promotes high engagement and readiness. Teachers seek a high level of accuracy in the initial practice stages to build confidence.
- **You Do:** In the independent application phase, students are set up for success to work independently, and the teacher moves around for checking and feedback.
- Recap and self-assessment/weekly and monthly reviews.

### Framing learning intentions and success criteria

In schools I have been in, it has taken different forms, but the premise is the same: the learning intention is made clear to students, and students are provided with success steps for achieving the learning intention, when learning new material. A daily review session would not require a learning intention, as it is a routine that occurs every day to revise previously learnt skills, concepts, vocabulary and content. However, a lesson in writing an introduction for a persuasive text, or applying phonics concepts to a text, or a lesson in syntax, would require the goals of the lesson to be very clear. An example may be as follows.

For a synthetic phonics lesson, after spending time explicitly teaching the alternate spellings for the /oo/ phoneme, an example learning intention may be:

> *By the end of this lesson, I will have sorted all of the /oo/ words by their alternate spellings.*

Success criteria may be:

1. Read the text out loud.
2. Highlight all of the words with the /oo/ sound.
3. Sort the /oo/ words into the columns of the alternate spellings 'ue', 'ew' and 'oo'.
4. Check my work with a partner.

## The importance of worked examples

One of the best examples of explicit instruction that considers both long-term memory and working memory is the instructional approach of a 'worked example' (Clark, Kirschner & Sweller, 2012). The approach applies to novice learners only, as expert learners do not require worked examples. This scaffolded approach involves the teacher showing students a problem/task that has already been solved, clearly showing how to do the task/skill on their own, with support and guidance. This reduces the burden on working memory, as only the solution requires comprehending – and students are not reliant on having to 'discover' the process, therefore directing the working memory resources towards storing what they are learning, into long-term memory.

## Worked example in action (for a lesson on teaching anaphoric reference)

For many students, anaphoric reference can be an obstacle to comprehension at the sentence level, particulary for students with EALD. Explaining to students why it is used in texts and teaching this micro skill using worked examples may be beneficial in supporting comprehension. Below is a worked example in action:

| Learning intention | I will be able to identify the pronouns in a paragraph and draw an arrow to show the anaphoric reference. |
|---|---|
| Success criteria/ steps | 1. Know what a pronoun is: he, I, she, they, me, you, this, it. |
| | 2. Underline the pronouns in a sentence. |
| | 3. Re-read the sentence and highlight each character/person in a different colour. |
| | 4. Highlight the pronouns to match the correct character (anaphora). |
| | 5. Draw an arrow from the pronoun to the character/person to show the anaphoric reference. |
| I Do | Today, we are learning about 'anaphora' – what a strange word. Anaphora is something that authors do when they write so they aren't always saying a person or character's name repeatedly. It relates to the characters and pronouns. Examples of pronouns are: he, I, she, they, me, you, this, it. |

| | |
|---|---|
| **I Do**<br>**(cont.)** | So, instead of saying:<br><br>**Sally** was hot. **Sally** went to the beach. **Sally** had a swim. **Sally** loved the water. **Sally** lay on her towel to dry off. Then **Sally** went home.<br><br>An author might write:<br><br>**Sally** was hot so <u>**she**</u> went to the beach. <u>**She**</u> had a swim.<br><br>**Sally** loved the water. <u>**She**</u> lay on her towel to dry off. Then <u>**she**</u> went home.<br><br>So, instead of just saying 'Sally' over and over again, the author has used the pronoun 'she' sometimes, to show reference to Sally. This is called anaphoric reference.<br><br>Sometimes, this anaphora is tricky and we need to work out who it is referring to, for example:<br><br>**Paul** took **Pablo** to work, as <u>**his**</u> car had broken down.<br><br>As both characters here are presumably male, we must decide who the 'his' is referring to. We need to infer that it is referencing Pablo, as his car has broken down.<br><br>I will draw an arrow to show the subjects and pronouns that are connected. This is called anaphoric reference.<br><br>Here is another example:<br><br>Listen to me read this passage, inspired by *The Grandest Bookshop in the World* (Amelia Mellor, 2020), and look for the anaphora. (I would recommend having the text on the interactive whiteboard for children to follow along.)<br><br>*Over the past week, something terrible made itself at home in Marty's brain. He tried to get it out but it kept creeping in like a mouse on a hunt for morsels. He tried to starve it but it was a pesky little scavenger, persistent in its quest for food. It kept finding rambling thoughts and odd details. Grandad's limp. The new huskiness in his storytelling at bedtime. A creaking door besides his walking cane, and a strange new neighbour. By Tuesday it was trapped inside his skull. Too large to ignore. Marty was on edge.*<br><br>What is going on in this passage? (Explanation: Marty is having rambling thoughts and they are playing on his mind. There is not really a mouse, but it feels like a scavenger is taking over his brain).<br><br>In this passage, can anyone tell me who the subjects are? (Marty; and rambling random thoughts including those about Grandad and the new neighbours.) |

| | |
|---|---|
| **I Do (cont.)** | I am going to underline the main subjects in this piece and link them back to their pronouns.<br><br>Over the past week, something terrible made itself at home in <u>Marty's</u> **brain**. <u>He</u> tried to get **it** out but it kept creeping in like a mouse on a hunt for morsels. <u>He</u> tried to starve **it** but **it** was a **pesky little scavenger**, persistent in **its** quest for food. It kept finding rambling thoughts and odd details. <u>Grandad's</u> limp. The new huskiness in <u>his</u> storytelling at bedtime. A creaking door besides <u>his</u> walking cane, and a strange <u>new neighbour</u>. By Tuesday it was trapped inside <u>his</u> skull. Too large to ignore. <u>Marty</u> was on edge. |
| **We Do** | Now I am going to give you another paragraph, and let's find the anaphora together. I am going to read the paragraphs, then you can read with me. Let's just recap – what are some pronouns again? (he, I, she, they, me, you, this, it)<br><br>Over the past week, *an unsettling force* took hold of both **Sarah** and <u>Ethan</u>, entwining *their* minds in an insidious dance. **Sarah** fought tirelessly to evict *it* from her thoughts, but *it* persisted, slithering through her consciousness like a shadowy serpent. **She** tried to ignore *it*, but *it* possessed a relentless hunger, scavenging morsels of **her** attention. *It* clung to the distant look in <u>Ethan's</u> eyes, the way <u>he</u> hesitated before speaking, and the cryptic notes <u>he</u> left behind. Meanwhile, <u>Ethan</u>, too, grappled with the same sinister presence, as if a mirror image of **Sarah's** torment. *It* exploited <u>his</u> fleeting memories, the disorienting changes in **Sarah's** behavior, and the mysterious whispers that echoed through the night. By Thursday, *the force* had become an inescapable resident in *their intertwined minds*, a palpable weight that left *them both* on edge, *their* paths converging as *they* sought to unravel the enigma that consumed *them*.<br><br>Let's make the pronouns for Sarah in **bold** first.<br><br>Talk to your partner, then I am going to choose someone at random (from the pop sticks) to tell me the pronoun referencing for Ethan. Let's underline the noun-pronoun references to Ethan (in the classroom, I would highlight the characters in different colours and draw arrows to show the referencing).<br><br>Are there any other characters in the passage? (Some students might pick up the 'it', which is referring to the thoughts in their minds and 'their', which is referencing Sarah and Ethan.)<br><br>Listen to paired discussions. Provide explicit feedback. Proceed to explicitly modelling highlighting these and showing the reference to these aspects of the passage. |

| You Do | Now you are going to have a go on your own in (mixed-ability) pairs. |
|---|---|
| | You are going to read the passage and underline and highlight the pronouns in different colours and draw arrows back to them. |
| | Have the success steps visible for students to refer to. |
| | While he appeared preoccupied with his task, Nebulon's perceptive nature alerted him to the fact that he was being observed. A sudden shift in his gaze revealed the source—a curious cat positioned at the far end of the street. Locking eyes with the feline, he sensed an unspoken connection, an understanding that transcended the visible realm. In that brief moment, their gazes met, and an unspoken understanding passed between them, bridging the gap between wizard and creature. |
| Plenary | Discuss with students the noun-pronoun referencing in the passage. Provide feedback to the whole class on independent level work and reteach where necessary. |
| | Ask students closing questions to reflect on their learning against the learning intention. What is something you learnt today? |
| | Self-reflection: *Thumbs-up, side, down formative assessment* |
| | *The latter three text examples in this lesson outline were generated through Chat GPT.* |

## Supporting cognitive load and working memory in reading (reflection and wait time)

Cognitive Load Theory (CLT) is the theory of how the brain learns and how it stores information in working memory and long-term memory. It is important to consider that there will most likely be students in every class with working memory difficulties, whether diagnosed or not. Students with poor working memory will often struggle with multistep instructions, writing, spelling multisyllabic words and reading comprehension. The key here is to anticipate these needs and plan for them as part of an inclusive classroom culture. Providing reflection and wait time during instructional time are two ways in which we can support working memory and cognitive load. Wait time alone plays a vital role in memory retention.

## Support for students with working memory difficulties (DSF, 2014)

- Break instructions into small steps/chunks.
- Provide wait and reflection time.
- Provide a visual demonstration/worked example in small steps.
- Check for understanding with the whole class before students begin a task, for example, ask: *What did I ask you to do? What do you need to do first?*
- Systematise routines to ease cognitive load. For example, teach students to use a diary for homework with dates indicated, have a streamlined system for stationery organisation, a clear morning routine for exchanging home readers.
- Highlight/pre-exempt what a child needs to listen for in a text.
- Underline key words and information while reading.
- Provide writing frameworks such as graphic organisers and editing checklists.

## Practical considerations for the classroom for explicit instruction

- Be very clear on your learning intentions and in your explanations. Avoid unnecessary teacher talk as "providing unnecessary information can be a major reason for instructional failure" (Sweller, 2016, p8).
- Display success criteria or steps to success clearly for students to refer to when needed, particularly for writing instruction.
- Check for understanding as an ongoing part of your practice within and at the end of lessons. This can be with simple formative assessments, such as thumbs-up, down, side, the use of mini whiteboards and/or exit slips.
- Use the Think, Pair, Share approach throughout the day. This approach provides opportunities for thinking time, oral language through student interaction and feedback to you as the teacher for ongoing formative assessment.
- Phonemic awareness and phonics: Explicitly teach phonics through physically modelling how to segment and blend phonemes using magnetic graphemes or magnetic Post-its. Provide daily opportunities for students to practise decoding with word lists, sentences and connected text, providing support and feedback as required.

- Phonemic awareness and phonics: Support students who find segmenting and blending to be difficult, to use continuant phonation – holding on to the letters that can be stretched, such as sssssssuuuuuuuun (sun). Showing students the movements of their mouths in a mirror can be a helpful support here, too (Ehri, 2022).
- Reading pairs: Establish clear, concise routines for lessons such as fluency pairs. Teach students the expectations for set-up and pack-away, so these routines become automated.
- Spelling: Provide phoneme-grapheme boxes (also known as Elkonin boxes) for sounding out individual phonemes in words when spelling in the early years, or for students that struggle to segment words into individual phonemes when encoding in the older years.
- Explicitly teach vocabulary in the context of rich texts. Show students the spelling of new words with an accompanying picture, provide a meaning, the word in the context of a sentence, as well as examples and non-examples. Review and practise on subsequent days so that students have many opportunities to apply the new vocabulary in a range of ways. Examples may include sentence stems, word associations, word relationships and developing their own meanings for the words.
- Reading: While reading a new text or novel, allow students to underline key words or jot down a key idea in the column as a summary reminder.
- Prior to reading a new text/picture book/novel to students, identify words, sentences and concepts that may be an obstacle to students' comprehension. Specifically address this when reading aloud and build in checks for understanding at these points. Open-ended queries such as *'What is happening here?'* or *'What is going on?'* at chosen places during the teacher read-aloud will provide valuable insight into student understanding or lack thereof.
- Writing: Provide visual scaffolds such as graphic organisers for writing tasks so students have a visual framework for the genre structure being taught.
- Provide examples of high-quality sentences and mentor texts when teaching sentence-level grammar and writing genres. For example, if working on narrative openings, provide examples of high-quality story openings for students to have a very clear picture of what they are striving towards.

- Provide opportunities to extend more able students through differentiated questioning and higher-level worked examples where appropriate in literature or writing instruction.
- Provide simple editing reminder charts for students to self-monitor their use of micro skills in written work, such as a COPS mnemonic framework (**C**apitalisation, **O**rganisation of sentences and paragraphs, **P**unctuation, **S**pelling).
- Although there are times when differentiating content is necessary, aim to differentiate instruction through questioning, support and outcome, rather than content, in an explicit teaching lesson. Far too often, the level of differentiation is far too high and therefore not providing students the opportunity to access year level curriculum.

## Summary

- Successful student outcomes in literacy requires teachers to be highly skilled in not just the content of reading science (the what), but also the pedagogical knowledge and practices that will make the greatest impact on student learning (the how). Neither one is sufficient alone.
- The human brain is not born wired to read, spell and write. These academic skills are not 'natural' or easily learned, and for most of us, need to be explicitly taught.
- Explicit teaching is not required all day, every day. Small-group or independent projects can be effective, but as a means of practising skills already learnt and not when learning new material.
- Visible learning ensures that every student is made aware of the learning intentions and the steps to get there, with clear, explicit feedback throughout the learning process.
- At the heart of visible learning, effective teachers are evaluators of the impact of their teaching (Hattie & Zierer, 2010)
- Anita Archer identifies explicit teaching as consisting of six key steps: Review, Presentation, Guided practice, Corrections and feedback, Independent practice, Weekly and monthly reviews.
- One of the best examples of explicit instruction that considers both long-term memory and working memory is the instructional approach of a 'worked example' (Clark, Kirschner & Sweller, 2012).
- Support cognitive load and working memory in reading by providing multiple opportunities for reflection and wait time during lesson instruction.

## Professional discussion

- What is an agreed definition of 'fully guided instruction' across your school? Once this has been developed, articulate how this looks in terms of the structure of each lesson.
- How will you apply the elements of cognitive load theory in your classroom?
- To what extent is visible learning evident in your classroom/school?
- Discuss the concept of 'I assess the _impact_ of my teaching'.
- If we were watching a visible learning lesson, what would we see?
- Many high-performing schools that strive for a low variance curriculum develop instructional frameworks for explicit instruction. How might this look in your school?

*Hattie & Zierer (2017) references included in Hattie & Zierer (2018).*

## Visible learning self-reflection tool

With a rating of 1 to 5 – 5 being always, consistently or exceptionally well – to what extent do you promote visible teaching and learning?

| | Unsure | 1 | 2 | 3 | 4 | 5 |
|---|---|---|---|---|---|---|
| My mindset is 'What was the impact of my teaching?' rather than 'Did that lesson go well?' | | | | | | |
| I hold high expectations for every child | | | | | | |
| I know where students are at before teaching and use assessment *for* learning and not just assessment *of* learning | | | | | | |
| I have a deep understanding of what students already know and what they can do | | | | | | |
| I am an attentive listener to what students know and find out how they learnt something | | | | | | |

|  | Unsure | 1 | 2 | 3 | 4 | 5 |
|---|---|---|---|---|---|---|
| I am very clear about what is to be learnt and share learning intentions with the class at the start of every lesson | | | | | | |
| I clearly explain the steps for students to know how to achieve the learning intention | | | | | | |
| I have a high emphasis on encouragement of student strengths, encouraging confidence and self-belief | | | | | | |
| I limit teacher talk in each lesson | | | | | | |
| I have a high level of flexibility within a lesson and know when to intervene to advance the learning or reteach | | | | | | |
| My feedback is explicit and helps students know where they are going and where they need to go next | | | | | | |
| I utilise a range of high impact teaching strategies, including cooperative learning and explicit teaching of key skills | | | | | | |
| Students self-assess their learning towards the learning intention at the end of every lesson | | | | | | |
| I regularly examine the *impact of learning* for each child<br><br>I review the effectiveness of learning intentions and success criteria I set | | | | | | |
| I regularly celebrate small wins and achievements of student progress and achievement | | | | | | |

## Chapter 4

# DATA-INFORMED TEACHING

"Good practice without data is an event, and good data
without impacting practice is a research paper"

~ Dr Russell Quaglia (2015)

## Self-reflection

| Self-reflection | Give yourself a rating out of 5 |
|---|---|
| **I am very good at:** | |
| • Using data to inform planning and assess the impact of my teaching | |
| • Being explicit about learning intentions and success criteria | |
| • Using assessment for, as and of learning | |
| **My goal is always to:** | |
| • Use frequent formative assessment to allow agile and responsive teaching within my lessons | |
| • Use data to inform planning and decisions I make | |
| **I believe:** | |
| • Every child has the potential to improve | |

## Using assessment data to inform practice

Our core business as educators is to teach children and make an impact on their learning. But if we don't have useful data, or are using assessments that are not research based, or not using data effectively, then it is impossible to know that our teaching is impactful. Teaching without effective data is like going on a journey with no destination in mind. You may get somewhere good, but there's a high probability you won't.

Dr Russell Quaglia makes the connection between the use of data and our teaching, perfectly. He says that if we are not using data to inform our teaching, then a lesson is simply an 'event', and if we are not using data to inform our teaching and learning, then the data is nothing but a 'research paper'. I think that is so true, because if we are not using data effectively, then we aren't teaching a lesson, we are simply facilitating an event.

## What's the purpose of data?

Assessment data is information that we use to improve teaching and learning. It needs to have a clearly defined purpose, be collected systematically, responded to flexibly and responsively, and monitored rigorously.

Data across a school should take many forms: formative, summative, diagnostic and preventative. In terms of preventative approaches, universal screening is crucial.

Universal screening is used to identify students requiring early intervention. It involves schoolwide screening in the subskills of reading and spelling, three times per year. These assessments require predetermined benchmarks to identify students at risk, track progress and support the decision-making process around intervention and goal setting for whole-school improvement.

Our choices around the types of assessments we use matters significantly. If our assessments are only giving us a 'level' of reading, then I would ask: *What information is this providing about what a child can and can't do?* and *How will this 'reading level' inform next steps in teaching phonemic awareness, phonics, decoding and so on?* I will unpack this later in the chapter.

## Assessment techniques – *of, for* and *as* learning

There are three different techniques of using assessment – assessment *of, for* and *as* learning.

### Assessment *of* learning – summative assessment

The purpose of assessment here is summative and mostly used at the end of a unit of work. Summative assessments also include mandated national assessments, such as NAPLAN and Foundation year-entry assessments. Summative assessments may also include a diagnostic assessment to identify a specific student's strengths and needs.

### Assessment *for* learning – formative assessment

Formative assessment refers to brief, frequent and interactive assessments of students' progress and understanding to allow teachers to be flexible and responsive during lessons. These quick assessment check-ins are ongoing during the learning process. Students understand exactly what they are learning, with clear expectations and success steps, and are given feedback on how to improve. Formative assessment can be particularly powerful when teachers backward-map formative tasks from summative tasks. I will unpack formative assessment and some examples a little later.

### Assessment *as* learning – student self-assessment

This is a process where students are being reflective and metacognitive about their own learning. This is done through self or peer assessment, which is modelled by teachers. Students may also be reflecting on their progress using a success criteria or rubric, such as one I recommend in the chapter on fluency in Part 2.

## Examples of formative assessment

*"There is little evidence that standardised tests and/or exhaustive summative assessment regimes improve student achievement. However, there is compelling evidence that formative assessment techniques can significantly improve student learning and wellbeing outcomes, particularly when coupled with data-informed practice"*

~ AISNSW (2017, p4)

Although summative assessments, such as end-of-unit tests or mandated national tests, can provide some interesting and useful information, it is essential that assessment also serves a formative function. Formative assessment takes shape during class lessons and has a focus on improvement.

Educators who use formative assessment approaches and techniques are better prepared to meet the needs of a diverse student group. They can then effectively make use of the data to differentiate and adapt their instruction, creating greater equity of student outcomes (AISNSW, 2017).

Some examples of formative assessment include:

**Green, orange and red words:** This is a fantastic formative assessment tool where students can be taught to identify words as being either a green, orange or red word based on their vocabulary knowledge. A green word is a word that they know, can explain and put in a sentence, an orange word is a word they have heard and know it is something to do with…x, and a red word is a word they haven't heard or don't know.

**Entry and exit slips:** Students respond to questions or prompts at the beginning or end of learning. Exit slips are great at the end of a lesson just before leaving the room for recess or lunch. The teacher would pose a question and students record their answer on a slip of paper, handing it to their teacher as they walk out of the classroom.

**Gallery walk:** Students respond to prompts and questions to engage in the feedback and reflection process. Large pieces of butchers paper are placed around the room and students can walk around to each piece of paper in mixed-ability groups to record their understandings or answer questions posed.

**Mini whiteboards:** A simple, high impact device for students to show working out, write responses and/or ask questions. The teacher poses the question and students record their response on the whiteboard. When the teacher says, 'chin it', students hold the whiteboard up for the teacher to do a quick scan and assess for understanding. This is a great approach during daily review, synthetic phonics lessons and instruction.

**Observation:** Teachers observe and record evidence of student learning against a specific learning intention, success criteria and/or learning goals.

**Peer feedback:** Students use criteria or a rubric to review their peers' work. This is particularly powerful in daily mixed-ability fluency paired work.

**Quizzes and polls:** Students attempt questions that test knowledge about a topic and provide instant feedback. There are many great apps such as Kahoot!, to gain instant feedback from students that can be displayed on the interactive whiteboard.

**Rubrics:** Teachers and students use criteria along a continuum of proficiency to communicate and evaluate student learning. Students may use a fluency rubric to self-assess against the key elements of fluency, such as accuracy, pace, smoothness and phrasing.

**Strategic questioning and statements:** A deliberate way for the teacher to find out what students know, understand and can do.

**Student self-assessment:** Student self-monitoring, self-assessment and self-evaluation can help students take ownership of their learning. Very simple self-assessment approaches include using a traffic light system against the learning intention. Students ask themselves 'To what extent did I achieve this learning intention?' and on the top of their work indicate a simple circle to indicate a traffic light. Green means 'I got it', orange means 'I'm nearly there but still need some help' and red indicates 'I haven't got it yet'.

**Anticipation Guide:** One of my personal favourites is the Anticipation Guide. Anticipation Guides provide educators "with some understanding of the quality and quantity of prior knowledge students have about the ideas in the reading assignment" (Anders & Spitler, 2007, p171 in Hennessy,

2021, p158). Anticipation Guides are particularly useful when teaching subskills of language comprehension, such as background knowledge and syntax. In this approach, students read the statements and identify whether the statement is 'true or false', or 'agree or disagree'.

### Anticipation Guide example

**What do I know about tigers?**

| | True | False |
|---|---|---|
| Tigers are very fast swimmers | | |
| Tigers are carnivores and will eat whatever they can catch | | |
| Female tigers can have up to five babies at a time | | |
| Tigers can weigh up to 200kg | | |
| Tigers like to be on their own | | |
| The body length of a tiger is usually one metre long | | |
| Tigers usually hunt in packs | | |
| Every tiger has a slightly different striped pattern | | |
| Tigers are a critically endangered animal | | |
| Tigers live in Australia and America | | |
| There are now fewer than 500 Sumatran tigers left in the wild | | |
| Tigers can live up to a maximum of 10 years of age | | |

An example of an Anticipation Guide – a useful formative assessment tool for identifying student background knowledge before and after teaching a topic.

**KWL chart:** An acronym for **K**now, **W**ant to know and **L**earnt, KWL charts are a useful visual organiser for students to record what they know before starting a knowledge unit. They are also an effective starting point for discussion with peers about what they would like to know, as well as a scaffold for building connections and a way to show what they have learnt after a unit (Hennessy, 2021, p159).

## KWL chart example

| Year 5 First Nations History |
| --- |
| Prior to and after European settlement, what do we know about Indigenous Australian people's:<br><br>a.  culture and traditions?<br>b.  use of the environment? |

| What do I KNOW about Indigenous Australian people's culture and traditions? | What do I WANT to know about Indigenous Australian people's culture and traditions? | What have I LEARNT about Indigenous Australian people's culture and traditions? |
| --- | --- | --- |
| Before European settlement: | | |
| After European settlement: | | |

An example of a KWL chart for identifying student background knowledge before and after teaching a Year 5 First Nations unit on pre- and post-European settlement.

## What are the Australian minimum requirements for assessment?

In the Australian Institute for Teaching and School Leadership (AITSL) standards, Standard 5.1, at the Graduate standard, states that teachers are to:

> *"Demonstrate understanding of assessment strategies, including informal and formal, diagnostic, formative and summative approaches to assess student learning."*

A lead teacher is expected to:

> *"Evaluate school assessment policies and strategies to support colleagues with: using assessment data to diagnose learning needs, complying with curriculum, system and/or school assessment requirements using a range of assessment strategies"*
>
> ~ AITSL (2017)

## Effective use of data

To ensure teachers are meeting AITSL standards there are many considerations teachers must make to be data informed in their teaching. These include the following:

### Assessment must have a clear purpose

What is the purpose of the assessment? What information are you seeking and how will you use the data?

### Assessments must be evidence aligned

Assessments must be able to provide information about the subskills of skilled reading that are aligned with reading science. Subskills of reading include phonemic awareness (PA), alphabetic code knowledge, decoding skill, language comprehension and fluency proficiency.

Helpful questions to determine what assessments to use include:

- To what extent are the student's PA skills (phonemic blending, phonemic segmentation, phonemic manipulation) developed? A PA screener is essential here.
- To what extent are students able to identify the names and phonemes of the alphabetic code? A criterion-referenced phonics screener such as the Phonics Books Screening test or non-word spelling screener such as the Astronaut Invented spelling Test-2 (AIST-2 – Neilson) will identify these skills.
- To what proficiency can students decode words? Examples include: Vowel Consonant words (VC) such as 'in'; Consonant Vowel Consonant words (CVC) such as 'hot'; Consonant Vowel Consonant Consonant words (CVCC) such as 'hint'; Consonant Consonant Vowel Consonant words (CCVC) such as 'plum'; Consonant Consonant Vowel Consonant Consonant words (CCVCC) such as 'drink'; ai/ay/a-e digraphs; trigraphs; and multisyllabic words, etc. A non-word decoding screener is essential here, preferably one that will then support you in making decisions around what decodable texts might be appropriate at students' level of decoding skill for independent reading practice.
- What is the rate of oral reading automaticity of the students? Are students on a trajectory towards end-of-year expected oral reading fluency (ORF) measures? What is the fluency rate of non-word decoding, single-letter fluency, phonemic segmentation? A DIBELS® 8th Edition or Acadience ORF or Test of Word Reading Efficiency

(TOWRE) assessment, as well as the many subskill tests to assess the mini subskills, are great recommendations here, as is the MultiLit WARP. These are quick one-minute measures with a high reliability of risk indication.

- What is the students' proficiency in language comprehension (understanding of vocabulary, oral retell, language complexity, comprehension of language)? A language comprehension screener such as CUBED NLM Listening will provide excellent data on students' language comprehension skills.
- What areas of spelling does a student demonstrate proficiency, in terms of phonological, orthographic and morphological knowledge? Although we are not specifically addressing spelling in this book, it may be helpful to be aware of excellent non-word spelling assessments that will provide valuable diagnostic data about your students' spelling proficiency and needs. I highly recommend the Macquarie University MOTIf series, including the DiSTn (phonics) and the DiSTm (morphology) screener.

## Assessment data must be analysed and responded to promptly with rigour

Something I have noticed during my career is that collecting data is often not the problem – as this is often in abundance – but it is what is done with it afterwards that is lacking. Dr Matthew Burns (2022) articulates this well with his comment that "schools are data rich, but decision-making poor".

Schools are incredibly busy places and teachers have demanding roles, so something I strongly encourage is to not only map out when testing will take place throughout the year, but then also when the analysis of student data will occur. This way, it is scheduled and forms part of the essential underpinnings of the very busy calendar. This scheduling needs to occur as soon after the actual assessment as possible. I encourage school leaders to provide time for teachers to analyse this data, such as during staff meetings and professional learning committee meetings or collaborative times.

A powerful way to streamline data analysis is to use a disciplined dialogue approach. Disciplined dialogue is a systematic approach for analysing data with three guiding questions:

- *What is the data telling us?*
- *Why do we think this is so?*
- *What are we going to do about it?*

This approach provides a framework for really digging deep into the assessment data to identify student strengths, required differentiation, intervention and target setting for growth. I will elaborate on this framework with a template for teacher use later in this chapter.

## Moving away from 'benchmarking' and 'levels' of reading proficiency

> *"I have sought studies that would support the original contention that we could facilitate student learning by placing kids in the right levels of text. Of course, guided reading and levelled books are so widely used it would make sense that there would be lots of evidence as to their efficacy. Except that there is not"*
>
> ~ Shanahan (2011)

There is no scientific-based evidence behind benchmarking and giving students a 'reading level' (Shanahan, 2011). Benchmarking is aligned with the whole language approach to reading, which was debunked decades ago. Reading is a multifaceted and complex skill and, as such, assessment data needs to provide componential information about the subskills of reading, including PA, alphabetic code knowledge, decoding ability and fluency, not a level.

A running record also provides invalid and incomprehensive information about a child's reading ability. On many occasions, children may appear to be 'reading' at a level 16 or 20, for example, and yet after doing diagnostic assessments in decoding, they are unable to decode a non-word, meaning they have no word attack skills for unknown words. Dr Matthew Burns (2022) reported that a common reading benchmark system found in schools had a very poor accuracy rating in terms of validity and accuracy in levelling students in reading. He said:

> *"We found that the Fountas and Pinnell Benchmark Assessment System had about 54% diagnostic accuracy. It identified children as good readers and struggling readers about as accurately as if you were to flip a coin."*

If we go back to the Australian teaching standards for a moment, in the Assessment and Feedback standard – Standard 5.4, at the graduate level, teachers are expected to: *'Demonstrate the capacity to interpret student assessment data to evaluate student learning* and modify *teaching practice.'* At the Highly Accomplished teacher standard, teachers are expected to: *'Work with colleagues to use data from internal and external student assessments for evaluating learning and teaching, identifying interventions and modifying teaching practice.'* It is very clear here that teachers are expected to be able to *use data to evaluate student learning and teaching practice, identify appropriate intervention and MODIFY their teaching practice accordingly.* However, giving students a 'reading level' cannot support teachers to meet this requirement. This is because not only is the levelling system flawed, but it also provides no information to inform teachers of how to evaluate learning and modify their practice, close gaps or implement intervention. Therefore, I would argue strongly that the use of levels for reading is *against* the AITSL Standard 5.4, even at the Graduate standard.

I have recently coached two delightful teaching school leaders from a New South Wales school, who informed me that they had taken my advice and moved away from using reading levels. They replaced this ineffective approach with assessments that provide information about the subskills of reading. With this small tweak in assessment practice, they found they had a group of students that appeared to be at an appropriate 'level' for their year group, but when they administered evidence-based assessments, they could not decode a CVC non-word, meaning they were unable to decode unfamiliar words at the simplest level. In these instances, these students had learnt to memorise whole words – which is what poor readers do (Hanford, 2019). Reading is a multifaceted and complex skill and as such, it is not something that can be determined with a level (and a flawed levelling system at that).

## Evidence-based alternative to assessing reading skill

When I am supporting teachers to move away from benchmarking and levelling students, what I find is that it makes sense to them as to why we would do this, but understandably, the following thinking follows: "If we are not using levels, then what do we use?" I recommend the following two steps as a starting point.

1. Identify the proficiency of decoding accuracy. As you are teaching your systematic phonics code, monitor student progress in a chart like the one overleaf. This is a far more effective way to measure progress, it provides diagnostic data, can inform instruction and the types of texts (decodable for emerging readers) to practise the skills.

| Student names | Can decode VC words | Can decode CVC words | Can decode CVCC words | Can decode CCVC words |
|---|---|---|---|---|
|  |  |  |  |  |
|  |  |  |  |  |
|  |  |  |  |  |

2. The other shift is in how to change the language from a 'reading level' to data-informed language. Here is an example of how this looks:

| Levelled reading language | Data-informed language |
|---|---|
| Holly is reading at Level 16. | Holly is able to read CCVC words (for example, slim, flat, trot). Holly can decode words with ay/ai/a/a-e graphemes. Holly needs support to decode words with the ee/ea/ey graphemes. Holly will be engaged in a Tier 2 small group intervention three times per week for the next five weeks, to explicitly teach her how to decode single syllable words with the ee/ea/ey graphemes. |
| Holly is reading at Level 16. Gives no clue as to the subskills of reading, nor does it provide data on how the teacher can take the student forward or set a target for growth. | This is an easy and effective way to determine next steps in moving forward with decoding skills and in how to set targets for growth. |

## Streamlining the data-analysis process

Data analysis can be a bit overwhelming at times and it can be easy to get drawn into a rabbit hole with lots of interesting information. A solution for this is to adopt a disciplined dialogue approach. Disciplined dialogue provides a clear focus and framework for targeted analysis and action planning with three guiding questions:

1. What is the data telling us?
2. Why do we think this is so?
3. What (if anything) are we going to do about it?

Below is a template for you to use in group data chats. I suggest teachers have highlighters on hand for colour blocking, as it is so much easier to see patterns and trends when pertinent data is highlighted and blocked out. When colour blocking, I suggest you adopt the colour-coding approach of standardised assessments: blue (above benchmark), green (at benchmark), yellow (some risk) and red (at risk).

### Discussion guide for data chats

This guide is good enlarged to A3. Highlight data in four colours: green – at expected level, orange – area of growth, pink – area of concern, blue – above expected level. Choose one focus area at a time and follow the guiding questions below. A target is not necessary for each question, but at least one in each focus area is a good guide. Remember to always celebrate the good stuff!

| What is the data telling us? | Why do we think this is so? | What are we going to do about it? |
| --- | --- | --- |
| **Focus area** | | |
| What are the strengths? | What is the story behind the data? | Targets and next steps |
| What are the growth areas? | What is the story behind the data? | Targets and next steps |

| What is the data telling us? | Why do we think this is so? | What are we going to do about it? |
|---|---|---|
| What are the concerns? | What is the story behind the data? | Targets and next steps |
| What are the above expected progress areas for students? | What is the story behind the data? | Targets and next steps |

I like to break these questions down further into strengths, growth areas, concerns and above-expected level progress. Colour blocking is useful in quickly identifying trends. It also makes it easy to convert to percentages if you have colours to guide your focus. It is important to ensure you include enough time to analyse all areas and address all three questions. So, my recommendation is that if you and your team have 60 minutes allocated to analyse fluency ORF data, for example, set a timer for 20 minutes on each of the three questions for that time.

## Disciplined dialogue questions during data chats

The first question, *'What is the data telling us?'* is about looking at students or the group of students – at, below and above expected standard, norms or benchmark. With the second question the task is to delve into the story behind the data, asking *'Why do we think this is so?'* It is essential to investigate if it may be because the underlying issue is another subcomponent of reading, for example, poor PA or phonic gaps, or language comprehension deficits. In this case, further diagnostic assessments and investigation will be required to promptly identify and respond to the students' needs. It is also important to reflect on the quality of teaching. For example, have the students engaged in adequate explicit instruction or practise in the target area? Has the content covered been based on high impact, evidence-based research? Has the evidence-based synthetic phonics program been implemented with fidelity? This is an important time for teachers to reflect on the question: 'What is the impact of my teaching?'

The final question, *'What are we going to do about it?'* is when teachers plan the next steps and set targets. These targets need to be SMART (**S**pecific, **M**easurable, **A**chievable, **R**ealistic and **T**ime-bound) to be of any value. An example may be: *'By the end of Week 9, Term 3, 2023, 90% of Pre-Primary students will be able to segment and blend CVC words with satpin graphemes, with accuracy on nine out of 10 occasions.'*

## Decision-making around assessment data

Depending on the assessment type, it is essential that teachers are well equipped to make effective decisions around instructional and intervention needs of students. For example, when teachers are analysing standardised oral reading fluency data, they need to know that a fluency screen, while it is an accurate predictor of risk, will not provide the information needed as to why a student is not achieving an expected standard in reading automaticity. Teachers will need to know the cut-off benchmarks, and then for students identified in the 'some risk' yellow range and 'at risk' red range, that they conduct further Tier 2 diagnostic screening to identify the root of the fluency issue. To take a medical analogy, the ORF screener is the blood pressure check and the diagnostic screening is the blood work to identify the cause of the blood pressure being out of range.

### Example 1

Take an example of a small group of 11 Year 1 students in an end-of-year screen on the University of Oregon's DIBELS® 8th fluency assessment (see overleaf). By the end of Year 1, the expected ORF is 60 words correct per minute (WCPM). If we look at the third column, at a quick glance, we can see that three students have achieved this benchmark (green range) or above (blue range). Secondly, five students have been identified as needing intensive support, three students have been identified in the yellow 'some risk' range requiring strategic support. Here, the eight students identified with risk indicators require further diagnostic screening to identify the source of their fluency problems. Quite frequently, it is a PA or decoding difficulty that is underlying the lack of automaticity in reading, and these subskills of reading need to be addressed promptly with targeted intervention. Other considerations would be to check prosody, comprehension monitoring and oral language as contributors to the fluency concerns. Dibels® 8th and Acadience also contain subtests such as Phoneme Segmentation Fluency (PSF) and non-word reading (NWR) for the early years that can provide clues as to the cause of a child's fluency difficulties. I highly recommend administering these quick and useful subtests.

| Colour code | Oral reading fluency words correct per minute analysis | Number of students | Percentage |
|---|---|---|---|
| Blue range | Above benchmark | 1 student | 12.5% |
| Green range | At benchmark; minimal risk | 2 students | 25% |
| Yellow range | Some risk; strategic support required | 3 students | 37.5% |
| Red range | At risk; intensive support required | 5 students | 62.5% |

Analysis of a group of 11 Year 1 students on the University of Oregon's Dibels® 8th benchmark ORF assessment, 2020.

From a Tier 1, whole-class perspective, based on the minimal number of students reaching end-of-year proficiency, I would consider: *'Have these students had regular exposure to "at grade level" text reading through daily choral reading of teacher-led echo and repeated reading throughout the week to build reading fluency?'* If not, I would recommend these high impact approaches for the whole class. I would also be looking at the Tier 1 instruction of reading in a more general view in terms of the quality of explicit teaching of phonics, decoding and building of background knowledge as possible sources of the low number of students reaching benchmark.

### Example 2

Another example of analysing student data to inform next steps is the case study on page 64. This data is based on the responses of a Year 3 student, in a non-word decoding screener, similar to the Phonics Books Placement Test. This student had a spiky profile in that they had some difficulties at the single sound level, CVC level, CCVC and CCVCC level, yet they read whole, high-frequency words with a high level of accuracy and speed. This student had been taught in the early years of school with the ineffective approach of learning whole words with flash cards.

If we look at Part 5 in the table on the next page, you will see that the student read pseudo CCVC words brem as broom, stem as storm and flim as film; and in Part 6 they read stemp as stamp, grupt as grumpy and stonk as sink. These responses indicate the student was not using letter sound knowledge to decode these unfamiliar words, but instead was trying to approximate the unknown with familiar real words through guessing.

On further diagnostic screening to identify alphabetic code knowledge, I identified that this student did not know many of the common digraphs, such as ai, oa, o-e, and had significantly weak PA proficiency. After three months of intervention, many of the words that were a struggle had been remedied with the implementation of PA, synthetic phonics and writing intervention. The best outcome was that the student had completely moved away from the ineffective strategy of guessing unknown words and was utilising decoding skills of segmenting and blending to read unfamiliar words.

## Teacher confidence

Interestingly, international studies show that many educators do not feel adequately equipped or confident in using and analysing assessment data. Certainly, in personal conversations with teachers or even pre-service teachers embarking on their final practicum, questions that frequently pop up are:

- *What types of assessment tools do I use?*
- *What is formative assessment and how does it look in a lesson?*
- *How do I use the data to plan?*
- *If we don't do running records and benchmarking, then what do we do?*

In my experience, as a deputy principal and literacy consultant, I have spent much of my time coaching teachers in how to use evidence-aligned assessments and how to unpack assessment data to plan units of work.

## Case study: decoding assessment and analysis

| Part | Code knowledge | Decoding assessment material | Student response | Analysis |
|------|----------------|------------------------------|------------------|----------|
| 1 | Single sound knowledge | s, a, o, i, x, u, c | These letter sounds were unknown but were read as letter names | • Confused letter names with letter sounds<br>• Student needs intervention in identifying all alphabet letter sounds |
| | | j | Read as /g/ only | |
| | | o | Read as /oo/ | |
| 2 | Consonant digraphs | ll, ff, ss, zz | Read correctly | • Consonant digraphs in the assessment all known |
| 3 | CVC words | wug | weg | • CVC decoding not entirely secure |
| 4 | CVCC words | lant | land | • CVCC decoding not secure |
| 5 | CCVC words | brem<br>stem<br>flim | broom<br>storm<br>film | • CCVC decoding is not secure<br>• Student appears to be guessing or approximating real words |
| 6 | CCVCC words | stemp<br>grupt<br>stonk | stamp<br>grumpy<br>sink | • CCVCC decoding is not secure<br>• Student appears to be guessing or approximating real words |
| 7 | Digraphs | drain<br>bloat | dran<br>blot | • Digraph knowledge is not secure<br>• Assessment indicated unknown digraphs: oa, ai, |
| 8 | High-frequency words | who, people, world, talk, school, there, soccer | Read correctly with confidence and speed | • This profile is indicative of a student that has been taught reading in a whole-word approach |

## Data-informed practice audit

Something you might like to do in your school is an audit on data-informed practice. A starting point can be found at the end of this chapter. This could be done in teams or as a whole staff to reflect on what practices are working well and what might need a bit of tweaking. A quote from the Association of Independent Schools of NSW (AISNSW) sums up data-informed practice beautifully:

> *"Simply having data offers very little insight.* The value comes from being able to interpret what the data means for individuals, groups and whole classes of students, and then to use it to make decisions about classroom instruction and wellbeing interventions. *Data-informed practice is the systematic use of a variety of forms and levels of data by educators for this very purpose – improving student learning, classroom practice and overall wellbeing"*
>
> ~ AISNSW

## Summary

- Assessment data is information that we use to improve teaching and learning. It needs to have a clearly defined purpose, be collected systematically, responded to flexibly and responsively, and monitored rigorously.
- Data across a school should take many forms: formative, summative, diagnostic and preventative. In terms of preventative approaches, universal screening is crucial.
- There are three different techniques of using assessment: assessment *of, for* and *as* learning.
- Instead of a reading 'level', questions for teachers include: To what proficiency can students decode words? What is the student's oral reading rate for fluency?
- There is no scientific-based evidence behind benchmarking and giving students a 'reading level' (Shanahan, 2011).
- When moving away from benchmarking and levelling students, start by identifying the proficiency of decoding accuracy, PA ability and ORF against end-of-year ORF expectations.
- International studies show that many educators do not feel adequately equipped or confident in using and analysing assessment data.

## Professional discussion

- Using DIBELS® or Acadience fluency screening tools, what percentage of your students are in the blue, green, yellow and red zones in each subtest? This is the first step in analysing your data for universal screening three times per year.
- How well is data used to inform teaching and learning? How do you know?
- What evidence-based assessments are used across the school? Do they reflect a componential view of reading and spelling?
- How is data collated/analysed in your school? To what extent is this approach making an 'impact' on learning? How do you know?

## Data-informed practice audit

With a rating of 1 to 5 – 5 being always, consistently or exceptionally well – to what extent do you and your school demonstrate data-informed practice?

| | Unsure | 1 | 2 | 3 | 4 | 5 |
|---|---|---|---|---|---|---|
| Year level teams are established in the school for collaboration | | | | | | |
| Collaborative teams are effective and focused on knowing their impact | | | | | | |
| There is a clear framework of assessment and data-analysis dates embedded in the school calendar across the school year | | | | | | |
| Teachers have regular opportunities to plan collaboratively | | | | | | |
| There is a streamlined approach for data-analysis sessions based on disciplined dialogue questions | | | | | | |
| There is a strong culture of data-informed practice and language use in the school | | | | | | |

|  | Unsure | 1 | 2 | 3 | 4 | 5 |
|---|---|---|---|---|---|---|
| Staff has a strong understanding and application of explicit, immediate feedback for students | | | | | | |
| Visible learning approaches are embedded, including learning intentions and success criteria for every lesson | | | | | | |
| Teachers strive for challenge in students and not merely 'doing your best' | | | | | | |
| Teachers effectively build relationships and trust in classrooms, so children feel safe to make mistakes and learn from others | | | | | | |
| All staff believe that all students can improve | | | | | | |
| Teachers see assessment as informing their impact and next steps | | | | | | |
| Teachers use data effectively to inform planning, differentiation and intervention | | | | | | |
| Evidenced-informed Tier 1 assessments are utilised for universal screening followed by prompt analysis and action | | | | | | |
| We effectively use Tier 1 assessment data to track student progress and inform school decisions | | | | | | |
| We regularly celebrate small wins and achievements in terms of student progress and development of teacher capacity as a staff | | | | | | |

## Chapter 5

# RESPONSE TO INTERVENTION

"Without RTI practices, educators may overlook many children's reading difficulties, fail to address them properly, or even inadvertently exacerbate them by faulty instruction"

~ Louise Spear-Swerling (2015)

## Chapter overview

- Anticipation Guide
- Introduction
- What is Response to Intervention (RTI)?
- Why is it so important?
- The five key components of RTI
- High-quality, evidence-based classroom instruction
- Tiered instruction
- Ongoing student assessment – universal screening and progress monitoring
- Parent involvement
- Schoolwide RTI approaches
- How does instruction look in each tier?
- Guidelines for effective Tier 2 and Tier 3 intervention
- Writing effective SMART goals
- Reading difficulty profiles
- Summary
- Professional discussion

- Anticipation Guide answers
- RTI School Reflection Tool
- Example SMART goals for documented plans

## Anticipation Guide

| Anticipation Guide | True/ False |
|---|---|
| A school has RTI embedded if it has a phonics program in place for intervention | |
| Universal screening should occur across the school once per year | |
| Progress monitoring should occur every three to five weeks for Tier 2 instruction and every one to two weeks for Tier 3 intervention | |
| There are generally three broad categories of reading difficulty | |

## Introduction

I've included Response to Intervention (RTI) in the high impact instruction section of this book for a number of reasons, but I will touch on three now. The first is related to its effect size of 1.07 (Hattie & Zierer, 2018), which by all accounts, is huge.

The second reason is that we could be the most skilled educators, with reading science embedded in our structured literacy classrooms, but if we don't have schoolwide systems of prevention and response in terms of RTI, then we're not providing social equity for all students. For this equity to exist, RTI is essential in every classroom, in every school.

The third reason is that literacy is a fundamental right of every child. With RTI in place in every school, we avoid the potential lifelong consequences of a student experiencing social-emotional turmoil and missed opportunities, due to illiteracy or literacy struggle.

### What is Response to Intervention?

RTI sits under the umbrella term of a Multi-Tiered System of Support (MTSS), which is both preventative and responsive in nature. Based on the continuous cycle of teaching and learning, RTI involves ongoing reflection on the impact of teaching and intervention approaches. A common misconception about RTI is that it is an 'intervention program', rather than a schoolwide, systematic approach to supporting all students. It is not a one-size-fits-all approach and can look slightly different in every school.

## Why is it so important?

When considering the 'why' behind RTI, I like to think of schools without RTI as a bucket with a crack at the base. Like a leaky bucket in the real world, as water enters, there will always be a stream of water escaping. If we apply the analogy to a school, then without robust schoolwide processes and supports, there will always be students slipping through the cracks of education.

When students are provided whole-class, evidence-based instruction within an RTI system, 95% of these can be reading effectively by the end of Year 1 (Moats, 2010). Although, sadly, this is not the case for most schools.

RTI has the potential to close the gap between the students that *do* reach reading proficiency in this timeframe and *those that have the potential*. That is not to say we are forgetting our remaining 5% of students; as with our 5% of learners that require more intensive supports, RTI is also the key.

## The five key components of RTI

The five key elements in an effective RTI model are:

1. High-quality, evidence-based classroom instruction
2. Tiered instruction
3. Ongoing student assessment and progress monitoring
4. Parent involvement
5. Schoolwide RTI approaches

## High-quality, evidence-based classroom instruction

The first and arguably most important starting point for RTI is to be providing high-quality, evidence-based instruction for *all* students, also known as Tier 1 instruction. For this to occur, teachers need to be highly skilled in delivering educational practices that encompass a componential view of reading (Spear-Swerling, 2015). This involves having a strong conceptual and practical knowledge of all the subskills essential for skilled reading and writing, which we will explore in Part 2.

In addition to being highly skilled in what children need in terms of evidence-based instruction, we also need to be skilled in the 'how' of structured literacy instruction. A whole-school RTI framework requires a high level of teacher skill in explicitly teaching the essential subskills of reading and writing, along with high-rigour differentiation, with flexible pull-aside groups through the week to close learning gaps. Teaching and learning are also based on high expectations for every student, with quality assessment data-informing lesson and unit planning.

## Tiered instruction

RTI consists of a three-tiered approach to instruction, frequently illustrated as a triangle divided into three layers (see the diagram below).

### The three tiers of RTI

Increasing intensity and frequency

High-quality, whole-class instruction for all students

**Tier 1**
Effective, high-quality teaching based on scientifically proven research (approximately 80% of students)

Small-group, evidence-based intervention

**Tier 2**
Additional small-group intervention to provide opportunity to catch up (approximately 15% of students)

1:1 intensive support

**Tier 3**
Targeted intervention for individual children requiring intensive support, including learning disabilities (approximately 5% of students)

Tier 1 is depicted as the largest section, as it is preventative in nature, whereas Tier 2 is the middle section and Tier 3 the pointy end. Tier 1 instruction entails quality evidence-based instruction and high rigour, low differentiation, which when implemented with fidelity can meet the needs of 80% of students (De Bruin, 2021).

Students not making the expected progress in whole-class instruction will require supplementary support, such as small-group intervention. In a true RTI model, this support will typically be required for 15% of students. This additional support is aimed at catching students up to their peers. For most students this 'double dose' effect will be sufficient to close the achievement gap within a short timeframe. Intervention is always *in addition* to the regular classroom Tier 1 daily literacy instruction. Tier 2 interventions can be provided in class by the teacher while the rest of the class works independently, or it may be provided by a suitably qualified literacy support teacher or education assistant.

A small percentage of students, typically 5% – despite high-quality, whole-class Tier 1 instruction and the additional Tier 2 support – will require intensive, individualised support. These students are often diagnosed with a specific learning disorder in reading (dyslexia) or spelling and writing (dysgraphia). Schools without RTI, or in the early stages of embedding an RTI framework, will frequently have a higher percentage of students requiring Tier 2 and Tier 3 intervention until the robust processes and systems are firmly in place.

| Tier 1: Whole class | Tier 2: 15% of students | Tier 3: 5% of students |
| --- | --- | --- |
| • Daily, high-quality, evidence-based explicit teaching for the whole class<br><br>• High-rigour differentiation in terms of support, pull-aside groups, but not 'ability grouping' per se<br><br>• High expectations for every student<br><br>• Use of formative assessment, adjusting instruction to student needs<br><br>• Decodable texts in the early years that are aligned with a systematic phonics sequence | • Small-group intervention in addition to the literacy block (three to five students)<br><br>• Increased intensity and frequency (perhaps 3 × 30 minutes per week)<br><br>• Intervention is aligned to specific subskills of difficulty identified<br><br>• Clear, short-term targets and progress monitoring<br><br>• Frequent progress monitoring using standardised tools (every three to five weeks)<br><br>• Aim is to catch these students up and close the reading gap | • 1:1 or 2:1 intervention<br><br>• Clear plan with specific targets<br><br>• Often will involve a case management approach with school psychologist and will investigate underlying learning disabilities<br><br>• Longer duration of intervention/support<br><br>• Frequent progress monitoring using standardised tools (every one to two weeks)<br><br>• May be provided by allied professionals or specialised personnel |

## Ongoing student assessment

### Universal screening

The third key element of RTI involves ongoing student assessment, which includes universal screening and rigorous progress monitoring. To reference a medical analogy, universal screening is like a regular blood pressure check-up. A simple blood pressure reading doesn't tell us what the problem is, but does provide an indication of whether things are in the expected range. If the blood pressure reading indicates there is a problem, then further testing may be advised.

The same is the case for universal screening for all students. "Prevention and intervention are better, in both human and practical terms, than waiting until children's reading difficulties become severe, entrenched, and greatly compounded by behavioural or social-emotional factors" (Spear-Swerling, 2015).

Universal screening assessments are brief, norm-referenced, standardised tools that indicate if students are on track to reach end-of-year expectations. Educators employ screening of every student ideally three times per year in a range of literacy areas, including PA, decoding, language comprehension and ORF. Students identified at risk will then engage in further diagnostic screening in a componential approach to reading. This componential approach to diagnostic testing greatly facilitates early identification of reading problems (Spear-Swerling, 2015).

Of course, none of this is relevant or useful if we don't use the data promptly, with high rigour to inform decisions in terms of support, resourcing and instructional improvement. For example, if Year 1 screening data indicates that 50% of students require intervention in PA, then phonemic instruction in Foundation and Year 1 is problematic and needs to be improved. Likewise, if students that have been engaging in Tier 2 intervention are not making progress, then it is important to question the efficacy of the intervention implementation.

### Progress monitoring

Progress monitoring occurs in several ways. Following universal screening, each student's progress and achievement is monitored individually, and in comparison, with the peer group, at a classroom level and tracked at a leadership level. Decisions made regarding each student's instructional needs are based on multiple data points in context, over time. Rigorous progress monitoring can allow teachers to make informed decisions about student movement between the tiers of instruction.

Students who score below benchmark in the universal screeners require regular, brief assessment checks to ensure they are making good progress. The higher the needs of the student, the more frequent the monitoring. For example, students receiving Tier 2 intervention should be progress monitored every three to five weeks; and for Tier 3 intervention it would occur every one to two weeks. DIBELS® 8th and Acadience fluency screeners I have mentioned in this text include enough built-in progress-monitoring tools and reading passages to use in each year level on a fortnightly basis, for a whole year. These are invaluable resources for schools!

## Parent involvement

The fourth aspect of RTI is active engagement with parents. There is significant research on the impact of parent involvement on student achievement, attendance, social skills and behaviour, so it makes sense that schools strive to collaborate with parents and carers in keeping them widely informed of their child's goals and progress. In effective RTI models, parents and carers are kept informed of how students are tracking, and in the case that students require specific intervention, they are provided regular updates on student goals for the intervention/s, the staff providing the instruction, how often and when.

From a Tier 1 perspective, providing parents an outline of end-of-year expectations is a great way to keep parents involved in their child's learning journey. Another example of this collaboration is based on my personal experience as a deputy principal, where we provided regular opportunities for parents to engage in coffee chat sessions to learn about aspects of literacy throughout the year. Parental involvement in children's literacy experiences has been found to be more powerful in effect than any other background variables, including social class, level of parental education and family size (Flouri & Buchanan, 2004).

## Schoolwide RTI approaches

Due to the systemic nature of RTI, it requires effective school leadership with ongoing evidence-based professional learning for teachers. Of more than 1,300 studies, "teachers who receive substantial professional development – an average of 49 hours in the nine studies – can boost their student's achievement by about 21 percentile points" (Yoon et al, 2007).

As such, teaching and non-teaching staff need to have a thorough understanding of the language of RTI, how to implement reading science, including the pillars of reading (oral language, PA, phonics, fluency, vocabulary and reading comprehension), a strong conceptual understanding of the development of reading skills of typically developing children, risk indicators for students with learning difficulties and learning disorders, and how to set SMART (**S**pecific, **M**easurable, **A**chievable, **R**ealistic, **T**ime-bound) goals for those requiring additional support. Furthermore, schools with effective RTI approaches have a culture of data-informed planning and practice, with prompt and rigorous data analysis and response.

## How does instruction look in each tier?

### Tier 1: High-quality, whole-class teaching

- Evidence-based teaching approaches, including: a culture of high expectations for every student, explicit teaching, checking for understanding, effective questioning, ongoing formative assessment and timely, specific feedback.
- There are clear and explicit learning intentions and instructions in every lesson.
- High-rigour differentiation with pull-aside groups to reteach or target specific skills in Tier 1 instruction. Differentiation is focused on outcome and support rather than content as a general rule, but there are times when differentiated content is essential, such as the use of decodable readers based on individual decoding skill, for independent reading.
- Quality assessment data informs unit and lesson planning.
- Explicit teaching of phonemic awareness, phonics, vocabulary, fluency as well as the other subskills of language comprehension, through knowledge-rich units.
- Whole-school implementation of daily structured literacy blocks that are aligned with reading science.
- Evidence-based approaches to the teaching of writing, including the explicit teaching of sentence-level writing.
- *Daily*, structured, sequential synthetic phonics instruction for years F–2.
- Evidence-based, structured spelling instruction for Years 3–6, including explicit teaching of morphology and etymology.

- *Daily* high-quality texts, both fiction and non-fiction, are read to all students to build language comprehension, background knowledge and vocabulary – explicitly teaching up to 10 new words per week.
- Writing is preceded by oral language opportunities; taught explicitly with modelling, think-alouds and worked examples at the sentence and text level.
- Graphic organisers are provided as a visual scaffold for paragraph and genre level writing.

## Tier 2: Small-group intervention and additional support

- Evidence-based, small-group instructional support that targets specific student needs, with short-term targeted goals in place; shared with all stakeholders.
- Rigorous, regular progress monitoring enables teachers to ensure that students are making sufficient progress towards goals set.
- Support is increased in terms of frequency and intensity.
- Student progress is monitored in an ongoing capacity, with regular review (three to five weeks) of student's response to intervention.

## Tier 3: Individualised support

- Generally 1:1 or 2:1 intensive instruction, with increased frequency.
- Multiple sources of assessment will guide the decision-making process. This may include speech pathologist, psychologist or paediatrician involvement.
- Documented plans include SMART targets that are monitored regularly (ideally every one to two weeks).

## Guidelines for effective Tier 2 and Tier 3 intervention

Although most schools have some form of intervention approach, what differs is the quality of this intervention. Although approaches, strategies or programs may differ, there are a few essential considerations for intervention that should be evident in every context:

1. Evidence-based, universal screening and diagnostic assessments pinpoint the specific subskill/s of reading difficulty, not a reading 'level'. All aspects of difficulty are addressed.
2. Intervention programs are evidence-based or evidence-informed, and *in addition* to the literacy block.

3. The intervention plan is clear, with specific, measurable and time-bound targets that specifically address the subskill deficits of reading identified. There is an exit plan in place from the outset.
4. Intervention is sequential, cumulative and systematic – concepts and skills are taught in a step-by-step approach, following a sequence of progression, with ongoing review of previously learnt skills.
5. Rigorous progress monitoring is ongoing and communicated with all involved. For Tier 2 students this may be every three to five weeks and for Tier 3 students this would be every one to two weeks.
6. Staff engaged in the delivery of intervention are highly qualified in what they are teaching and have a clear understanding of student goals.
7. Responding to student difficulties is prompt, with intervention in place at the first sign of academic difficulties.
8. All stakeholders are well informed of the goals, the planned timeframe for intervention and how often progress monitoring will occur.

## Writing effective SMART goals

When setting goals for students – particularly those requiring intensive intervention – it is essential that we have clear goals in place. Although in my experience as a learning difficulties support teacher and deputy principal, goals for students were often either non-existent, lacking an end date or impossible to measure. I liken this approach to setting off on a destination with no end point or timeframe in mind. Or to a medical analogy, like prescribing an ongoing course of antibiotics for a patient.

If we are serious about implementing effective intervention for students, we must be clear on what we are putting in place and for how long, with a very clear process for monitoring progress, just as we would do in the medical world.

Below is a template I have used with teachers to scaffold the process to ensure goals are SMART. When setting goals for students, it is important to consider the following:

- What are the student's strengths, needs and interests?
- What data do you have about the student? Assessment results?
- What are the student's motivators or 'carrots'?
- What do you ultimately want the student to achieve by the end of the year? Then backward map the steps to achieve this standard and break it down into subskills and goals.

- Have you consulted parents on prior assessments or reports from allied professionals or previous schools? Can previous teachers provide useful data or information?
- What do you see as expected achievement each week towards the goal – is it realistic, yet challenging?

Then frame the goals using the following sentence prompts:

| | |
|---|---|
| **Time bound**<br><br>By the end of...<br>By Week, Term, Year... | *Example:*<br>*By the end of Week 9,*<br>*Term 3, 2023* |
| **Specific/Realistic/Achievable**<br><br>'Student' will be able to...<br>identify/blend/read/write/spell... | *Example:*<br>*John will be able to segment*<br>*CVC words orally from Unit 2 of*<br>*the Sounds-Write program* |
| **Measurable**<br><br>...with accuracy on 9/10 occasions<br>...with fluency on 9/10 occasions<br>...with 90% accuracy | *Example:*<br>*...with accuracy on 9/10 occasions* |

Worked example of the targets above:

> *By the end of Week 9, Term 3, 2023, John will be able to segment CVC words orally from Unit 2 of the Sounds-Write program with accuracy on nine out of 10 occasions.*

Additional examples of SMART targets can be found at the end of the chapter.

## Reading difficulty profiles

As there are so many facets to skilled reading, there are many factors that can underlie a child's struggles. However, research indicates that there are generally three broad categories of reading difficulty (Sleeman, 2021). Understanding the general profile of reading difficulty can provide a starting point for understanding what may be going on for a student and, in turn, know what supports and intervention to put into place (Spear-Swerling, 2015). These reading difficulty profiles are based on the Simple View of Reading (SVR):

Decoding × Language Comprehension = Reading Comprehension
(D × LC = RC)

In this empirically validated model, there are two constructs that students need to be developing at the same time, with increasing proficiency; and the product of these two skills lead to reading comprehension. The three profiles are based on this model and consist of the: word reading difficulty profile, reading comprehension difficulty profile or mixed reading difficulty profile. The type of intervention a child will require will depend which category of difficulty the student is experiencing.

## Word reading difficulty profile

The word reading difficulty profile is the first of the poor reader profiles. Students with this profile tend to have at least average oral language and language comprehension skills. However, just like the decoding (or word recognition) strand of the SVR, students with this profile may have difficulties in any or all the reading subskills of phonological awareness, phonics, decoding and sight word (orthographic) knowledge of familiar words.

Students with this profile may exhibit trouble decoding or 'lifting the words off the page', but have strong oral language abilities, vocabulary and comprehension when being read *to*. Although these students may have poor reading comprehension when reading independently, the core of the reading comprehension problem is attributed to their word recognition skills. A child with this reading difficulty profile requires remediation in PA, synthetic phonics, decoding and/or fluency.

## Specific learning disorder in reading

There is a small proportion of our students that exhibit the word reading difficulty profile that may be diagnosed with dyslexia – a learning disability of neurological origin. While the term 'dyslexia' has been removed from the *Diagnostic Statistic Manual of Mental Disorders (DSM-5)* and replaced with 'specific learning disorder in reading', the fact remains that we have many students that struggle with reading, many of whom are not attributable to neurological origins. However, the response must be the same: swift, data-informed, evidence-based intervention, with rigorous progress monitoring, that is targeted to individual gaps in learning.

Chapman and Tunmer (2019) explain this perfectly: "Official use of the term *dyslexia* is as much a hindrance to change, as a rallying point for more effective reading instruction... Instead, we argue that the focus ought to be on effective classroom instruction and remedial intervention for *all* students who experience reading difficulties, regardless of the assumed causes."

## Reading comprehension difficulty profile

The second reading difficulty profile is related to language comprehension or the ability to understand spoken language. A child with a reading comprehension difficulty profile has average or better word-recognition skills (PA, phonics, decoding, sight word knowledge), but their difficulties in comprehending written text is attributed to a deficit in their language comprehension skills. This may involve gaps in any aspect of the language comprehension strand, including oral language, background knowledge, vocabulary, language structures (such as understanding of syntax, anaphora, structure of genre) and verbal reasoning (metaphor and inference).

Students with this reading difficulty profile may or may not require speech and language therapy, but may also significantly benefit from building background knowledge and explicit teaching of vocabulary, explicit teaching of sentence level skills in reading and writing, and micro skill instruction such as anaphoric reference (linking the pronoun to he/she in sentences) or explicit teaching of the different meanings of conjunctions and connectives (such as but, because, so, however, unfortunately). Students with this profile often don't exhibit difficulties until middle elementary (primary years) or beyond (Spear-Swerling, 2015).

## Mixed reading difficulty profile

Children with a mixed reading difficulty profile have word-recognition difficulties combined with core comprehension weaknesses that impairs reading comprehension. This profile may be apparent in the early years before students are reading or it may be apparent in Year 3 or later. Students with this profile require intervention to address both word recognition and reading comprehension gaps. Determining their specific underlying weaknesses in each of these constructs is the essential first step in remediating the reading problem.

## The case for a widespread understanding of reading difficulty profiles

Effective intervention in schools (and private practice) is essential in achieving equity and closing the literacy gaps between students. However, if the intervention in place is not addressing the specific reading difficulty profile of the student, then we are not going to achieve the level of literacy progress that we seek.

This starts with schools allocating time to develop teacher knowledge in the SVR, Scarborough's Reading Rope and the big six of reading, which are the fundamental skills required for skilled reading, in addition to an understanding of the reading difficulty profiles. This way, teachers will have a starting point for understanding what may be going on for a student experiencing reading difficulty and, in turn, know what supports and intervention to put into place.

Louise Spear-Swerling (2015, p215) sums up this concept and the importance of RTI in general: "Using RTI/MTSS approaches in conjunction with poor reader profiles is not perfect policy – in fact, it is a messy, imperfect policy, fraught with challenges. Still, it is the best approach we have, by a very long way, for preventing and solving children's reading problems."

## Summary

- RTI sits under the umbrella term of a MTSS, which is both preventative and responsive in nature. It has an effect size of 1.07 when implemented with fidelity.
- With RTI in place in every school, we avoid the potential lifelong consequences of a student experiencing social-emotional turmoil and missed opportunities, due to illiteracy or literacy struggle.
- RTI is not an 'intervention program', but a schoolwide, systematic approach to supporting all students. It is not a one-size-fits-all approach and can look slightly different in every school.
- When students are provided whole-class, evidence-based instruction within an RTI system, 95% of them can be reading effectively by the end of Year 1 (Moats, 2010).
- The five key elements in an effective RTI model are: high-quality, evidence-based instruction, tiered instruction, universal screening and progress monitoring, parent involvement and schoolwide RTI approaches.

- Tiered instruction consists of evidence-based daily structured literacy instruction for every student, which should meet the needs of 80% of students. Some 15% of students will require catch-up, small-group intervention and 5% of students will require intensive 1:1 or 2:1 support in addition to the literacy block.
- Universal screening is like a blood pressure check to identify students at risk three times per year.
- Setting goals for students needing additional support should be rigorous and SMART.
- There are generally three broad categories of reading difficulty (Sleeman, 2021). Understanding the general profile of reading difficulty can provide a starting point for understanding what may be going on for a student and, in turn, know what supports and intervention to put into place (Spear-Swerling, 2015).

## Professional discussion

Considering that 95% of students can be proficient readers by the end of Year 1 when evidence-based preventative and responsive approaches are in place, what is the proportion of students that meet this standard by the end of Year 1 in your school?

- What percentage of students require remediation, catch-up support or external intervention in your school? If there is more than 20%, then there is a problem with the Tier 1 instruction. Discuss.
- To what extent do you and your colleagues feel upskilled and supported in each of the components of RTI?
- How effectively are the reading difficulty profiles utilised as a starting point for understanding a student's reading struggles?

## Anticipation Guide answers

| Anticipation Guide | True/False |
| --- | --- |
| A school has RTI embedded if it has a phonics program in place for intervention | False. RTI is a systemic, whole-school approach to preventing and responding to literacy difficulties |

| Anticipation Guide | True/False |
|---|---|
| Universal screening should occur across the school once per year | False. Universal screening should take place three times per year – at the beginning, middle and end of year |
| Progress monitoring should occur every three to five weeks for Tier 2 instruction and every one to two weeks for Tier 3 intervention | True |
| There are generally three broad categories of reading difficulty | True |

## RTI School Reflection Tool

- To what extent does our school have aspects of RTI embedded?
- What aspects are making an impact on student progress and achievement?
- What do we already do well in terms of the RTI components?
- What components are areas of growth?

*The National School Improvement Tool (NSIT, ACER) is an excellent starting point for school review.*

| High-Quality Evidence-Based Literacy Instruction |
|---|
| <ul><li>Strong oral language focus throughout the school</li><li>Phonemic awareness and structured synthetic phonics</li><li>Explicit teaching of vocabulary through daily rich text read aloud</li><li>Daily fluency instruction</li><li>Language comprehension for reading and writing through knowledge-rich units</li><li>Consistent structured literacy practices within consistent literacy blocks</li></ul> <ul><li>Consistent approaches across the school with low variance scope and sequences</li><li>High rigour, low differentiation across the school</li><li>Immediate feedback to students</li><li>High expectations for every student – evident in complexity of content provided, dialogue with students and explicit feedback</li><li>Ongoing evidence-based professional learning to support teachers</li></ul> |

| Ongoing Student Assessment and Progress Monitoring | Tiered Instruction | Parent Involvement |
|---|---|---|
| • *Universal screening – three times per year utilising assessments aligned with reading science* <br><br> • *Planned dates for streamlined data analysis* <br><br> • *Teachers are skilled in data-informed practice* <br><br> • *Students identified at risk engaged in fortnightly or monthly progress monitoring* | • *Teachers are confident to identify student needs and implement in class intervention* <br><br> *Tier 1 whole-class instruction* <br><br> *Tier 2 small-group intervention* <br><br> *Tier 3 individualised intervention* | • *Ongoing communication with all stakeholders about student learning, progress and target setting* |

## Example SMART goals for documented plans

SMART: Specific, Measurable, Achievable, Realistic, Time-bound

| Phonemic awareness | *By Week 9, Term 3, 2023, Jenny will be able to orally blend individual sounds in CVC words consistently on five consecutive occasions, when given three phonemes in robot talk by an adult.* <br><br> *For example: /d/ /o/ /g/ = /dog/ /p/ /e/ /t/ = /pet/ /ch/ /i/ /n/ = /chin/* |
|---|---|
| Synthetic phonics | *By Week 9, Term 3, 2023, John will be able to read words with spellings of 'ai', 'ay' and 'a–e' graphemes, with accuracy on five consecutive occasions.* |
| Decoding | *Jenny will be able to decode CCVCC words (for example, stamp, plump, trust) consistently on five consecutive occasions by Week 5, Term 3, 2023.* <br><br> *John will read Moon Dog decodable books at the CVC level by segmenting and blending the words read, with fluency and accuracy on nine out of 10 occasions.* |

| Writing | John will improve the quality of his sentence writing by using a range of conjunctions (for example, because, but or so) by combining two simple sentences to write a compound sentence in four out of five writing lessons by Week 5, Term 3, 2023. |
|---|---|
| | At the completion of a writing task, Jenny will use a self-regulatory framework such as COPS to edit her writing accurately on four out of five occasions. |
| Reading comprehension | By Week 9, Term 3, 2023, Jenny will accurately summarise the ideas of a Year 6 non-fiction progress monitoring DIBELS® or Acadience reading passage. |
| | By the end of Week 5, Term 3, 2023, John will be able to demonstrate self-monitoring skills (such as: Do I understand what I am reading? How does this connect to what I already know? What do I think might happen next?) with 90% accuracy when reading a Year 5 level text. |
| Reading fluency | When reading a Decodable Readers Australia nonfiction level 3 book, John will be able to read with 60 words correct per minute (WCPM) by Week 8, Term 3, 2023. |
| | When given a decodable text such as Phonics Books Talisman Unit 5, Jenny will read 110 words accurately in one minute, by Week 8, Term 3, 2023. |
| Vocabulary | By the end of Week 4, Term 4, 2023, John will be able to state the vocabulary terms and meanings in a Vocabulary Knowledge Scale on nine out of 10 occasions in two subsequent class-based rich text units. |

# Part 2
# EVIDENCE-BASED LITERACY INSTRUCTION - AKA THE SCIENCE OF READING

"There can be no equity, no social justice, without literacy"

~ Kareem Weaver (2021)

## Chapter 6

# INTRODUCTION TO THE SCIENCE OF READING

**"We have to do a neurological backflip to teach our brains to read"**

~ Carolyn Strom

## Chapter overview

- Anticipation Guide
- Introducing the science of reading
- International inquiries on how children learn to read
- Reading and the brain
- The Simple View of Reading
- Scarborough's Reading Rope
- Science of reading fundamentals for sharing with families
- Summary
- Professional discussion
- Anticipation Guide answers

## Anticipation Guide

| Anticipation Guide | True/False |
|---|---|
| The science of reading is based on the explicit teaching of phonics | |
| The Simple View of Reading is a visual metaphor developed to show parents the aspects required for successful reading acquisition. It involves two strands of word recognition and language comprehension that when intertwined leads to skilled and fluent reading | |
| Learning to read is not an innate ability | |
| Three international inquiries from 2000 to 2006 identified the same key findings about what is required for children to become successful readers: oral language, phonemic awareness, phonics, fluency, vocabulary and comprehension | |
| Three systems are required for reading: phonology, orthography and semantics. These three systems need to be bonded in memory, so when a child sees the orthographic representation of a word (its spelling), they know how it sounds (the phonemes and pronunciation) and what it means (semantics, context and meaning) | |
| An equal amount of time needs to be spent each day on teaching the subskills of language comprehension as the subskills of word recognition | |
| When learning to read, the brain needs to recycle the part of the brain that recognises faces and build new neural pathways | |

## Introducing the science of reading

For the past few decades, there has been an abundance of research into how children learn to read, why some struggle, how to effectively teach and assess literacy, and how to prevent and remediate literacy difficulties. This scientific study of reading instruction has been coined 'the science of reading.'

> *"The body of work referred to as the 'science of reading' is not an ideology, a philosophy, a political agenda, a one-size-fits-all approach, a program of instruction, or a specific component*

*of instruction. It is the emerging consensus from many related disciplines, based on literally thousands of studies, supported by hundreds of millions of research dollars, conducted across the world in many languages. These studies have revealed a great deal about how we learn to read, what goes wrong when students don't learn, and what kind of instruction is most likely to work the best for the most students"*

~ Moats (2020, para 3) in Wheldall, Wheldall & Buckingham (2023, p4)

My first encounter with the reading science was in 2008, as Support Teacher Learning Difficulties for what was then known as the Centre for Inclusive Schooling (now SSEND) for the Department of Education, Western Australia. In this team, we supported schools state-wide in professional learning and consultancy in embedding consistent whole-school approaches and RTI frameworks in literacy and numeracy. It is during this time that my team leaders shared with us the three international inquiries into how children learn to read. These inquiries, from the United States, Australia and UK from 2000 to 2006, form the underpinnings of the science of reading.

## International inquiries of how children learn to read

Prior to the year 2000, a crisis in reading achievement in the United States prompted a national inquiry into the most effective approaches into how to teach reading. This inquiry headed up by the National Reading Panel published its findings.

A few short years later, similar student assessment findings were evident in Australia with the failure of whole-language approaches, and so a national inquiry led by the late Ken Rowe resulted in the 'National Inquiry into the Teaching of Literacy'. The following year, in 2006, the United Kingdom published its own report, published by Jim Rose entitled, the 'Independent Review of the Teaching of Early Literacy'.

All three independent inquiries came to the same conclusions in terms of what students require to be effective readers – often referred to as the Big Five. The consensus was that "all students learn best when teachers adopt an integrated approach to reading that explicitly teaches PA, phonics, fluency, vocabulary knowledge and comprehension" (Rowe, 2005). All three papers provided clear recommendations on best practice in the teaching of early reading and in teacher training.

Recent research also indicates that there should in fact be a sixth element – oral language, as it is the foundation of all literacy success. A strong foundation in oral language and instructional approaches in the classroom are an essential element of reading instruction, as learning to read requires the ability to map the symbols of the alphabetic code to the speech sounds of spoken language.

## Reading and the brain

Decades of research in cognitive and neuroscience has graced us with knowledge around the structure of the brain and how reading is mapped and measured with brain imaging. From this research, we know these things:

1. Learning to read is not an innate capability, as the human brain is not built with the capacity to learn to read. Unlike spoken language, which is a natural capacity, the brain is not born with the structural architecture for reading, as it is a relatively new invention.
2. When learning to read, the brain needs to recycle the part of the brain that recognises faces (the visual cortex) and build new neural pathways.
3. There are three systems that are required for reading: phonology, orthography and semantics. These three systems need to be bonded in memory, so when a child sees the orthographic representation of a word (its spelling), they know how it sounds (the phonemes and pronunciation), and what it means (semantics, context and meaning) (Brown, 2022).
4. From brain imaging, we know that when a *skilled* reader reads, three areas of the brain are engaged and connected: the visual cortex that sees the printed word, the part of the brain responsible for spoken language and pronunciation, as well as a pathway for the meaning of the word (Dehaene, 2010). In this way, the left side of the brain lights up from the back to front.

Let's take the word 'cat', for example.

cat = /k/ /a/ /t/

When we read the printed word 'cat', it is recognised in the visual cortex, which then connects to the part of the brain that is responsible for speech where it maps the individual phonemes (sounds) of the word in the auditory (phonological) part of the brain. This is also connected to the language centre that makes sense of the meaning of the word – in this case, a fluffy feline.

Although this sounds simple, it is not a natural process, as the brain has to recycle the part of the brain that recognises faces and turn it into what is referred to as the brain's 'letterbox', which stores the letter representations that are mapped to the speech sounds. The key here is that this brain activation is how 'skilled' readers read, so it is essential that teachers are aware of the importance of making the explicit connections between speech, print and meaning to enable this rewiring process to occur. When we consider that, as teachers, we are on the front lines of building children's brains (through teaching them how to read), then we should know a little bit about how this occurs in the brain (Strom, 2020).

## The Simple View of Reading

The science of reading is underpinned by two theoretical frameworks: the Simple View of Reading (SVR) (Gough & Tunmer, 1986) and Scarborough's Reading Rope (2001).

$$D \times LC = RC$$

The SVR is a theoretical construct that explains the reading process. In this algorithm, the symbols in the algorithm are as follows:

$D$ = Decoding,
$LC$ = Language Comprehension and
$RC$ = Reading Comprehension

The SVR postulates that reading comprehension is the product of two complex, separable, but interlinked dimensions: decoding and language comprehension. The key here is that both decoding and language comprehension play *equal* importance, so a student that is efficient in one area and not the other will experience faulty reading comprehension. As such, this is an essential consideration for classroom instruction and intervention.

Another way to consider the SVR, and the importance of supporting students to be skilled in both dimensions, is to view it like a mathematical algorithm, such as: $1 \times 1 = 1$ (Parker, 2021).

If a child is skilled in decoding, but has no language comprehension, then the equation would look like this, with a factor of zero for reading comprehension:

$$D \times LC = RC$$
$$1 \times 0 = 0$$

Likewise, if a child has strong language comprehension and no decoding ability, then the equation would look like this, again with a value of zero for reading comprehension:

$$D \times LC = RC$$
$$0 \times 1 = 0$$

In both cases, if one part of the equation is lacking, then reading comprehension will be hindered.

## Scarborough's Reading Rope

The second theoretical framework underpinning the reading science is Scarborough's Reading Rope, developed by Hollis Scarborough as a visual metaphor for explaining to parents how children learn to read. Following on from the SVR, the Reading Rope unpacks the eight sub-strands of the two key components of language comprehension and word recognition.

The top strand of the rope – language comprehension – consists of: *background knowledge, vocabulary, language structures, verbal reasoning and literacy knowledge.* Whereas the lower strand – word recognition – entails: *phonological awareness, decoding* and *sight recognition* (of familiar words). As these skills are developing, they become increasingly strategic and automatic, and intertwine to develop into fluent and skilled reading and text comprehension.

## The many strands that are woven into skilled reading

**Language comprehension**

Background knowledge
(facts, concepts, etc)

Vocabulary
(breadth, precision, links, etc)

Language structures
(syntax, semantics, etc)

Verbal reasoning
(inference, metaphor, etc)

Literacy knowledge
(print concepts, genres, etc)

**Word recognition**

Phonological awareness
(syllables, phonemes, etc)

Decoding (alphabetic principle,
spelling-sound correspondences)

Sight recognition
(of familiar words)

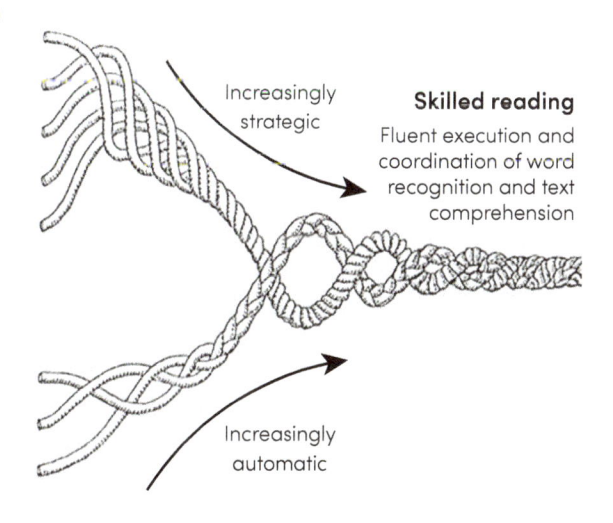

Increasingly
strategic

**Skilled reading**

Fluent execution and
coordination of word
recognition and text
comprehension

Increasingly
automatic

The image, courtesy of the author, originally appeared in: Scarborough, HS (2001). 'Connecting early language and literacy to later reading (dis)abilities: Evidence, theory, and practice.' In Neuman, S & Dickinson, D (Eds) *Handbook for research in early literacy* (pp97–110). New York, NY: Guilford Press. Reprinted with permission of Guilford Press.

So, how do we ensure decoding and language comprehension both develop concurrently? Stephen Parker in Snow (2019) proposes that the daily PA and phonics lesson is split in half, where half of the time is spent explicitly teaching children the alphabetic code; while the second part of the lesson is spent reading high-quality rich texts *to* students, explicitly teaching the skills of language comprehension. This way, both essential elements of decoding and language comprehension develop daily, in unison.

## Science of reading fundamentals for sharing with families

There are many ways in which we can engage parents of our students in successful literacy acquisition, and in my experience, this partnership is vastly underutilised. Sharing snippets of information about the underpinnings of how children learn to read as well as simple things they can be doing at home can be hugely beneficial for our students. As a deputy principal, teacher and parent, the following simple foundations are some of the common things parents have wanted to know:

- The importance of starting with letter sounds, rather than letter names when learning to read
- How to pronounce the 44 sounds of English correctly
- Successful home-reading approaches
- The 'why' behind the use of decodable readers in the early years
- The importance of reading high-quality texts *to* children and asking 'queries' throughout, to check for understanding
- Types of queries and questions parents can be asking their children about texts read aloud
- The two key dimensions of the SVR to achieve reading comprehension: decoding and language comprehension
- The first step in tackling an unknown word is by segmenting and blending graphemes and phonemes
- Building topic knowledge through podcasts, documentaries, visits to museums and talking to children about a range of topics and experiences
- Ongoing opportunities for oral language after reading to their children, such as five-finger retells, oral innovations of texts read, like changing a character's name or setting
- Sharing with parents the current alphabetic code knowledge, morphology or key vocabulary students are currently learning in class
- Sharing with parents the end-of-year expectations for literacy
- How to support their child to improve decoding and reading fluency

## Summary

- The scientific study of reading instruction has been coined the 'science of reading', and 'structured literacy' is the application of this scientifically based research.
- Three international independent inquiries between 2000 and 2006 came to the same conclusion that "all students learn best when teachers adopt an integrated approach to reading that explicitly teaches phonemic awareness, phonics, fluency, vocabulary knowledge and comprehension" (Rowe, 2005).
- Recent research also indicates that there should in fact be a sixth element: oral language, as it is the foundation is all literacy success.

- Reading is not a naturally acquired skill. Unlike spoken language, human beings are not born with the structural architecture for reading.
- When learning to read, the brain needs to recycle the part that recognises faces and build new neural pathways.
- There are three systems that are required for reading: phonology, orthography and semantics. These three systems need to be bonded in memory so that when a child sees the orthographic representation of a word (its spelling), they know how it sounds (the phonemes and pronunciation), and what it means (semantics, context and meaning) (Brown, 2022).
- The science of reading is underpinned by two theoretical frameworks: the Simple View of Reading (Gough & Tunmer, 1986) and Scarborough's Reading Rope (2001).
- Sharing snippets of information about the underpinnings of how children learn to read as well as simple things they can be doing at home, with our parent community in school, can be hugely beneficial for our students.

## Professional discussion

- To what extent are the key elements of the science of reading underpinned in our school, in terms of the six essential subskills of reading, SVR and the Reading Rope?
- There are two separable, yet interlinked dimensions of the SVR and the Reading Rope. Is there an equal amount of instructional time paid to each in every classroom?
- To what extent do we engage our parent body in understanding the reading science and providing information to support the learning journey of our students?

# Anticipation Guide answers

| Anticipation Guide | True/False |
|---|---|
| The science of reading is based on the explicit teaching of phonics | False, this is only one part of it |
| The Simple View of Reading is a visual metaphor developed to show parents the aspects required for successful reading acquisition. It involves two strands of word recognition and language comprehension that when intertwined leads to skilled and fluent reading | False, this is referring to Scarborough's Reading Rope. The SVR refers to the algorithm D × LC = RC |
| Learning to read is not an innate ability | True |
| Three international inquiries from 2000 to 2006 identified the same key findings about what is required for children to become successful readers: oral language, phonemic awareness, phonics, fluency, vocabulary and comprehension | True |
| Three systems are required for reading: phonology, orthography and semantics. These three systems need to be bonded in memory, so when a child sees the orthographic representation of a word (its spelling), they know how it sounds (the phonemes and pronunciation), and what it means (semantics, context and meaning) | True |
| An equal amount of time needs to be spent each day on teaching the subskills of language comprehension as the subskills of word recognition | True, this explains the algorithm of the SVR: D × LC = RC |
| When learning to read, the brain needs to recycle the part of the brain that recognises faces and build new neural pathways | True |

## Chapter 7

# ORAL LANGUAGE

"Oral language and early literacy experiences are the foundation
of all literacy achievement"

~ Deslea Konza (2014)

## Chapter overview

- Anticipation Guide
- The why behind oral language instruction
- Bridging the gap between spoken and written language through oral storytelling
- What is the macrostructure and microstructure of a narrative?
- How to incorporate oral storytelling into the classroom
- General oral language teaching strategies and principles
- Recommendations for teacher language
- Oral language instruction in the primary years
- Assessment and intervention of oral language
- Developmental Language Disorder
- Summary
- Professional discussion
- Anticipation Guide answers

# Anticipation Guide

| Anticipation Guide | True/False |
|---|---|
| Early oral language development has a significant impact on the development of reading | |
| Teaching oral storytelling has an impact on social and emotional development | |
| Assessment for oral language is recommended in schools once per year from four years of age | |
| Developmental Language Disorder affects approximately one in five people in the community | |
| One way to bridge the divide between conversational oral language and academic written language is through explicit teaching of oral storytelling | |
| A narrative microstructure includes compound and complex sentences, coordinating and subordinating conjunctions and adverbial phrases | |

## The why behind oral language instruction

"Oral language skills refer to the ability to understand the spoken language of others and the ability to express oneself verbally by putting words and ideas into sentences and engaging appropriately in different social situations" (Snow & Ashman, 2019).

Between 2000 and 2006, three international inquiries into the essential elements of teaching early reading identified five essential components as being critical to the development of early reading:

- Phonemic awareness
- Phonics
- Vocabulary
- Fluency
- Comprehension

However, the one critical aspect not identified was oral language. Konza (2014) recommends that the 'Big Five' become the 'Big Six' and states the importance of teachers being aware of the underlying importance of oral language in the development of reading and ensuring a strong focus on oral language in the classroom.

To understand the long-term impact of language development in the early years, we can look to the work of Hart and Risley (1995), who tracked the growth of 42 children from seven to nine months until the age of three. They found there was an enormous discrepancy between the number of words children heard in the home, with some children being exposed to 30 million more words than others. The children were tracked until ages nine and 10 and they found that vocabulary use at age three was strongly correlated with scores in receptive vocabulary, language skill (in terms of listening, speaking, semantics and syntax) and reading comprehension (Hart & Risley, 2003, in Konza, 2014).

Further to this, early oral language skills are one of the best predictors of later social skills (Pace et al., 2018) and difficulties expressing one's self is linked to behaviour problems (Chow et al., 2018, in Spencer & Pierce, 2022). In addition, competency in oral storytelling is also a protective factor for students who, in the event that they may be exposed to abuse, are equipped with the oral language tools to be able to relay these events to an adult.

## Bridging the gap between spoken and written language through oral storytelling

"Children who are surrounded by, and included in, rich and increasingly complex conversations have an overwhelming advantage in vocabulary development, in understanding the structures of language, and in tuning into the sounds of English. As children engage in these early interactions, they are immersed in various aspects of language that will ultimately support their reading development" (Konza, 2014).

From birth, children who are fortunate to be surrounded by rich language, vocabulary and a variety of conversations arrive at school on the first day with a significant advantage over their less language-rich peers. However, even with our more fortunate students, when beginning school, there is a divide between young students' oral language capacity (speaking abilities) and written language (such as in texts and books). The missing piece in this divide is often referred to as 'academic language' (Spencer & Pierce, 2022).

Incorporating intentional oral language repertoires, including vocabulary, grammar and syntax, and text structures to develop oral academic language, is essential in closing this gap (Cervetti et al., 2020; Phillips Galloway et al., 2020, in Spencer & Pierce, 2022). This is due to the need for students to have established proficient 'academic oral language' before they are expected to produce it in written form, as students are not going to be able write what they can't yet say.

One of the vehicles for bridging the divide between conversational oral language and academic written language is through explicit teaching of oral storytelling. This is an effective approach and highly achievable as both conversational narrative and written narratives share similar features, including word level, sentence level and discourse level patterns (Pinto et al., 2015, in Spencer & Pierce, 2022).

These consistent internal patterns and structures refer to the *macrostructure* and *microstructure* of oral and written narratives (or stories). In terms of end of school year expectations, Spencer and Pierce (2022) identify that by the end of Year 1, neurotypical children are expected to be able to correctly tell or retell an oral narrative with five main elements of a narrative macrostructure. See the story grammar framework with end-of-year expectations for ages four to eight on page 108.

## What is the macrostructure and microstructure of a narrative?

In Western cultures, narrative *macrostructure* generally includes:

- A setting (character, time and place)
- An initiating event or problem
- A character response (emotions and plan)
- A series of attempts, action and/or events
- An ending (resolution and consequence)

Narrative *microstructure* includes:

- Compound and complex sentences
- Coordinating and subordinating conjunctions
- Adverbial phrases
- Pronouns and referencing
- Elaborate noun phrases
- Cognitive (for example, felt, thought, desired) and linguistic verbs (yelled, whimpered)

(Carrow-Woolfolk, 1988; Cortazzi & Jin, 2007; Greenhalgh & Strong, 2001; Peterson, 2010; Stein & Glenn, 1979; Westby, 1985 in Glisson, 2022)

An example of how that can look is as follows.

| Simple story macrostructure for oral retelling | |
| --- | --- |
| Example: *The Way Back Home* ~ Oliver Jeffers | |
| **Setting and character** | Once there was a boy and one day, he found an aeroplane in his cupboard. |
| **Initiating event or problem** | He thought he would take it out for a fly right away. The aeroplane ran out of petrol, and he landed on the moon. He met an alien whose engine had broken down. They were both stuck on the moon. |
| **Response or feeling** | They were all alone in the dark. They could hear noises and were very scared. |
| **Attempts/ action/event** | Both the boy and the Martian thought of ways they could help each other to get back home. The boy needed petrol for his aeroplane and the Martian needed his engine fixed. |
| **Resolution or consequence** | The boy had a plan to go back home and get the things they would need. He returned with the things they needed, and they fixed their machines. They said goodbye and wondered if they would ever meet again. |

## How to incorporate oral storytelling into the classroom

Children love to hear stories and engage in storytelling, and the primary classroom is a wonderful place for developing children's oral language development through this medium. Below are six suggestions on how to incorporate storytelling into the classroom.

### 1. Teach using retelling

The act of retelling a personal event or fictional story requires both listening comprehension and the ability to express this understanding verbally.

Modelling retelling a personal event to students and then asking, "Think of a time when this has happened to you, then tell your partner about it" is a great place to start in building skill in oral retelling. As students become proficient in orally retelling personal experiences, this will be a good foundation for generalising this skill into retelling of fictional stories read to them.

## 2. Model identifying the macrostructure and retelling of simple stories

Once students have had many experiences in retelling personal stories or events, with key elements included, teachers can model retelling simple stories to the students. The aim here is to initially choose stories that are beyond what students can decode, but not as complex as a story that adults would typically read to them. Carefully choose short, simple narratives that follow a clear sequence of events to begin with to avoid overloading students, and as proficiency develops, choose stories with more complex story structure, sentence complexity and vocabulary.

For young children, students with EALD and students with learning disabilities, it is recommended to start with a narrative of about 50–70 words. This short narrative should have the main narrative macrostructure grammar features such as: character, problem, feeling, action, consequence. Model identifying these macrostructure features to students. When students can retell a narrative with these five main parts, then the expectation can be raised to include the setting and ending (Spencer & Pierce, 2022).

## 3. Scaffold retelling with visuals such as a story mountain

"Many short stories and picture books lend themselves to children drawing the story map and moving onto drawing a story mountain, graph or flow chart that shows the key scenes. This helps to unpick the plot pattern" (Corbett, 2003).

A simple way to scaffold retelling is to begin with modelling the key events in a story map. From here, teachers can evolve this scaffold into a story mountain to show the complication of the narrative at the summit of the mountain. Once this has been demonstrated many times by the teacher, and students are comfortable with retelling a familiar story using the mountain as a visual scaffold, you may like to incorporate a story mountain retelling corner into the classroom. This can be a space where students have access to a board with butchers' paper and they can draw their own story mountain to retell their own stories to their peers.

Example story mountain of *The Three Little Pigs*

## 4. Scaffold retelling with a five-finger story retell

From the early years of schooling, another supportive scaffold for oral retelling is through a five-finger story retell. Once the key events have been identified in the story orally, teachers can explicitly teach students that we can retell these simple tales with each finger on one hand and time connectives to retell the story. The great thing about this approach is that not only are students learning how to sequence and summarise key events, which supports comprehension, but they are also supported to use time connectives in their oral retell. When you hear a five-year-old student use the word 'unfortunately' in their oral retell, it is pretty exciting, but maybe that's just me! This approach is similar to the Five Sentence Story in Talk for Writing and can be found in Pie Corbett's teaching guide for progression in writing year by year (see www.talk4writing.com/wp-content/uploads/2018/12/1-overview-Grammar-progression-new.pdf).

For example,

> *Long ago...*
> *First...*
> *Next...*
> *Unfortunately...*
> *Finally...*

Five-finger story retell example with time connective prompts

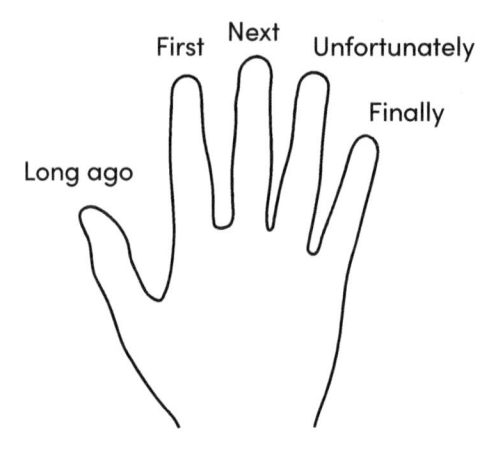

## 5. Storytelling with substitution

A fun way to adapt story retelling is to substitute the name of a character or setting. I have done this many times with my own children and instead of the main character's name, I substitute it with my child's name, or we substitute a part of the story such as the setting or main event. There is something very exciting about children hearing their name in a story and it lends itself to a fun adaptation to the art of oral storytelling.

An example is instead of *The Tiger Who Came to Tea*, it was *The Rhino Who Came to Tea*. Instead of the main character being Sophie, I would replace Sophie with my son or daughter's name. This approach is also found in the Innovation stage of the Talk for Writing approach, advocated by Pie Corbett as an effective way for young learners to develop their understanding of a narrative structure.

## 6. Model and explicitly teach story grammar

Before students can write detailed narratives with all the episodic features and narrative discourse structure, they need to be able to do this orally. Teaching students the story grammar framework explicitly (see opposite) will support this development. When students are taught the key elements of a story, teachers can begin prompting students to use longer complex sentences and replace common or generic words.

The story grammar framework opposite outlines the year level expectations for students aged four to eight years old, as well as example mini narratives as a guide for modelling to students. It is recommended that in the beginning of teaching this approach that visuals or icons are provided for each of the episodic features as a visual scaffold. These icons are generic in nature so that they can be used for any narrative storytelling. It is important to note, though, that these should be faded as quickly as possible to avoid dependency and prepare students for the higher academic demands of reading and writing (Spencer & Pierce, 2022).

### Story grammar framework
*Age-related expectations (Spencer & Pierce, 2022)*

| Macrostructure | | | | |
|---|---|---|---|---|
| Four-year-olds | Five-year-olds | Year 1 | Year 2 | Year 3 |
| Problem | **Character** | Character | Character | Character |
| Action | Problem | **Setting** | Setting | Setting |
| Consequence | **Feeling** | Problem | Problem | Problem |
| | Action | Feeling | Feeling | Feeling |
| | Consequence | Action | **Plan** | Plan |
| | | Consequence | Action | Action |
| | | **Ending** | Consequence | **Complication** |
| | | | Ending | **Feeling** |
| | | | **End** | **Plan** |
| | | | **Feeling** | **Action** |
| | | | | Consequence |
| | | | | Ending |
| | | | | End |
| | | | | Feeling |

Once students have had many exposures to the basic story grammar structure, teachers can introduce other story plots. Pie Corbett (2003) breaks these down beautifully, into examples such as, a Wishing Tale, Warning Tale, Conquering the Monster Tale or Rags to Riches tale. In these cases, I highly recommend using high-quality rich texts that have been modified to explicitly teach the plot structure. Over the page are examples of these types of Generic Story Plots kindly shared by Pie Corbett and adapted by Maria Richards (2013) (see www.talk4writing.com/wp-content/uploads/2013/08/Adapted_Generic_Story_Plots_MR2.pdf).

| Wishing Tale | Generic structure |
|---|---|
| Opening | Main Character (MC) wants something badly |
| Build up | MC tries to get it |
| Problem | MC is prevented by some sort of difficulty |
| Resolution | MC overcomes the difficulty |
| Ending | MC gets what they want (Was it worth it?) |

| Warning Tale | Generic structure |
|---|---|
| Opening | MCs are warned not to do something |
| Build up | MCs do what they are warned against |
| Problem | Something goes wrong and the MCs are in trouble |
| Resolution | MCs are eventually rescued |
| Ending | MCs are told off/punished for not listening to the warning |

| Conquering the Monster Tale | Generic structure |
|---|---|
| Opening | Introduce the MCs – all is well |
| Build up | A monster appears and causes problems |
| Problem | The monster is difficult to defeat |
| Resolution | MCs defeat the monster |
| Ending | All is well again; MCs get a reward |

| Rags to Riches Tale | Generic structure |
|---|---|
| Opening | Introduce the MC |
| Build up | MC is sad, lonely/treated badly |
| Problem | MC has to face difficulties because of their situation |
| Resolution | MC overcomes the difficulties/is helped to overcome the difficulties |
| Ending | MC achieves happiness/wealth/recognition |

For a range of quality model texts, see www.talk4writing.com/resources/planning.

## General oral language teaching strategies and principles

There are a range of other high-quality approaches teachers can use to benefit the oral language development of all students, including:

- Teach active listening – teach students to listen for specific information and vocabulary.
- Build on student language – extend conversation through questioning, reinforce through repetition, model self-talk and teach age-appropriate skills such as eye contact.
- Build oral language development into daily routines and games.
- Provide opportunities for social interaction – Think, Pair, Share with peers, small group work, buddy classes, teacher to student interactions.
- Read stories often – use planned, open-ended questions to check for understanding and monitor listening and language comprehension.
- Consider the language demands of each lesson and explicitly teach new vocabulary.
- Don't be afraid to 'correct' children's communication – recast what students say if their language is incomplete or incorrect (Konza, 2011). For example, if a child says, "Me go toilet", respond by saying, "Are you telling me you need to go to the toilet?"
- Build oral language across all the year levels and throughout all curriculum areas.
- When posing questions to students, allow a wait time of three to five seconds to provide thinking and processing time, thus limiting the burden on working memory.

## Recommendations for teacher language

As role models of high-quality language use, I think it is good practice to intermittently consider to what extent we are demonstrating this, including asking ourselves the following:

1. Am I modelling clear and correct use of oral language?
2. Am I building in frequent checks for understanding and monitoring student understanding frequently throughout lessons?
3. Do I adjust language, simplify or repeat oral language when needed?

4. Do I adjust language according to student need?
5. Do I give clear and concise instructions?
6. Do I avoid sarcasm or irony when speaking to students? (Which can cause difficulty for students with Developmental Language Disorder.)

## Oral language instruction in the primary years

Below are a few practical suggestions for incorporating oral language into the primary classroom.

**Four- and five-year-olds:**

- Oral personal or class recounts – using a specific topic each week with a modelled structure. Spending five minutes at the end of the day recounting the events of the school day is a great starting point for practising sequencing events, while also providing a recap of what students learnt, to share with their families.
- Topic-based group news telling – provide a specific focus for each week, such as a description of a favourite toy, sport or event. Small group news telling is far more efficient on time and provides many more opportunities for students to have their turn.
- Use prompts such as five-finger storytelling, story mountains or icons for retelling simple texts.
- Incorporate nursery rhymes/chants and multiple opportunities for whole-class recitation.
- Explicit teaching of vocabulary from the stories read to children.
- Incorporate a storytelling corner into the classroom with books, props and costumes of stories previously read to students.
- Revitalise the classroom book corner. Ensure many of the books that have already been read to children, including fiction and non-fiction texts, are accessible for students to 'read' over and over again.

**Semester 2:**

- Begin introducing oral procedural retells. It could be as simple as an oral retell on making a honey sandwich for a teddy bear's picnic, after making them in the classroom. Oral rehearsal in small groups and building it up is a key part of the Imitation stage of the Talk for Writing approach outlined in pages 18–19 of *Creating Storytellers* (2017).
- Begin introducing oral reports on a shared experience such as an excursion/incursion.
- Think, Pair, Share throughout each day.

### Year 1:

- Begin teaching oral retell of simple fictional stories read to students.
- Explicit teaching of recount, from oral to written.
- Oral presentations – object-based news in small groups.
- Oral informational reports such as an animal report based on what has been taught in class. Oral reports will move into written forms.
- Procedural writing – oral procedural retells before moving into written forms.
- The main focus for writing will be on explicit teaching of complete sentences.
- Use barrier games as a way of refining oral language skills.
- Think, Pair, Share throughout each day.

### Year 2:

- Fiction texts – oral and written.
- Persuasive texts – oral and written.
- Procedural writing – oral and written.
- Informational reports – oral and written.
- The main focus for writing will be on explicit teaching of complete sentences.
- Use barrier games as a way of refining oral language skills.
- Think, Pair, Share throughout each day.

### Years 3–6:

- All writing should entail an oral language component first – to generate ideas, plan, sequence thoughts, to scaffold less proficient language learners.
- Set up small group debating for discussing persuasive text points of view.
- Teach students to be active listeners with note taking from visual or auditory texts with a specific focus.
- Oral presentations – related to knowledge-rich topics covered in class Students will be very clear on expectations and use rubrics to support self-assessment of their own progress.
- Ask students to pose questions or provide positive feedback on peer oral presentations to encourage active listening skills.
- Provide opportunities for cooperative learning through graphic organisers such as Anticipation Guides and KWL charts to encourage peer interactions while also activating background knowledge in cross-curricular areas.
- Think, Pair, Share throughout each day.

## Assessment and intervention of oral language

Without the foundational oral language skills firmly established, students struggle to acquire successful reading and writing repertoires (National Center for Education Statistics, 2011 & 2019, in Spencer & Pierce, 2022).

As part of a preventative, systemic RTI framework in schools, it is highly recommended that students engage in universal screening three times per year. In terms of oral language, I recommend the CUBED NLM Listening Assessment from four-year-olds up to Year 3. This would ideally take place at the start of the year, middle of year and end of year. For Australian contexts within a four-term school year, this may occur at the following times to coincide with end-of-semester reporting:

- Term 1, Week 2
- Term 2, Week 5
- Term 4, Week 5

Students identified at risk in this assessment would be recommended to engage in Tier 2 oral language intervention; and students identified at significant risk would be referred to a speech and language pathologist for a full speech and language assessment as early as possible. Further recommendations for Tier 3 assessment tools can be identified in the Primary Reading Pledge (Five from Five, Auspeld & Learning Difficulties Australia, 2020) at www.fivefromfive.com.au/primary-reading-pledge

Recommended intervention programs include:

- The Oral Narrative Intervention Programme (the ONIP Version 2) –
  an oral narrative intervention program for five- to six-year-old children
  with oral narrative difficulties. Developed by Glisson, Leitao and
  Claessen (2022), it is available at www.trackstoliteracy.com
- Language Lift – by MultiLit. Available at www.multilit.com/programs/
  languagelift-program
- Story Champs® – A multi-tiered language intervention curriculum.
  Available at www.languagedynamicsgroup.com/story-champs. This
  program is also an excellent tool for Tier 1 whole-class instruction in
  the early years.

## Developmental Language Disorder

Many students with difficulties processing and using spoken language and reading social and linguistic cues have what is referred to as Developmental Language Disorder (DLD). Although it is estimated that one in 14 people experience this – which is equivalent to two children in the regular classroom (The DLD Project, 2023) – it remains frequently unknown or goes unnoticed as it is often masked by other things, such as noncompliant or disruptive behaviour. Sadly, if left undiagnosed, the repercussions can be wide ranging. It is estimated that 50–60% of people in contact with the criminal justice system have undiagnosed DLD (Snow & Ashman, 2019).

On completion of school-based universal screening in language, if a student is identified in the 'at risk' range, a referral to a speech language pathologist/speech language therapist for a full language assessment is recommended. Depending on the outcome of the assessment, and if the student is identified as having DLD, a report with a recommended intervention plan would follow.

Intervention would include evidence-based procedures to assist with the aspects of language that are difficult for the child and may include: spoken and written language comprehension, conversational skills, work in forming sentences (syntax), morphology and grammatical rules, inferencing skills, figurative language, pragmatics, vocabulary, word retrieval and writing (Bowen & Snow, 2017).

The earlier the intervention the better. One of the many reasons for this includes research on the link between untreated language difficulties and memory. McKean et al. (2015 in Bowen & Snow, 2017) identified that students who experience language difficulties at five years of age were likely to have less advanced memory skills than their peers.

## Summary

- Oral language skills refer to the ability to understand the spoken language of others and the ability to express oneself verbally.
- It is important that teachers are aware of the underlying importance of oral language in the development of reading.
- Children who are exposed to language rich environments as infants in the family home have an overwhelming advantage over peers from less language-rich homes.
- One of the vehicles for bridging the divide between conversational oral language and academic written language is through explicit teaching of oral storytelling.
- In Western culture there is generally a consistent macrostructure and microstructure in oral and written narratives.

- It is recommended that students are screened for oral language difficulties three times per year as part of a systemic RTI approach.
- Teaching students to be proficient in oral retelling is not only supportive of reading and writing development, but also has significant social-emotional benefits.
- One in 14 people have DLD and 50–60% of people in contact with the criminal justice system have undiagnosed DLD.

## Professional discussion

- How could you incorporate explicit teaching of oral storytelling into your daily classroom routines?
- What can you learn about your students' language capabilities from the oral stories they generate?
- Considering the number of students that are in our schools with undiagnosed DLD, what are some things you can be doing at a whole-class level to support these students?

## Anticipation Guide answers

| Anticipation Guide | True/False |
| --- | --- |
| Early oral language development has a significant impact on the development of reading | True |
| Teaching oral storytelling has an impact on social and emotional development | True |
| Assessment for oral language is recommended in schools once per year from four years of age | False – recommended to be done three times per year |
| Developmental Language Disorder affects approximately one in five people in the community | False – one in 14 |
| One way to bridge the divide between conversational oral language and academic written language is through explicit teaching of oral storytelling | True |
| A narrative microstructure includes compound and complex sentences, coordinating and subordinating conjunctions and adverbial phrases | True |

## Chapter 8

# PHONEMIC AWARENESS AND SYNTHETIC PHONICS

*"A child's level of phonemic awareness is the strongest single determinant of the success that she or he will experience in learning to read - or conversely, the likelihood that she or he will fail"*

~ Adams (1990); Stanovich (1986)

## Chapter overview

- Anticipation Guide
- Introduction
- What is phonemic awareness?
- Why teach phonemic awareness with graphemes?
- What is synthetic phonics instruction?
- Linguistic terminology and concept knowledge
- Examples of SSPPs
- The superiority of synthetic phonics over analytic phonics
- Instructional routines for PA and phonics instruction
- Decodable vs predictable and levelled texts
- Getting to the bottom of PA and phonics difficulties early
- Universal screening and intervention
- Progress monitoring
- Moving away from literacy rotations and Look, Cover, Write, Check
- Starting points for PA and phonics instruction

- Summary
- Professional discussion
- Anticipation Guide answers
- Self-reflection – teaching synthetic phonics

## Anticipation Guide

| Anticipation Guide | True/False |
|---|---|
| Synthetic phonics involves teaching students a target grapheme and then students brainstorming words with that grapheme | |
| Synthetic phonics has a high effect on student progress when taught at the whole-class level rather than ability grouping | |
| Consonant clusters/adjacent consonants such as sl, bl, tr are taught explicitly as complete units | |
| Phonemic awareness is ideally taught in an 'oral only' approach in addition to the phonics lesson | |
| Synthetic phonics should be taught at a rapid pace | |

## Introduction

Phonemic awareness (PA) and synthetic phonics are included in this chapter together as, although they were identified as separate skills in the international inquiries of 2000–2006, they are dependent of one another for skilled reading. Linnea Ehri in Brown (2022) refers to this as "reciprocal causation".

Learning to read involves three fundamental systems: phonology (the sounds of, and within, words), orthography (the printed representations of these sounds and words) and semantics (the meanings of words). As such, teaching students' PA devoid of orthography (the graphemes or letter and letter combinations) does not maximise the learning opportunities for students, hence why I have combined them in this chapter.

## What is phonemic awareness?

"Phonemic awareness is what makes phonics instruction meaningful. Without a comprehensive knowledge of the separate sounds in words, our alphabetic script will make no sense to children" (Torgesen, 2004).

PA is the ability to segment, blend and manipulate individual phonemes in words. It is critical for proficient reading and spelling, and yet is an area that is sometimes not explicitly taught – or if taught, frequently not taught through the most efficient approach. PA not only helps students tune into the sounds of words, but has also been proven to improve decoding skills (Schuele & Boudreau, 2008). Students who can't isolate phonemes will struggle as readers (Brown, 2022).

There are three essential PA skills for learning to read: blending, segmenting and manipulation.

- **Blending:** Phonemic blending is the ability to hear the individual phonemes in a word, and blend the sounds together to say the word, for example: /s/ /a/ /d/ = sad, /s/ /c/ /ar/ /f/ = scarf. This subskill is typically mastered by late Foundation, early Year 1.

- **Segmenting:** Phonemic segmentation is the ability to break down words into individual phonemes, for example: hand = /h/ /a/ /n/ /d/, fish = /f/ /i/ /sh/. This subskill is typically mastered in Year 1.

- **Manipulating:** Phonemic manipulation is the ability to change, modify or delete the phonemes in a word to make a new word. For example:
  - *Say ship without the 'sh' (ip)*
  - *Say hat without the 'h' (at)*
  - *Say twist without the 's' (twit)*
  - *Write dam, now change dam to dash, change dash to dish*

It is pertinent to note, that although there has been recent debate about the need to include 'advanced' phonemic manipulation tasks, Dr Kathleen Brown (2022) cites: "There are still no published studies in high quality peer refereed journals supporting the use of advanced phonemic awareness curriculum in classrooms towards reading and spelling development."

## Why teach phonemic awareness with graphemes?

A personal anecdote about when I first learnt the impact of combining PA with phonics was back in 2008, when engaging in a professional learning day at Dyslexia-SPELD Foundation (DSF) with Mandy Nayton. I still recall Mandy explaining that teaching PA with graphemes is like providing students with a visual coat hanger for which to hang the sound. This analogy has always stuck with me, and I still share this analogy when working with teachers as a simple visual metaphor for this reciprocal partnership. Johnston and Watson (2007) support this analogy by explaining that: "Phonemes are a very abstract concept, but when taught with letters and print, children have concrete visual representations of the sounds and these support their learning."

PA outcomes are greater when taught alongside graphemes within an explicit synthetic phonics approach. In the first two months of a longitudinal study in Clackmannanshire, Scotland, there was a 35% improvement in PA and additional seven months increase in reading ability compared to the oral-only approach (Johnston & Watson, 2007).

The National Reading Panel (2000) also found that children progressed fastest when they were taught through a combination of PA and phonics. Dr Kathleen Brown (2022) states that programs that don't tie PA to the orthography (written code) are "not effective or efficient". This is despite many popular programs being marketed and taught in this way.

## What is synthetic phonics instruction?

Synthetic phonics refers to the instructional approach of explicitly teaching children to 'synthesise' sounds to read and spell. It is an aspect of structured literacy, which is teacher-led, taught explicitly and systematically in a fast-moving approach. It teaches students the link between phonemes in words and the graphemes they represent (orthography). It also involves the explicit teaching of decoding where students are taught to use phonic knowledge to derive phonemes focusing on speech sounds and their pronunciations, utilising phonic-controlled (decodable) readers, in the novice reading period. However, decoding is a skill that continues to be important across the lifespan (Gough & Tunmer in Snow, 2017).

During synthetic phonics instruction, in the first year of full-time schooling, depending on the synthetic code being followed, children may learn the first four to six phonemes such as 's' 'a' 't' 'p' 'i' 'n' in the first two weeks. These phonemes are taught by explicitly teaching the link between the phonemes and their orthographic representation (the graphemes), by blending them together to make words, therefore decoding and encoding from the outset. I have broken down a few essential elements of synthetic phonics instruction.

**Structured approach:** The synthetic phonics code is taught in a structured approach with clearly established high impact routines in the subskills of PA and synthetic phonics. It builds on previously taught code knowledge and incorporates review into each lesson.

**Teacher-led:** Synthetic phonics instruction is teacher-led, which enables educators to provide prompt, targeted feedback in response to student error (Spear-Swerling, 2019). At the whole-class level, students are explicitly taught how to blend sounds to read (decode) and segment words to spell (encode).

**Explicit instruction:** Teachers clearly explain and model key skills in a gradual release of responsibility model. When teaching or reviewing previous content, teachers model correct letter formation and orientation of new graphemes and provide multiple opportunities for student practice, with prompt feedback.

**Systematic:** The systematic component refers to a well-organised sequence of instruction, with important prerequisite skills being taught before more advanced skills. For example, students are taught to decode and encode CVC words such as 'pit' *before* more complex short vowel words with adjacent consonants such as 'flat' and 'stamp'. Teachers also follow a carefully developed phonic code sequence taught in combination with PA, with accompanying decodable readers that support students to practise the code they are learning. A select few high-frequency words are taught alongside the phonics program and at the outset students are shown that although some may be tricky to read and spell, they can in fact still be decoded.

## Linguistic terminology and concept knowledge

Effective Structured Synthetic Phonics Programs (SSPP) provide guidance for teachers, including linguistic terminology and conceptual knowledge for instruction. It is important that we use this correct terminology with students to ensure consistency across the school.

Linguistic terminology

| | | Example | Examples in words | Non-examples |
|---|---|---|---|---|
| **phoneme** | Smallest unit of sound in English | /th/ | thin, bath | bl, tr, st |
| **graph** | One letter, one sound (phoneme) | s, a | sat, mast | x (this letter has two phonemes: /k/ /s/ ) |

| | Example | Examples in words | Non-examples |
|---|---|---|---|
| **digraph** Two letters, one sound (phoneme) | ch, oy | chop, chemist, toy | |
| **trigraph** Three letters, one sound (phoneme) | dge, ere | bridge, here | |
| **quadraph** Four letters, one sound (phoneme) | ough | through, bough | rough (ough in this instance has two phonemes: /u/ /ff/ ) |

## Consonant digraphs, blends and adjacent consonants

| Correct term | consonant digraphs | adjacent consonants |
|---|---|---|
| **Examples** | ff, ss, pp | bl, tr, st, sl |
| **Also known as** | double letters | blends, consonant blends |
| **How should they be taught?** | As two letters, one phoneme, in the context of teaching CVC words (such as puff, buzz) when consonant digraphs are introduced in your synthetic phonics code | As two letters, two phonemes, in the context of teaching consonant, consonant vowel consonant words (CCVC – flat, plum) and consonant vowel consonant consonant words (CVCC – jump, mist) words in your synthetic phonics code |
| **How many phonemes?** | One | Two |

## Conceptual knowledge

| Concept | Examples |
|---|---|
| **One phoneme** can have **many spellings** | /e/ for example, bread, fed, said |
| **One spelling** can have **many pronunciations** | 'ea' (bread, great, read) |

| Concept | Examples |
|---|---|
| Some words have **schwas** – the **unstressed short vowel** sound in a word – sometimes referred to as the 'lazy' sound. This is a particularly important concept to teach to EALD students.<br><br>One way to teach students how to identify (or look out for) schwas is to segment a word into its syllables, then locate the dominant syllable in a word. This is helpful as a schwa is frequently located in the subsequent less dominant syllable/s (Walker, 2020). | moment – the 'e' is pronounced as /uh/<br><br>teacher – the 'er' is pronounced as /uh/<br><br>doctor – the 'or' is pronounced as /uh/<br><br>dominant – the 'i' and 'a' are pronounced as /uh/<br><br>op \| to \| me\| trist<br><br>In the word 'optometrist', the dominant syllable is 'to', which is followed by a schwa in 'e' and 'i' which we pronounce as /uh/ |
| A **phoneme** can be spelt with one, two, three or four letters and are referred to as **graphs**, **digraphs**, **trigraphs** and **quadraphs** | a (pat)<br><br>ea (bread)<br><br>igh (fright)<br><br>ough (through) |
| In addition to phonemes and graphemes, words are made up of **meaningful parts (morphemes and morphographs)** | 'rupt' (to break)<br><br>'dis' (apart/not) |

## Examples of SSPPs

A SSPP will incorporate reading instruction that begins with the introduction of a small number of letter-sound correspondences, and explicitly and gradually teaching children how to blend, segment, insert and delete sounds to produce different words (Snow, 2017).

Ideally, schools will implement a schoolwide evidence-based or evidence-informed SSPP, with ongoing professional learning and support for teachers. However, for teachers or schools that have not had this direction, two SSPP recommendations include:

- Sounds-Write
- InitiaLit

For recommended evidence-based SSPPs, DSF provides excellent information, including SSPP code sequences. Find out more at www.dsf. net.au/CMSPages/GetFile.aspx?guid=7ce6a8da-6f3e-418c-ac2f-13e7a86dc44a

If your school is not ready to embark on a whole-school approach, and you need a place to start in your classroom, the Speld NSW Phonics and Morphology Scope and Sequence is a great starting point, which is freely available online.

## The superiority of synthetic phonics over analytic phonics

Findings from the seven-year study undertaken by Johnston and Watson (2005) clearly indicate the superior efficacy of synthetic phonics instruction (Rowe, 2005).

In a synthetic phonics approach, teachers start with the sounds and move to the word. For example, *"These are the graphemes that represent the phonemes in the word 'pat': /p/ /a/ /t/. What is the first phoneme you hear in the word 'pat'? What is the middle phoneme you hear in 'pat'? What is the final phoneme?"*

However, an analytic phonics approach focuses initially on the word, through a whole-to-part approach. Children are then taught to analyse letter-sound relations once the word is identified. For example, a teacher might ask students to think of as many words as possible that start with the letter 'p' and then brainstorm these words on the board.

In the Clackmannanshire seven-year study mentioned earlier, Johnston and Watson (2007) studied 300 children from mostly disadvantaged areas and compared the results of analytic phonics, synthetic phonics and mixed instruction. For 16 weeks, Primary 1 students (five-year-old equivalent) engaged in 20 minutes of their designated group's instruction. After the first 16 weeks of instruction, there was a 32.3% improvement in students engaging in analytic phonics instruction, and 56.9% improvement for students engaging in synthetic phonics instruction.

## Instructional routines for PA and phonics instruction

A synthetic phonics lesson that incorporates PA includes a daily 25- to 30-minute lesson. This lesson would include a series of routines, always beginning with explicit teaching, followed by guided practice, to independent practice. From Year 2 to Year 6, when students have been taught the alphabetic code, the focus would switch to a greater emphasis on morphology and vocabulary.

Below is a series of instructional routines that target the essential subskills of phonics and PA.

## Initial teaching of the basic code: Word Construction

**Skill/s: segmenting and blending with graphemes, encoding, orientation and formation of letters**

Whole-class explicit instruction (15 minutes) where all students have a mini whiteboard with lines, whiteboard marker and eraser. On the main whiteboard, the teacher will have the graphemes written on individual, coloured magnetic boxes, out of order, for example:

| i | t | s |
|---|---|---|

**Teacher script:**

1. *These are the letters that represent the sounds in the word 'sit.' Say 'sit.'*
2. *What are the sounds you can hear in the word 'sit'? Let's tap them out.*
3. Gesturing – *what is the first sound you hear in the word 'sit'?* Pull the coloured magnet with 's' down.
4. Gesturing – *what is the next sound you hear in the word 'sit'?* Pull the box with 'i' down.
5. Gesturing – *what is the final sound you hear in the word 'sit'?* Pull the 't' down.
6. *Let's sound out the word together – gesturing: /sssss/ /iiiiiiii/ /t/ = sit*
   Where possible, use continuant phonation to blend the word rather than segmenting each phoneme out in isolation. Continuant phonation is more effective than segmented phonation. Students who are taught to hold sounds – rather than break the sounds while blending – learn to decode easier. It is also essential that students do this out loud to connect the graphemes to their pronunciation, as this is the glue of orthographic mapping (Ehri, 2022).
7. *Let's spell 'sit.' Watch me.* Model correct letter formation and orientation and spell 'sit.'
8. Students write 'sit', saying each sound *out loud* as they do. Provide immediate, explicit feedback on letter formation, orientation and continuant phonation.
9. Repeat with the next word. In this routine, about six to eight words can be explicitly taught per day.

*Basic code: Word Construction (Example – CVCC words)*

Learning intention: to blend and segment phonemes to read and spell words.

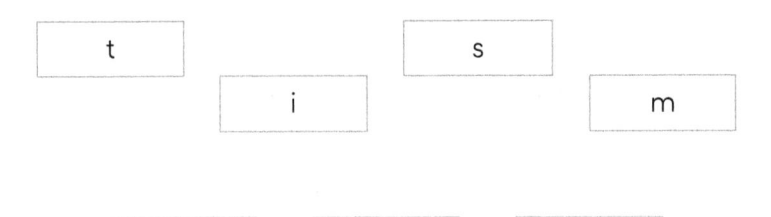

| t | | s |
| | i | m |

## Teaching the advanced code: Word Construction

**Skill/s: segmenting and blending with digraphs, encoding, orientation and formation of letters**

Whole-class explicit instruction where all students have a mini whiteboard with lines, whiteboard marker and eraser. On the main whiteboard, the teacher has the graphemes written on individual, coloured magnetic boxes, out of order, for example:

| ai | n | r |

**Teacher script:**

1. *These are the graphemes that represent the sounds in the word 'rain.' Say 'rain.' Sometimes phonemes have one letter, but they can also consist of two letters like this: 'ai.'*
2. *What are the phonemes you can hear in the word 'rain'? Let's tap them out on our hand.*
3. Gesturing – *what is the first sound you hear in the word 'rain'?* Pull the coloured magnet with 'r' down.
4. Gesturing – *what is the next (middle) phoneme you hear in the word 'rain'?* Pull the box with 'ai' down.
5. Gesturing – *what is the final phoneme you hear in the word 'rain'?* Pull the 'n' down.
6. *Let's sound out the word together* – gesturing: */rrrrrrrrrr/ /ai/ /n/ = rain* Where possible, use continuant phonation to blend the word rather

than segmenting each sound out in isolation. *Let's spell 'rain.' Watch me.* Model correct letter formation and orientation and spell 'rain'.

7. Students write 'rain', saying each sound *out loud* as they do. Provide immediate, explicit feedback on letter formation, orientation and continuant phonation.

8. Repeat with the next word, introducing 'ay'. In this routine, about six to eight words can be explicitly taught per day. The idea here is to show students that although the phoneme is the long 'ae' phoneme, it can be spelt in many ways. This supports students to develop skills in orthographic choice.

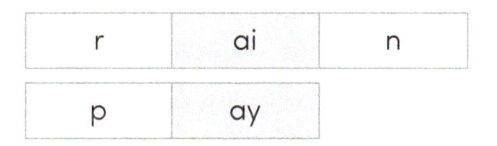

| r | ai | n |
|---|----|---|

| p | ay |
|---|----|

## Explicit teaching of phoneme manipulation: Sound Switching

**Skill/s: phoneme manipulation, encoding**

Whole-class explicit instruction – five minutes.

Using the current code knowledge children are learning, the teacher calls out a predetermined list of words and pseudo words, changing one phoneme each time. Pseudo words (non-words) are used to ensure children are tapping into their phoneme knowledge and not recalling whole words.

For example, at the CCVC level with the code previously taught, using the graphemes listed, the words may be as follows:

Sounds needed: a, b, i, l, o, p, r, sh

*prop- prip- rip- hip- blip- blib- blish- blash- blosh  losh  lash  plash  plish  plit*

1. The teacher tells the students to write down the graphemes they need.
2. Say the first word and tell them to change one sound to write the next word.

## Phoneme-grapheme mapping

**Skill/s: phoneme segmentation, encoding**

Phoneme-grapheme mapping is a scaffolded approach where students practise saying/hearing the individual phonemes in words and map them out in individual Elkonin boxes. For example, for the word 'ship', the phoneme /sh/ would be written in one box as it is a digraph with two letters, one phoneme, and 'i' and 'p' would be recorded in their own individual boxes. This is ideally supported by an adult to provide feedback.

This is also a good approach for home spelling practice, if parents have a clear explanation on how students do this successfully. It can be done in a brisk game-like fashion which many children find engaging (Spear-Swerling, 2022). This is far more effective than the Look, Cover, Write, Check approach, which I will discuss later in the chapter.

Example of phoneme-grapheme mapping:

| a | r | ou | n | d | = around |
|---|---|----|---|---|----------|
| s | w | a | ll | ow | = swallow |

## Dictation

**Skill/s: transcription skills, encoding, simple sentence structure, handwriting**

Dictation of a few sentences two to three times per week is a recommended approach for transcription skill development. Sentences for dictation should be directly aligned to the code knowledge students have been taught, and there should be no surprises in terms of letters/sounds/spelling rules that students have not yet learnt. This is also an excellent diagnostic tool for end-of-the-week assessment.

It is crucial to note, however, that it is only a valuable tool if we analyse the types of errors children are making and then reteach or address these mistakes. For example, you may find that one or two students frequently add a 't' instead of the 'ed' suffix, which can be addressed in class to rectify this misconception.

1. Teacher reads the sentence to students.
2. Students repeat the sentence back.
3. Teacher reads the sentence in phrase chunks for students to write.
4. Teacher moves around the room, providing support as needed and prompt feedback on letter formations and other skills.
5. Model writing the sentence(s) for students, providing immediate whole-class feedback.
6. This could be up to a small paragraph for students as their transcription skills increase.

### Explicit teaching and practice of decoding

**Skill/s: decoding, fluency**

Use of decodable: readers, passages, words, sentences, question and answers

### Whole class

Daily decoding practice within the daily review (for previously learnt code) and current level code is essential for putting new code learnt into practice. Whole-class choral reading is recommended with a passage, or part of a text on an interactive whiteboard. Choral reading, or reading in unison as a whole class, is an excellent approach for closing the gap between the strongest and weakest readers.

It also provides a supportive environment for the weaker readers, as they can practise decoding at a year level expectation, while being supported in a whole-class context. Decoding practice can consist of word, sentence and connected text level reading, depending on the age of students.

## Decodable vs predictable and levelled texts

In the early stages of learning to read, students should be provided with connected texts that provide opportunities to practise decoding based on code knowledge they have been explicitly taught. Introducing students to predictable readers or texts that have graphemes and multisyllabic words that they have not yet been taught provide a breeding ground for guessing and frustration. Once students have learnt the code, which is typically in the first two years of school, with a good structured synthetic phonics program, then students are able to access any text, as they will have the foundational skills for decoding unknown words. Recommended decodable readers, free and otherwise, include:

- Decodable Readers Australia
- Sounds-Write
- Phonic Books UK
- SPELD SA decodable readers – freely available online
- Little Learners Love Literacy

For catch-up readers for older students, I highly recommend Phonic Books UK.

## Getting to the bottom of PA and phonics difficulties early

A personal anecdote from my early years as a deputy principal was when I first arrived. In both schools, in the initial months, I was inundated with the number of student referrals from Years 3, 4 and 5 as having difficulties in what teachers deemed to be based on '*reading comprehension*'. To identify the cause of the problems, I supported the teachers in doing additional individual diagnostic assessments.

On analysis of the assessments, I often found that the core problem was not comprehension but decoding (identified through non-word reading and spelling assessments) or more often, a lack of PA. Although necessary, and never too late, putting intervention in place at this late stage in primary schooling was so much harder. Had there been a robust RTI framework in place, these difficulties would have been identified and rectified much earlier. It is crucial that students are identified with phonemic awareness deficits early and receive the intervention required, as unless these difficulties are corrected, additional reading progress will be minimal at any age (Bruch, 1992, Truch, 1994, in Kilpatrick, 2015).

## Universal screening and intervention

It is recommended that students in Foundation to Year 3 engage in universal screening three times per year in PA, decoding and phonic knowledge. For Australian contexts, this may occur at the following times to coincide with end-of-semester reporting:

- Term 1, Week 2
- Term 2, Week 5
- Term 4, Week 5

The types of screeners used will ideally be linked to the SSPP adopted in your school, as these assessments will link directly to the scope and sequence you are following. However, if you do not yet have a sequence or SSPP, some recommended assessments are listed opposite. Students identified at risk in these screeners may also need to undertake further diagnostic screening to identify specific needs for goal setting and intervention.

For a comprehensive list of evidence-based assessment tools, a fantastic resource is the Primary Reading Pledge (Five from Five, MultiLit, 2020), which is freely available online.

Most states in Australia have now been directed to assess all students in a phonics screener at the end of Year 1. Students scoring below a cut-off of 80% accuracy in these phonics screeners should engage in further diagnostic assessments, and depending on the outcome of the data, engage in Tier 2 or Tier 3 intervention. However, apart from the mandated phonics screening tools, I strongly recommend additional screeners to be undertaken earlier in the year as part of a whole-school RTI framework.

Recommended PA and phonics universal and diagnostic screeners that are not aligned to any SSPP include:

| Phonemic awareness | • Acadience First Sound Fluency (FSF) and Phoneme Segmentation Fluency (PSF) or DIBELS® 8th Australasian subtests<br>• CUBED DDM Phonemic Awareness screener – phoneme segmentation, first sounds, phoneme blending<br><br>Diagnostic:<br>• Astronaut Invented Spelling Test (AIST-2) – this assesses both encoding and phonemic awareness |
| --- | --- |
| Phonic knowledge/ decoding | • Acadience Nonsense Word Fluency (NWF) – letter sounds, letter names or DIBELS® 8th Australasian subtests<br>• CUBED DDM Decoding, Word Identification<br><br>Diagnostic:<br>• Phonics Books Placement Test – linked to decodable readers<br>• UK Year 1 phonics screening test |

In terms of PA and phonics intervention, intervention may be 'evidence based' (intervention program that is scientifically validated through efficacy trials) or 'evidence informed' (based on scientifically validated research but not necessarily a program). The latter may be beneficial for a student that has some code knowledge and decoding ability but has missed PA instruction and has gaps in this skill. In this instance, as the teacher, you may develop specific SMART targets and an intervention plan based on these areas of need, at the Tier 2 or Tier 3 level.

Example goals and strategies (based on a Year 1 student's profile) of a Tier 3 intervention plan includes:

| Goals | Strategies and resources |
|---|---|
| **Decoding – word level:**<br><br>By Week 9, Term 4, 2023, Max will be able to accurately decode CCVCC words on nine out of 10 occasions. | • Explicit teaching of segmenting and blending phonemes with education assistant for 10 minutes per day in addition to 30 minutes of whole-class instruction in PA and phonics.<br>• Daily reading aloud of CCVC, CVCC and CCVCC word cards each day to a teacher or education assistant for five minutes.<br>• Daily practice of reading CCVCC words on speed read display folder and study cards (home). |
| **Decoding – text level:**<br><br>By Week 9, Term 4, 2023, Max will be able to accurately decode any decodable text consisting of CCVCC code knowledge with accuracy on nine out of 10 occasions.<br><br>For example: *twist, grunt, trust, twist, strap* | • Daily home reading practice of a decodable text.<br>• Nightly home reading of an additional decodable text with previously learnt code knowledge – for one week to build fluency and confidence.<br>• Repeated reading of a dictation passage to be read each day for a week at school and home to build reading fluency. |
| **Phonics/spelling:**<br><br>By Week 4, Term 4, 2023, Max will be able to spell any CCVC or CVCC words with accuracy on nine out of 10 occasions.<br><br>By Week 9, Term 4, 2023, Max will be able to spell any CCVCC word with accuracy on nine out of 10 occasions. | • Explicitly teach Max the three forms of every new word he is taught – the phonology (sounds), the orthography (the spelling) and the meaning.<br>• Phoneme-grapheme mapping for all spelling practice at school.<br>• Provide immediate feedback for adjacent consonant errors, for example: *spelling slim for sim*<br>• Remind Max to sound each phoneme *out loud* when spelling at school and say each phoneme precisely.<br>• Daily dictation of current week's spelling foci with decodable sentences. (Three sentences per day and increasing as his writing stamina increases.) |

| Goals | Strategies and resources |
|---|---|
| **Phonemic awareness:**<br><br>By Week 9, Term 4, 2023, Max will be able to manipulate phonemes in any CCVCC word with accuracy on nine out of 10 occasions. | • Nonsense sound swapping activity five minutes per day with mini whiteboard at school, changing only one phoneme each time, for example:<br><br>*crin- cran- dran- dram- drim- drims- frims- froms- roms- croms- crams- rams- ams- am- fam- fim- frim- frims* |
| **Handwriting:**<br><br>By Week 9, Term 4, 2023, Max will be able to correctly form and orientate the following letters:<br>g b f j k p d y o | • Explicit teaching of the handwriting following the Write-Start K sequence.<br>• Daily practice at school/home on the letters identified.<br>• Use of laminated charts to show the starting points of letters.<br>• As he practises each letter, remind Max to say the sound as he does to increase the memory-motor link.<br>• Raised tactile handwriting paper to scaffold writing inside the lines. |

For a full list of evidence-based recommended phonics intervention programs, see Five from Five's Primary Reading Pledge.

## Progress monitoring

The way in which student assessment data is recorded and tracked will range from school to school, but a simple and effective approach is to identify the expected standard for the year level in each of the subskills of reading and then backward map the smaller goals for each term and half term, such as the following:

- Grapheme/phoneme knowledge:
    - Can identify the phoneme represented by each grapheme listed.
- Phonemic awareness:
    - Can segment CVC words with 'satpin' graphemes.
    - Can blend 'satpin' graphemes to decode CVC words.
    - Can manipulate phonemes in CVC words to change one phoneme to make a new word each time.

Decoding:
- – Can read CVC words with 'satpin' graphemes with 90% accuracy by Week 10, Term 1.
- Spelling and simple punctuation:
  - – Can write a dictated sentence with accuracy based on the graphemes of ... with a capital letter and full stop.

| Goals: Students can identify the phoneme represented by each grapheme listed | | | | | | | |
|---|---|---|---|---|---|---|---|
| Student names | s | a | t | p | i | n | o |
| Student A | | | | | | | |
| Student B | | | | | | | |

SPELD South Australia has freely available downloadable tracking tools, including: class trackers, individual student trackers for phonics, letter formation, high-frequency word knowledge and a term-by-term breakdown for Foundation to Year 2.

## Moving away from literacy rotations and Look, Cover, Write, Check

Despite their prevalence and popularity, literacy rotations have no evidence base. Traditional literacy rotations generally refer to students being grouped according to ability and each day they work in a small group doing a phonemic awareness or phonics game or activity. For part of the lesson (or in most cases, one day each week), each group will have a turn with the teacher engaging in explicit instruction of some kind.

This form of instruction is a waste of crucial learning time. Just from a time on task engaging in explicit instruction perspective alone, consider the number of minutes per week students are exposed to high-quality teacher-led instruction per week as opposed to the literacy rotations approach.

Look, Cover, Write, Check (LCWC) is also an ineffective method of practising spelling words, as it focuses on the whole word, not its phonemes or meaningful parts (morphemes). Typically, in this approach, children practise lists of spelling words, but often have no knowledge of the pronunciation or meaning of the words and are simply copying the word as a whole. This approach does not activate the three systems required for orthographic mapping: phonology, orthography and semantics/meaning. This is the reason why so many students do well on spelling tests but then don't transfer these spellings to their writing.

In addition to explicit teaching of spelling, linking to context and morphology across the week, replace the LCWC approach with the following routines:

**For emerging readers:**

1. Read and say the word.
2. Segment out loud, write and map the phonemes into Elkonin boxes (phoneme-grapheme mapping).
3. Blend the phonemes and say the word.
4. Say the meaning of the word.

**For Years 3+:**

1. Read the word out loud.
2. Break into syllables or meaningful parts (morphemes), for example, dis rup tive
3. Spell each meaningful part, for example, dis rupt ive
4. Say the meaning of the word.

## Starting points for PA and phonics instruction

- Tweak your instruction to align with scientific, evidence-based research. If it is not high impact and evidence based, it is not serving your students.
- Choose a SSPP to follow.
- Follow the SSPP code and program with fidelity. If it is not a commercial SSPP program, then explicitly teach the instructional routines as outlined in this chapter.
- Ensure that you are teaching in a structured, systematic approach with whole-class instruction, daily for 25 to 30 minutes.
- Use high-quality assessments such as a PA screener and non-word decoding screener to identify risk and monitor progress.
- Use assessment data to inform your planning, differentiation and intervention, but ensure that *all* students receive access to the PA and synthetic phonics code at 'year level' expectation. Any students that are needing additional support or intervention should be receiving a double dose, or they will never catch up to their peers. This is essential!

- Monitor student progress with formative assessment throughout the week. Students receiving Tier 2 intervention should be monitored every three to five weeks.
- Implement Tier 2 and Tier 3 interventions early!

## Summary

- PA is the ability to segment, blend and manipulate individual phonemes in words. It is critical for proficient reading and spelling.
- Teaching PA with graphemes is far more effective than an oral-only approach.
- Synthetic phonics refers to explicitly teaching children to 'synthesise' sounds to read and spell. Synthetic phonics instruction is an aspect of structured literacy, which is teacher-led, taught explicitly and systematically, in a fast-moving approach.
- Synthetic phonics has been proven to lead to higher achievement than analytic phonics approaches.
- Decodable texts provide novice readers with the opportunity to practise decoding using texts consisting of code knowledge they have previously learnt in the classroom.
- As part of an RTI framework, it is recommended that students engage in universal screening in PA, decoding and phonic knowledge three times per year.
- Students scoring below a cut of 80% accuracy in Year 1 phonics screeners should engage in diagnostic assessments, and depending on the outcome of the data, engage in Tier 2 or Tier 3 intervention.
- A simple and effective way to record and monitor progress is to identify the expected standard for the year level in each of the subskills of reading and then backward map from the end-of-year goal to smaller goals for each term.
- Literacy rotations have no evidence base and are a waste of precious learning time.

## Professional discussion

- To what extent are you and your school using universal and diagnostic screening tools to identify students at risk in PA, phonics and decoding?
- What instructional routines can you incorporate into your literacy block to reflect high impact instruction in PA and synthetic phonics?
- How could you incorporate a Tier 2 intervention group into your weekly routine to boost student learning for students not responding to your whole-class instruction?

## Anticipation Guide answers

| Anticipation Guide | True/False |
|---|---|
| Synthetic phonics involves teaching students a target grapheme and then students brainstorming and sorting words with that grapheme | False |
| Synthetic phonics has a high effect on student progress when taught at the whole-class level rather than ability grouping | True |
| Consonant clusters/adjacent consonants such as sl, bl, tr are taught explicitly as complete units | False |
| Phonemic awareness is ideally taught in an 'oral only' approach in addition to the phonics lesson | False |
| Synthetic phonics should be taught at a rapid pace | True |

# Self-reflection – teaching synthetic phonics

What aspects of synthetic phonics instruction are your strengths and areas for review and/or tweaking?

| During PA and phonics lessons in my class: | Strengths | Areas to tweak |
|---|---|---|
| Phonemic awareness is taught **with visual representations** (single letters/graphemes) and **not** orally only | | |
| I teach students to 'synthesise' a small group of phonemes from the outset by explicitly teaching them how to blend these phonemes to read the whole word, then model spelling these words, immediately followed by students spelling the words | | |
| There is a short daily review of previous code knowledge for students to build automaticity in PA and phonics knowledge and skills | | |
| New knowledge is taught systematically, in a logical, sequential way. I follow the structured synthetic phonics program and sequence with fidelity | | |
| There is daily 'explicit teaching' at the whole-class level, providing practice, guidance and immediate, specific feedback | | |
| A select few high-frequency words are taught alongside the phonics program each week; and from the outset students are shown that although tricky, they can in fact still be segmented and decoded like other unknown words | | |
| I am consistent in the instructional sequence of teaching PA and phonics | | |
| It is taught in a fast-moving, teacher-led approach, building on previously learnt code knowledge | | |
| Adjacent consonants (such as bl, sl, st, fr) are not taught as 'blends' but rather as individual phonemes that they are | | |

| During PA and phonics lessons in my class: | Strengths | Areas to tweak |
|---|---|---|
| **Conceptual knowledge**<br><br>Students are explicitly taught (with multiple practices and repetition) that:<br><br>One sound can have many spellings: /e/ (for example, bread, fed, said) | | |
| **Conceptual knowledge**<br><br>Children are explicitly taught that:<br><br>One spelling can have many sounds: 'ea' (for example, bread, read) | | |
| **Conceptual knowledge**<br><br>Children are explicitly taught that:<br><br>Some words have schwas (unstressed vowels) | | |
| Tier 2 and Tier 3 PA and phonics intervention for students needing additional support takes place outside (and in addition to) the whole-class explicit instruction | | |
| Dictation of previously taught code knowledge is included during the week to build written transcription skills and as a diagnostic tool for formative assessment | | |
| Students who are emerging readers (still learning how to decode) are provided decodable texts for home reading practice that are based on code knowledge they have learnt and their decoding skill proficiency, for example, ability to decode at a CVC, CCVC, CVCC, CCVCC level | | |

## Chapter 9

# VOCABULARY AND MORPHOLOGY

"The simple act of reading aloud is not enough to provide
consistent results to support the connection of reading
aloud and vocabulary learning"

~ Beck, McKeown & Kucan (2013)

## Chapter overview

- Self-reflection
- Why the explicit teaching of vocabulary?
- Three tiers of words
- Four stages of word knowledge
- Three forms of every word
- Principles of teaching vocabulary
- Identifying Tier 2 words in texts
- Before, during and after vocabulary instruction routine
- Example activities for applying the new vocabulary
- Morphology and etymology
- The importance of teaching morphology
- Layers of the English language
- Where to start with morphology in the early years
- Example lesson: prefixes
- Graphic organisers: morphological awareness
- Word-building routine for multimorphemic words

- Assessing morphology
- Assessing vocabulary
- Vocabulary difficulties and intervention
- Morphology intervention
- Summary
- Professional discussion
- Common morphemes

## Self-reflection

| Self-reflection | Give yourself a rating out of 5 |
| --- | --- |
| **I have a thorough understanding of:** | |
| • How to plan and implement high impact vocabulary instruction | |
| • Why vocabulary instruction is so important | |
| • How to identify Tier 2 words for instruction | |
| • How to assess and monitor progress in vocabulary instruction and learning | |
| **My goal is always to:** | |
| • Choose up to 10 high-quality Tier 2 words per week to teach | |
| • Review previously taught vocabulary words in an ongoing cycle | |

## Why the explicit teaching of vocabulary?

A longitudinal study from birth to five years of age found that there is a 1.4-million-word discrepancy, in the cumulative number of words exposed to, between a child who has never been read to and a child who has been read to every night (Logan et al., 2019). This huge gap between students creates an uneven playing field for many children when embarking on their entry into full-time schooling. The only way we, as educators, have any chance of closing this gap is through the explicit teaching of vocabulary from the first day of school.

Vocabulary is a strong predictor of reading comprehension and fluency. If students do not have sufficient vocabulary knowledge, they may indeed learn to proficiently 'lift the words off the page' when decoding, but not understand the meaning of the words they are reading, leading to impaired reading comprehension. This strong correlation is a predictor of not only reading success in primary school, but also into high school (Beck & McKeown, 2013).

## Three tiers of words

With approximately 88,000 words in English it is difficult to know where to start in what words to teach. When planning vocabulary instruction, there are three categories of words to consider (Beck, McKeown & Kucan, 2013). Tier 1 words are the most basic words that appear in general conversations. These are words that children are readily exposed to at an early age and include words such as *warm, cat, girl, swim, bath* and *hot*. These are not words that are generally needed to be explicitly taught unless there are gaps in language. Of course, students with EALD, however, may need support and explicit teaching of these words.

Tier 2 words are frequently used in mature language speakers and are typically found in written text. Examples include *emerged, glittering, precede, gnashed* and *alight*. These Tier 2 words are the words we need to explicitly teach to students. A recommended goal for instruction is to teach 400 words per year (Beck, McKeown & Kucan, 2013), or equivalent to 10 new words per school week in Years 5–6. These words are taught through rich texts we read *to* students each week.

Tier 3 words are those of least frequency and tend to be of Greek origin. Examples include *photosynthesis, cyclone, polygon, tentacles* and *oxygen* and are typically related to science and specific units of study. These words also require explicit teaching, but in the context they are being taught, such as HASS, science or maths lessons. Tier 3 words are ideally taught in planned, sequential topic units to build schema and background knowledge, essential for reading comprehension (Smith, Serry, Snow & Hammond, 2021).

| | Tier 1 words | Tier 2 words | Tier 3 words |
|---|---|---|---|
| When and where used/ found | Everyday language use; students usually know these words well by the start of schooling | Used in mature language speakers; typically found in texts | Rarely used; related to science and units of study |
| Example words | warm, cat, girl, swim, bath, hot | emerged, glittering, precede, gnashed, alight, extraordinary | photosynthesis, cyclone, tentacles, oxygen, polygon |
| Explicitly teach when? | If there are gaps in language; for students learning English as an Additional Language | Daily, explicit teaching of Tier 2 words chosen from high-quality rich fiction and non-fiction texts read *to* students | In context within planned, sequential topic units |
| How many words per week? | | Foundation to Year 2: two to five words<br>Years 3–4: seven to eight words<br>Years 5–6: 10 words | |

When choosing Tier 2 words, the following considerations may be helpful:

- Would children be able to explain these words using words they already know? Such as 'sibling' – relating it to their sisters and brothers.
- Are these words useful for writing?
- Would they appear in texts somewhat frequently?
- Could I also teach these words in a continuum to show shades of meaning? (for example, dark – dim – dull – well-lit – bright) Although not an essential consideration, this can be helpful for teaching the link between related words and building schema in the long-term memory.

## Four stages of word knowledge

In terms of word knowledge, it is not a case of students either knowing a word or not, but instead word knowledge exists in a continuum of understanding. Dale (1965) refers to this as four stages of word knowledge.

To demonstrate how the four stages of word knowledge apply to us as adults, consider the words in the table below and identify where you would place yourself on the Vocabulary Knowledge Scale (VKS).

1. Never heard of the word.
2. Heard of it but don't know what it means.
3. Know the word has something to do with... X
4. Know it well and can explain it in context.

| | 1. Never heard of the word | 2. Heard of it but don't know what it means | 3. Know the word has something to do with... X | 4. Know it well and can explain it in context |
|---|---|---|---|---|
| dolphin | | | | |
| photosynthesis | | | | |
| winch | | | | |
| acissmus | | | | |

One helpful formative assessment approach linked to the four stages of word knowledge is to pair it back to three stages and assign a colour to each stage. For example, teach students that if they have never heard of a word, it is a red word. If they have heard of it but don't know what it means, it is an orange word; and if they know the word and its meaning, it is a green word. This simple colour-coding system can be used when discussing words with students, and students can indicate with a thumbs-up, hand up or on their mini whiteboard to what extent the words are familiar or well known. This three-point VKS can be done orally or in written format with three columns, including the following:

1. Never heard of the word (red word)
2. Heard of it but don't know what it means (orange word)
3. Know it well and can explain it (green word)

## Three forms of every word

When explicitly teaching vocabulary, it is important to make explicit the three forms of every word. Effective vocabulary instruction involves not just explaining the meaning of a word, but also making the connections between a word's phonology (phonemes and syllables), orthography (how it is spelt) and their meanings (morphemes and their meaning and the overall definition of a word). This enables students to develop a strong foundation to each word to enable the process of storing words in long-term memory.

For example, the word 'ship' can be broken down into at least three forms.

1. **Phonology** – one syllable, three phonemes: /sh/ /i/ /p/
2. **Orthography** – four letters: s, h, i, p
3. **Semantics** – noun, a large boat; one root word with one morpheme
4. **Morphology and etymology** – root word, Anglo-Saxon origin

## Principles of teaching vocabulary

A few years ago, when my school was looking to implement whole-school approaches to the teaching of vocabulary, I was on the hunt for a whole-school scope and sequence. My literacy team and a nearby school engaged in a whole-day professional learning session on vocabulary instruction and from there I changed my thinking, as the more research I did, the more I realised that the most effective approach was to teach vocabulary in the context of teacher read-alouds of quality texts. In retrospect, this made a lot of sense, as rather than teaching a word from a list out of context, the words chosen are taught within the context of a rich text, giving students a strong context for instruction.

However, although students do learn words through oral language and texts read to them, "the simple act of reading aloud is not enough to provide consistent results to support the connection of reading aloud and vocabulary learning" (Beck, McKeown & Kucan, 2013). The key here is that teaching vocabulary in the context of texts read requires explicit instruction, identifying the three forms of every word, with application and review; this is what makes the difference.

## Identifying Tier 2 words in texts

To familiarise yourself with how to identify Tier 2 words, consider the text below, which sits nicely within an ocean sustainability topic.

### Sandy the Cheeky Dolphin

Deep <u>beneath</u> the <u>glistening</u> waters of the *Indian Ocean* lived a family of *bottlenose dolphins*. Mother and Father Dolph had six dolphins: Splish, Slash, Splosh, Aqua, Marine and the <u>youngest</u> of them all was Sandy.

The dolphins <u>spent</u> their days <u>frolicking</u> in the water, <u>spinning</u> and <u>twisting</u> their bodies in the air, playing seaweed soccer, <u>leaping</u> through hoops, and <u>diving</u> for <u>tasty</u> fish <u>morsels</u>. All the <u>siblings</u> were happy doing dolphin things, <u>except</u> for Sandy. Sandy was <u>bored</u>.

As a <u>result</u>, Sandy was always up to <u>mischief</u>. He liked to swim around Oliver Octopus so fast that he would get <u>tangled</u> up in his *tentacles*. He loved starting trouble with the *reef sharks* and was often <u>naughty</u> at Dolphin School. Sandy was very <u>cheeky indeed</u>.

The selected underlined words are consistent with Tier 2 words – words that are likely to be found in texts that are typically familiar with mature language speakers but require explicit teaching for students. The words in italics – for example, 'Indian Ocean' and 'tentacles' – are considered Tier 3 words.

## Before, during and after vocabulary instruction routine

As discussed earlier, vocabulary instruction is most effective when it is taught: a) in the context of rich texts through teacher read-alouds, and b) within planned, sequential knowledge-rich units. In later chapters, we will explore the notion of topic units, but for this chapter our focus will be on the instructional sequence for teaching vocabulary through rich text, and the preceding planning stage.

During the planning stage, there are a few key considerations I would suggest. The first is the type of rich text. It is important to select a range of fiction and non-fiction texts. This can be picture books, novels, articles, model texts for writing, diary entries, etc. For a class read-aloud, the key here is that it is at a level above the reading ability of most of the students so that they are exposed to high-level language, syntax and text structures.

It is also highly recommended that initially you read the chosen text a couple of times to yourself. The first read is to get the general gist of the text and the second time to identify main events (in fiction texts), and key knowledge or understandings to teach (in non-fiction texts), to build background knowledge. The next step is to highlight the chosen Tier 2 and Tier 3 words to explicitly teach. Taking time to select the pause points to check for understanding is also highly recommended.

The next step is to develop a system for planning out the vocabulary sessions.

At the start of a vocabulary session through a teacher read-aloud:

1. Activate prior knowledge related to the text at the start of the lesson.
2. Provide a quick overview of the text prior to reading. For example, if it was in relation to Sandy the Cheeky Dolphin, you might say, this is a story about a dolphin that was bored of his dolphin life and went on an adventure on his own. This quick summary can be a helpful scaffold for students with language difficulties and students with EALD.
3. Read the story aloud to the students, pause at predetermined places and monitor comprehension by posing queries throughout. I use sticky notes to mark these places in the texts.

Instructional sequence for teaching vocabulary after the read-aloud:

1. Introduce the targeted Tier 2 words with a picture visual, with the context of the text. Use of a PowerPoint template is ideal here.
2. Say the word, and students repeat the word orally.
3. Teacher models and students repeat – clapping out the syllables (or segmenting orally), then tapping the phonemes. Mark out syllables with upright strokes and phonemes with dots and dashes. The Sound Buttons font can do this for you.
4. Explain the meaning of the word.
5. Provide a sentence to build context, related to the visual.
6. Break it into root words and affixes; and identify their meanings.
7. Provide examples and non-examples. Non-examples are helpful for solidifying understanding of the examples.
8. Ask students to say the word and its meaning in their own words with a partner.

### PowerPoint slide examples

*(for explicit teaching of new Tier 2 vocabulary after the initial teacher read-aloud)*

### Slide 1

- The first slide shows the syllabification and the phonology of the targeted word. The teacher says the word and the students repeat. The whole class (with or without clapping) syllabifies the word orally.
- The whole class segments the word into its phonemes (with or without tapping the fingers).

### Slide 2

- The next slide shows an example sentence with the targeted word.
- The teacher explains a student-friendly definition and the type of word. Alternate definitions would be introduced as the week goes on.
- The teacher identifies the morphemes and origins and writes it in a Word Sum (more detail on page 156).

| Sentence | Meaning | Morphology |
|---|---|---|
| The old man was **agitated** as he thought some of his toys were missing. | **Agitated** means to feel troubled, worried or nervous; or to 'stir up'. It is an adjective. | agitate + d = agitated (past tense)<br><br>(Latin) |

### Slide 3

- This slide shows examples and non-examples of the targeted word.
- As the week goes on, the teacher would ask students for other examples and non-examples.

Examples and non-examples

On subsequent days after the initial teaching of the words, multiple reviews and applications of the words are required for long-term memory transfer. Suggestions include:

1. Re-read the text to students.
2. Review the Tier 2 or Tier 3 words with the approach on page 147.
3. Apply the vocabulary in sentences and change them to a statement, question, command or exclamation and/or add appositives (*The Writing Revolution* is a great resources for this).
4. Utilise a word jar for new words – use this throughout the day as an exit slip.
5. Introduce the concept of 'Magpie Books' (as in the Talk for Writing approach) for students to 'be like magpies' and record new words they come across to refer to during writing.
6. Apply the vocabulary words by completing sentence stems, using: because, but, so conjunctions.
7. Word association activity. Which word do you associate with...? Why?
8. Word relationship activity. *Does a relationship exist between these words?*
9. Review and repeat!

The need for repetition and review of the words cannot be underestimated. Children generally need to hear a word 15 times before it is well known and understood (Marzano, 2004). For a student who is struggling, this increases from 15 to 40 repetitions, and for a child with a learning disorder in reading, the repetitions required could increase to between 40 and 200 times (Montgomery, Ilk & Moats, 2012).

## Example activities for applying the new vocabulary

**Word association activity:** This activity is about making connections to things students know about the world. Choose one of your target words and ask students to come up with a movie, famous person or a common experience that they can associate and ask students to explain the connection they see.

| Word | Associations | Reason |
|---|---|---|
| stormed | An angry teenager thundering to their room | Because they are not getting their own way in going to a party |
| extravagant | Movie stars | Throwing lavish parties |

**Because, but, so:** This routine requires students to apply the target vocabulary into sentences using conjunctions. Not only is it fantastic for improving syntax skills, it is a great approach for knowledge building in cross-curricular units.

| Tier 2 or 3 vocabulary words | Sentence stems – because, but, so |
|---|---|
| glared | The thoughtful vet **glared** at the lady shouting at her dog *because*... |
| | The thoughtful vet **glared** at the lady shouting at her dog *but*... |
| | The thoughtful vet **glared** at the lady shouting at her dog *so*... |

**Card shuffle:** For older students, a card shuffle is a great way for students to work cooperatively to match vocabulary words to their definitions.

**Beat the clock quiz:** Providing older students with opportunities to race against the clock for two or five minutes, to match words with their meanings, or to complete a grid by identifying the phonemes, syllables, morphemes and definitions, is a great motivator for many students that love the element of competition. This could be a good mixed-ability activity.

**Word jar:** A word jar using a recycled flour container is a wonderful way to store and review the Tier 2 and Tier 3 words you teach throughout the year.

## Morphology and etymology

*"Morphemic knowledge greatly expands children's vocabularies because familiarity with common morphemes facilitates understanding of many interrelated words"*

~ Spear-Swerling (2015)

It is important that children are taught the interrelation between morphology, phonology and etymology, as when we combine all three areas, it teaches children how our writing system works. In its simplest form, it is the study of the structure of words and their meanings. Morphological instruction, however, should never replace a structured synthetic phonics approach and should be taught alongside the phonics/spelling instruction.

# Morphology definitions

| morpheme | The smallest unit of meaning within a word. Morphemes are classified as either being a base or root word (bed, stand, rupt) or an affix (a bound morpheme that occurs before or after a base or root word) |
|---|---|
| morphology | The study of words, word parts and their meanings |
| morphological awareness | "The ability to recognise the meaning of parts of words such as roots, affixes (prefixes and suffixes) and grammatical endings such as -s, -ed, -ly and -ing" (Kilpatrick, 2015) |
| morphograph | The orthographic representation of a morpheme – prefix, suffix, root or base word, used in teaching spelling |
| etymology | The origin and historical development of a linguistic form, tracing its language from one to another. It is the study of the origins of words and the way they have changed in history. |
| affix | A bound morpheme that comes before or after a base or root word (prefix or suffix) |
| prefix | A bound morpheme that comes before a base or root word (dis- pre- un-) |
| suffix | A bound morpheme that comes after a base or root word (-ly -ing -ed) |
| root word | A morpheme that cannot be broken down into a smaller meaning, for example, head, happy |
| bound root | A morpheme that does not stand alone, for example, rupt, astro, ject, mit, pute; also referred to as a base word |
| inflectional morphology | Changes the number, tense or aspect of a word, for example, 's' (adding 's' to pig, changes from one pig to more than one pig: pigs); '-ed' (adding -ed to 'walk' changes it from walking presently to in the past) |
| derivational morphology | Changes the form – from an adjective to a noun, for example, 'electric' is an adjective; when adding -ian, it changes to 'electrician', a noun) |

## The importance of teaching morphology

There are many reasons for the explicit teaching of morphology. Some of these reasons include:

- Morphemic knowledge is necessary for encoding, as if a student only encodes using grapheme-phoneme correspondences, they would likely spell words like knowledgeable and photographer as nolijabul and futogriffer respectively (Spear-Swerling, 2015).
- It is of particular benefit for students with language and literacy deficits. Wolter and Green (2013) cites, "Explicit instruction regarding the morphological structure of words may be of particular importance for children with language and literacy deficits, given that they may not have the foundational morphological knowledge that would typically aid in successful reading and spelling."
- By teaching children about the connection between phonology, morphology and etymology, it helps students understand how our language works.
- Improves – phonological awareness, vocabulary and non-word reading (Goodwin & Ahn, 2010).
- Some studies have found that explicit teaching of morphology can have a positive impact on reading comprehension, including significant progress for students with EALD (Amirjalili & Jabbari, 2018).
- Morphological awareness provides students with knowledge of the meanings of parts of words (such as a root word or prefix) that can aid reading comprehension even if it is a word they have never seen before.

Here is an example. Consider the following word:

aquaduotractist

As educated adults, who have never seen this word before, we could ascertain the rough meaning of this word and have some level of comprehension by breaking it down into the morphemes and distinguishing each meaning, such as:

aqua = water
duo = two
tract = to pull
ist = one who does (a particular form of work)

From this morphological analysis we could estimate the meaning that it is perhaps an underwater tractor for two people! I say 'estimate' as this is not a real word, yet we could use our morphological awareness to make assumptions of its meaning based on our previous knowledge of the morphemes it contains. This is an example of why teaching morphology to students is so impactful.

## Layers of the English language

The English language has a deep orthography. In contrast, languages like Spanish have a shallow orthography, meaning that each grapheme is fairly consistent in representing one phoneme. English is not like this. We have 26 alphabet letters representing roughly 44 different phonemes, meaning that much of our language is not pronounced as it reads. English is also a multimorphemic language with three layers: Anglo-Saxon, Latin and Greek.

1.  **Anglo-Saxon morphemes** contribute to 20% of English and usually consist of one-syllable words: for example, book, yard, rain, head, -ly, -ing or compound words such as yardstick, backyard, bookworm.
2.  **Latin morphemes** contribute to approximately 55% of English and are usually multisyllabic words, including bound roots such as: dent (tooth), pro- (before/in favour of), struct (build), rupt (break).
3.  **Greek morphemes** contribute to approximately 11% of English words and usually involve words related to science, school or the arts and many of our more complex spellings, such as: 'c' as in cyclone, 'ch' as in chemist, 'ph' as in phone and 'ps' as in pseudo.

The three layers of English as a multimorphemic language

**Greek** — Specialised words – especially in science, for example, photosynthesis

**Latin** — Technical, sophisticated words used in formal settings, for example, textbooks or literature

**Anglo-Saxon** — Common, short, everyday words used frequently in ordinary situations, for example, book, yard, rain, head

Adapted from M Henry, 1987; After Calfee & Associates, Stanford University Percentages, in Van Cleave, 2012

## Where to start with morphology in the early years

During systematic phonics instruction in the early years, students can be taught the function of morphemes in reading and spelling by introducing simple plural suffixes such as 's' when reading and writing known CVC words. For example: *pet = one pet; pets = more than one pet.* A few starting points include:

- Start with words with one base word (one morpheme only), for example, CVC words such as sit, pig, jump, and teach simple suffix plurals such as 's', and show how they change the meaning (cat, cats = two cats).
- Teach students how prefixes can change the meaning of words incidentally, such as *misuse = use the wrong way/badly; tie a shoelace/untie a shoelace.*
- Introduce morphology as it fits in the phonics code sequence, for example, the suffix 'ing' can be introduced when students are taught the digraph <ng>.

## Example lesson: prefixes

Here is an example of a six-step explicit instruction lesson in teaching morphology:

| Learning intention | We will understand the meaning of the prefix 'dis' and use it to read, write and understand many new words. |
|---|---|
| I Do | 1. **Write** the morphograph (prefix) dis- on the board. |
| | 2. **Explain the meaning:** dis- is often found at the beginning of a word. It is a prefix. It means 'the opposite of', 'away' or 'not'. |
| | 3. **Word building:** I am going to build a word with dis- as a prefix. When we see a word that starts with dis- we know that part of the meaning is about either: not/away/opposite of. This prefix is of Latin origin. Here is my word: |
| | dis rupt ive = disruptive |
| |     dis = not/apart<br>    rupt = to break<br>    ive = tendency to |
| | 'disruptive' means a tendency to break apart or away. |

| We Do | 4. **Word generation:** Can we think of other words that begin with dis-? Model generating a list. I will start (as a think-aloud). *dislike* *disappear* *disrupt* |
|---|---|
| You Do | 5. **Word generation:** Let's make some more words with dis- (in mixed-ability pairs), using a Word Web. Students could use magnetic morphographs to do this as a scaffold. Extension: Ask students to look at each word and use the morphographs that they know to work out the literal meaning of each word. |
| Review | 6. Think about what you have learnt about the prefix 'dis'. What can you tell me you have learnt today? Put 'dis-' in the class word jar. Follow-up activities/review in subsequent days/weeks such as Word Sums, Word Matrices and Word Webs. |
| Self-assessment | To what extent did I achieve the learning intention? *Thumbs up, side, down formative assessment.* |

## Graphic organisers: morphological awareness

The following are three recommended graphic organisers for supporting students in developing morphological awareness: Word Webs, Word Matrices and Word Sums.

**Word Webs:** are a great tool for practising previously learnt morphemes and are ideal as part of daily review.

### Word Web – Morphology

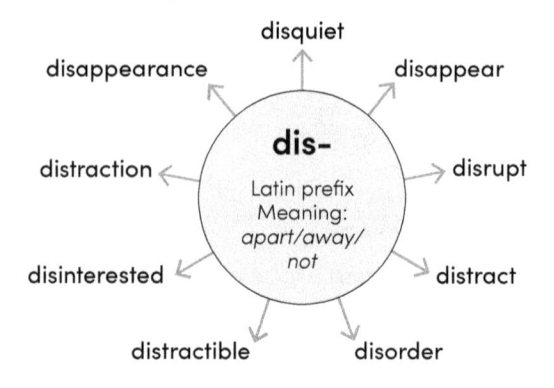

## Word Webs routine

1. Explicitly teach the new morphograph and its definition.
2. Students work in mixed-ability pairs to list as many words as they can with the target morphograph.
3. Pairs share their words with the class. Students need to be able to explain the meaning of the words listed. The website Etymonline may be used as a support.
4. The pair with the highest number of words in the Word Web is the winner.

## Word Matrix routine

A Word Matrix is a fantastic scaffold for identifying the underlying morphographic structure of a word. The root or base word is highlighted in the middle and students use their knowledge of other words to develop the matrix following explicit teaching of many worked examples by the teacher. Students can move from left to right only, taking one morphograph from each box, but can indeed start from the centre root word and move to the left from there. An example that is highlighted in the matrix below is as follows:

re + con + struct + ive = reconstructive

| re<br>de | con | | ure | al | ly |
|---|---|---|---|---|---|
| | | | | s | |
| | | | ing | | |
| in | do | **struct**<br>from Latin base 'stru'<br>meaning 'build' | ive | | |
| ob<br>in | | | s<br>ing<br>ion<br>or<br>ed | | |

An example Word Matrix for the base word 'struct'

1. Explicitly teach the new morphograph and its definition, such as the root word 'struct'.
2. Students work in mixed-ability pairs to create as many words as they can with the target morphograph in a list first and then in a Word Matrix. The key here is to use only one morphograph in each box when reading from left to right.
3. Pairs share their words with the class. Students need to be able to explain the meaning of the words listed. The website Etymonline may be used as a support or to extend students.
4. The pair with the highest number of words that can be created in the Word Matrix is the winner.

*This is also an excellent routine for independent practice at the end of a week after explicit teaching through worked examples.*

### Word Sums routine

Word Sums are another high impact approach to highlighting the underlying structure of a multimorphemic word. Students simply use an addition number sentence to break down the morphographs in a word.

| help + ful + ness = helpfulness |
| --- |
| + + = |

## Word-building routine for multimorphemic words

Below is an example lesson outline for word building.

| Learning intention | I know the meanings of the morphemes in 'disruptive' and can create a Word Matrix with the base word 'rupt'. |
| --- | --- |
| I Do | These are the morphographs that make the word disruptive: |
| | dis- rupt -ive |
| | Teacher builds the word: 'disruptive' using magnetic wipe-its. One morpheme is on each magnet. Write it as a Word Sum: dis + rupt + ive = disruptive |

| I Do (cont.) | Explain the meaning of each morphograph. Explain the literal meaning of the word 'disruptive' based on its morphemes: dis- not/apart, rupt- to break, ive- tendency to = a tendency to break apart/away. This has a Latin origin. |
| --- | --- |
| | *For differentiation, you may need to model segmenting the morphemes into phonemes.* |
| We Do | Here is a sentence with the word 'disruptive'. |
| | Can you think of another sentence for 'disruptive'? Tell your partner (mixed-ability pairs): Think, Pair, Share. |
| | Show the word with alternate prefixes and suffixes using the Word Matrix graphic organiser. |
| | Let's create other words using the morphemes in 'disruptive'. I'll start. Write examples to show students. |
| | Tell me another word (for example, disrupting, erupt) with 'rupt' at the base and model write these words on the Word Matrix. |
| You Do | In your mixed-ability pairs, create your own Word Matrix using 'rupt' as the base word. Move around the room providing explicit feedback. |
| Plenary | Review the lesson and extent to which students have achieved the learning intention. |
| Review | Follow up activities/review/word jar in subsequent days/weeks. |

## Assessing morphology

One highly recommended assessment tool is the Diagnostic Spelling Test – Morphology (DiST-m) that assesses a person's ability to apply morphological regularities in spelling. Developed by Dr Saskia Kohnen, the DiST-m forms part of the evidence-based Motif series. The Dist-m is designed for assessing students from Year 3 to secondary school and, in my experience, can be used within the whole class or for remediation purposes.

I have found it particularly useful for Tier 3 instruction to pinpoint specific spelling difficulties that are over and above phonic knowledge. The DiSTm consists of 28 morphologically complex non-words (for example, 'trocked') that the teacher reads to the students. It also has an excellent analysis tool to identify common error patterns to support teachers with planning, target setting and intervention. This can be found at www.motif.org.au/distm

## Assessing vocabulary

Because vocabulary knowledge is so closely linked to background knowledge, it is difficult to find vocabulary assessments that are not biased. The National Reading Panel identified that teacher-developed tests are best for assessing vocabulary, as the more closely assessment matches the instructional context, the more appropriate the conclusions about the instruction will be (NICHD, 2000, 4.26). Below are some examples of assessments that teachers can adapt to their vocabulary instruction.

### Vocabulary Recognition Task

The Vocabulary Recognition Task (VRT) is a formative assessment that is done pre- and post-learning of a knowledge unit. Selected Tier 3 words are listed on paper and students circle the words that have something to do with the unit they will be learning about/have learnt about. For example, if students are learning about the life cycle of frogs, students will need to identify (by circling) the words that they believe are vocabulary related to the unit. At the conclusion of the unit, the same sheet will be used, and students can show their vocabulary progress using a different colour pencil.

Example of a VRT

### Life cycle of frogs

We have been learning about the life cycles of frogs. Put a circle around the words that you can read and are sure have something to do with this unit.

| | | |
|---|---|---|
| tadpoles | vertebrate | flies |
| larvae | mammal | eggs |
| nest | amphibian | |

### Concept Web

Another example of a formative assessment for vocabulary is through a concept web. Like the VRT, students use a graphic organiser to list vocabulary related to the knowledge topic being taught in class before and after a knowledge unit. An example of this type of graphic organiser is below on mammals.

| Mammals | |
|---|---|
| Types of mammals | Features of mammals |
| Mammal body parts | Non-examples of mammals |

## Vocabulary quiz

An oldie but a goodie, is a vocabulary quiz to determine knowledge learnt in relation to the vocabulary being taught in a knowledge or rich text unit.

| Vocabulary words | Definition | Example of how the word might be used/sentence |
|---|---|---|
| emerged | | |
| tempestuous | | |
| morsels | | |

## Vocabulary difficulties and intervention

If a student has strong decoding skills, good verbal skills, yet poor comprehension, a comprehensive vocabulary assessment might be investigated. A school or clinical psychologist could administer the Peabody Picture Vocabulary Test; vocabulary and similarities subtest (from Wechsler Abbreviated Scale of Intelligence) and a speech pathologist would also be recommended for a full language assessment.

## Morphology intervention

Tier 2 morphology intervention may be beneficial in the following circumstances:

- Difficulty decoding multisyllabic words
- Vocabulary deficits
- EALD students with reading difficulties
- A student who appears to have good comprehension but poor decoding/phonics skills at the multisyllabic level
- A reader who reads accurately but without automaticity

This type of intervention might consist of additional, explicit instruction in the following:

- Recognising affixes and root/base words in words
- Teaching students to look out for prefixes and suffixes
- Understanding the meaning of morphemes (affixes and base words)
- Identifying patterns and morphemic word families
- Creating multimorphemic words by word building
- Word Sorts

## Summary

- English words can be divided into three tiers of language complexity: with Tier 2 and Tier 3 words being most critical for explicit instruction. This is not to be confused with the tiers of instruction in RTI.
- Tier 2 and Tier 3 words are best taught through read-alouds of rich texts, within planned, sequential topics of knowledge.
- It is important for teachers to make visible the connection between all forms of a word: phonology, orthography, meaning and morphology.
- Students need to be learning 10 new words per school week by Years 5–6, seven to eight words in Years 3–4, and two to five words in Foundation.
- It is essential that after teaching new vocabulary, these words are applied in different ways and reviewed often.
- Class-based vocabulary assessments are recommended, as when assessments are aligned with instruction, there is greater validity in terms of the judgements that can be drawn.
- Morphology knowledge is necessary for encoding (spelling).

## Professional discussion

- To what extent is our current vocabulary, morphology instruction and assessment in line with best practice?
- What changes can we make that are low-yield actions that could result in high impact, quick wins?
- What consistent vocabulary routines can we implement to ensure high-quality vocabulary instruction is in place?

## Common morphemes

| Prefixes | Meaning | Examples |
| --- | --- | --- |
| in- | into; not | into, incomplete |
| un- | not | undo, untie |
| mis- | wrong | mistaken, misunderstand |
| dis- | away, separate, not | discolour, disappear |
| de- | down, away from | deescalate, depend |
| pre- | before | prejudice, preview |
| a- | not, in, on, without | atypical, aside |
| pro- | in favour of, positive, in front of | professional, proactive |
| con- | together, with | connect, confident |
| com- | with, together | compliment, command, company, committee |
| re- | back again | replay, recycle |
| sub- | under | submarine |
| ex- | out, away from | extension, extraordinary |

| Suffixes | Meaning | Examples |
| --- | --- | --- |
| -s | more than one | cats, eats |
| -er | one who does; more | teacher, banker, shorter |
| -ly | in a certain way | quickly, naughtily |
| -ed | in the past | walked, cried |

| Suffixes | Meaning | Examples |
|---|---|---|
| -ing | an action or result | painting |
| -less | without | boneless |
| -ship | how something is, to do with status | friendship |
| -y | a state of being | bony, shiny |
| -ible | ability | flexible |
| -ful | having qualities of, full of | beautiful |
| -ion | a process, state or result | decoration |
| -able | able to be | inflatable |
| -est | most | biggest |
| -ish | a little | childish |

| Root/base words | Meaning | Examples |
|---|---|---|
| hope | to anticipate with pleasure | hoping, hopeful, hopeless |
| play | to move at a brisk pace, move with joy | playful, player, playing |
| able | ability | unable, disable, ability |
| port | to carry | transport, porter, reporter |
| ject | to throw, to throw down | inject, interject, subject |
| rupt | to break | disrupt, interrupt |

## Chapter 10

# READING FLUENCY

"If readers do not develop adequate levels of fluency, they can become stuck in the middle of the bridge, able to decode words but with insufficient automaticity to adequately facilitate comprehension or enjoy the process of reading"

~ International Literacy Association (2018)

## Chapter overview

- Self-reflection
- Defining fluency
- Accuracy
- Reading rate
- Prosody
- Progressions of fluency development
- Orthographic mapping and reading fluency
- Assessing accuracy and reading rate
- Suggested assessment tools
- High impact opportunities for teaching fluency
- Progress monitoring
- Identifying and responding to fluency difficulties
- Fluency intervention approaches
- Summary
- Professional discussion

## Self-reflection

| Self-reflection | Give yourself a rating out of 5 |
| --- | --- |
| **I have a very thorough understanding of:** | |
| • All components of reading fluency | |
| • How to determine and implement useful assessments for reading fluency | |
| • The rate of reading expected for the students I teach | |
| • How to implement fluency routines in the literacy block, including fluency pairs, repeated reading and choral reading | |
| • How to assess and monitor fluency progress | |
| **My goal is always to:** | |
| • Model fluent reading in a range of texts and teach fluency on a daily basis | |
| • Assess words correct per minute (oral reading fluency) three times per year to track progress and respond appropriately to students below expected standard | |
| • Set high expectations for all students in fluency development and set individual goals based on specific need, for example, grapheme, word, paragraph or text level fluency | |

Reading fluency is a complex and multifaceted construct (Hudson, Pullen, Lane & Torgesen, 2009; Hudson et al., 2009) and is essential for reading proficiency. For analogy's sake, reading fluency is like the bridge that runs between word recognition and language; and reading comprehension. Without fluency, it is near impossible to avoid reading comprehension being hampered, as fluency and comprehension are interdependent of one another. "Fluency can only occur if the reader comprehends the material as it is read, in order to pause and phrase groups of words appropriately. Similarly, if reading is hesitant and disjointed, meaning is lost. The two elements support each other" (Konza, 2011).

## Defining fluency

Hasbrouck and Glaser (2019) define fluency as *reasonably accurate reading at an appropriate rate*, with suitable expression, that leads to accurate and *deep comprehension* and *motivation to read*. Wolf and Katzir-Cohen (2001) elaborate further by identifying a componential structure of fluency development in students, based on integrated progressions of development, with the following explanation:

> "*In its beginnings, reading fluency is the product of the initial development of accuracy and the subsequent development of automaticity in underlying sublexical processes, lexical processes, and their integration in single word reading and connected text. These include perceptual, phonological, orthographic, and morphological processes at the letter-, letter-pattern, and word-level, as well as semantic and syntactic processes at the word-level and connected text-level. After it is fully developed, reading fluency refers to a level of accuracy and rate where decoding is relatively effortless; where oral reading is smooth and accurate with correct prosody; and where attention can be allocated to comprehension.*"

## Accuracy

The foundation of reading fluency is accurate word reading (Hasbrouck, 2021). To achieve this, in the early years of schooling, the focus must be on PA and teaching the alphabetic code through explicit and systematic synthetic phonics. Once students have moved past the decoding stage and they are able to instantaneously recognise words by sight (and know the meaning of these words), then these words become 'orthographically mapped', becoming part of the reader's 'sight vocabulary'. The greater the number of words that are understood and recognised on sight, the greater the range of texts accessible to students (Konza, 2011).

So, how accurate is '*reasonably*' accurate? When students are reading texts independently, we need to be aiming to provide texts that are read with 95% accuracy, and 97–98% accuracy for emerging or beginning readers. A good way to determine if a text is suitable for independent reading is through a simple 100 word check. If there are more than five errors for every 100 words, then the text is not suitable; as when accuracy falls below 95%, reading comprehension will be affected (Hasbrouck, 2021). A 100 word check, as recommended by MultiLit (2007), is a simple template for assessing whether the text is at the appropriate level for 'reasonable' accuracy, for independent reading.

## 100 word check

Date:                Book and unit:                                    Total errors:

|  |  |  |  |  |  |  |  |  |  |
|--|--|--|--|--|--|--|--|--|--|
|  |  |  |  |  |  |  |  |  |  |
|  |  |  |  |  |  |  |  |  |  |
|  |  |  |  |  |  |  |  |  |  |
|  |  |  |  |  |  |  |  |  |  |
|  |  |  |  |  |  |  |  |  |  |
|  |  |  |  |  |  |  |  |  |  |
|  |  |  |  |  |  |  |  |  |  |
|  |  |  |  |  |  |  |  |  |  |
|  |  |  |  |  |  |  |  |  |  |
|  |  |  |  |  |  |  |  |  |  |

Adapted from the MultiLit Reinforced Reading 100 Word Sample (www.multilit.com/wp-content/uploads/2020/03/RR-100-word-sample.pdf).

## Reading rate

The speed at which readers can access connected text has been found to be almost as important as word reading accuracy (Kuhn & Stahl, 2000). When a reader is both accurate and rapid, it means that the word identification processes have become automatised – meaning they no longer require conscious attention, freeing cognitive space for higher-order comprehension processes (Konza, 2011). However, although developing an efficient reading rate is essential, students need to understand that there are other key aspects to reading fluency than speed alone.

## Prosody

Prosody, often referred to as reading expression, is the third core element of fluency. Prosody refers to the rise and fall of pitch, syllable prominence, phrasing and rhythm while reading. Prosodic features are essential for reading stories aloud, making oral reading meaningful.

## Progressions of fluency development

As discussed earlier, fluent reading is a product of many sub-lexical progressions of the phonological, orthographic and morphological systems. Consequently, at the classroom level, effective instruction must consist of a systematic approach to building fluency at the letter, letter pattern, word, sentence and text level.

In terms of classroom instruction, this means that when teaching students the subskills of word recognition, we need to be providing systematic instruction at each stage to the point of accuracy, and then reading rate.

For example, in the Foundation year of schooling when systematic synthetic phonics instruction is taking place, it is beneficial for students to be practising fluency skills at the single sound level, alongside PA, and then into the word level, decodable sentence level and so on, according to the alphabetic code sequence being taught. Some examples of how this may look in a simple PowerPoint slide are below. This approach is ideal as part of the daily review component of the literacy block as students require repeated opportunities to read previously learnt letters, letter combinations and words.

### Fluency practice

1. Teacher/EA/parent models reading the graphemes or words (I Do)
2. Teacher/EA/parent and child do it together (We Do)
3. Child does it independently (You Do)

### Phoneme-grapheme correspondences

| a | e | s | t | w |
|---|---|---|---|---|
| y | a | i | u | c |
| g | a | t | i | x |
| o | m | a | e | g |

CVC words

| ant | tan | pit | sin | sit |
|-----|-----|-----|-----|-----|
| pan | his | yup | box | peg |
| rag | not | ump | lap | pat |
| pug | win | imp | pen | tag |

/ee/ words

| steam | peel | sticky | me | beach |
|-------|------|--------|-----|-------|
| happy | cream | we | please | treats |
| seed | weed | green | be | sunny |
| street | beach | these | wobbly | she |

## Orthographic mapping and reading fluency

Typically, developing readers need to be exposed to an unfamiliar word one to four times before it is permanently learnt. However, children with reading disabilities often do not 'store' a word even after 12 to 16 times (Ehri & Saltmarsh, 1995, Martens & De Jong, 2008, in Coalla et al., 2014). The difference between these is the skill of orthographic mapping. Ensuring students have proficient orthographic mapping skills is the best approach to addressing fluency (Ehri, 2005a, 2005b, Torgesen, 2004a, 2004b, Torgesen, Rashotte, Alexander, Alexander & MacPhee, 2003, in Kilpatrick, 2015).

Based on the work of Linnea Ehri (2014) orthographic mapping is the process all successful readers use to become fluent readers. If you consider every word has three forms: its phonology, orthography and meaning, orthographic mapping is the mental process that integrates all these forms, then permanently stores them in long-term memory as 'sight words'. When students have a large 'sight vocabulary', the quicker and easier it becomes for them to read text without having to decode unfamiliar words. This is, however, not to be confused with learning 'sight words' by rote.

To provide an example of orthographic mapping in action, consider these three words. Can you read these words effortlessly? And if so, why?

| wump | flaich | splotch |
|------|--------|---------|

As skilled readers, we can read these words effortlessly and yet you will never have seen them before as they are pseudo words. The reason we can read them is because we have developed effective orthographic mapping skills. We know the phonemes represented by each of these letters and letter combinations, and have a solid orthographic understanding of the digraph and trigraph of 'ai' and 'tch' respectively, and consequently, can automatically read these words with ease.

## Assessing accuracy and reading rate

Reading fluency rate is generally measured by words correct per minute (WCPM) or ORF. Using ORF as an assessment tool is like a thermometer check of reading proficiency (Hasbrouck, 2021). A 60-second ORF assessment can provide an accurate indication of whether a child is on the right track in reading fluency. But like a thermometer check in the real world, it is only an *indicator*, as it doesn't break down the subskill(s) that may be causing the fluency difficulty.

The following table identifies the 25th to 75th percentile range of reading fluency for students in Years 1–6. The range refers to the expected WCPM at the end of each term. The column on the right-hand side highlights the 50th percentile goal of reading fluency, for end-of-year expectations.

### Fluency rate and accuracy – ORF norms

|  | End Term 2 WCPM | End Term 3 WCPM | End Term 4 WCPM | WCPM 50th percentile goal |
|---|---|---|---|---|
| Year 1 | NA | 16–59 | 34–91 | 60 |
| Year 2 | 30–84 | 59–109 | 72–124 | 100 |
| Year 3 | 59–104 | 79–137 | 91–139 | 112 |
| Year 4 | 75–125 | 95–143 | 105–160 | 133 |
| Year 5 | 87–153 | 109–160 | 119–169 | 146 |
| Year 6 | 112–159 | 116–166 | 122–173 | 146 |

This table shows the *expected range* of reading fluency accuracy and speed per minute, for Year 1 to Year 6 at the end of Terms 2, 3 and 4 adapted to the Australian context (Hasbrouck & Tindal, 2017).

Although the 50th percentile seems low and is not usually something we aim for, in the case of a fluency analogy, the 50th percentile is the benchmark to which the door to reading fluency is opened. There is no research that very high rates of reading fluency improve reading comprehension and, in fact, in some cases, it is detrimental to comprehension outcomes (Hasbrouck, 2021).

Calculating a student's ORF in an ongoing capacity throughout the year is highly effective as part of a RTI framework. Administering a simple ORF assessment three times per year is a quick and effective way to identify and respond to students at risk and monitor whole-school reading fluency attainment and progress.

## Suggested assessment tools

Recommended evidence-based tools for assessing reading fluency in terms of reading rate and accuracy are DIBELS® 8th and Acadience.

### Assessing prosody

Prosody is not as easily assessed as reading rate and accuracy, however, rubrics such as the Fluency Rubric 1234 (see opposite) is useful for tracking progress in this subskill.

The Fluency Rubric 1234 is a diagnostic tool for categorising the different elements of prosody and fluency. The scale rates reader fluency based on expression and volume, phrasing, smoothness and pace. Scores range from 4 to 16 and generally a score of 10 or less indicates that fluency may be a concern. This rubric can also be utilised as a success criterion – to show students the elements we strive for as a fluent reader. It can also be used by students to provide feedback when listening to a peer read orally. Thank you to Tim Rasinski for kindly allowing this rubric to be republished here.

As this tool is diagnostic in nature, before using the rubric, it is helpful to provide opportunities for students to have read the text they are reading before assessment. As mentioned earlier, the text should be read with 95% accuracy or 97–98% accuracy for emerging readers.

### Assessing reading motivation

A simple reading questionnaire such as the Motivation for Reading Questionnaire MRQ-R (Wigfield & Guthrie, 1997) is a great way to provide teachers with a snapshot of the affective factors of a student's reading experiences. Providing opportunities for student voice and feedback is a powerful motivator for learning and engagement (Quaglia, 2015).

# Fluency Rubric 1234

| 1 | 2 | 3 | 4 |
|---|---|---|---|

**Expression and volume**

| 1 | 2 | 3 | 4 |
|---|---|---|---|
| Reads in a quiet voice as if to get words out. The reading does not sound natural like talking to a friend. | Reads in a quiet voice. The reading sounds natural in part of the text, but the reader does not always sound like they are talking to a friend. | Reads with volume and expression. However, sometimes the reader slips into expressionless reading and does not sound like they are talking to a friend. | Reads with varied volume and expression. The reader sounds like they are talking to a friend with their voice matching the interpretation of the passage. |

**Phrasing**

| 1 | 2 | 3 | 4 |
|---|---|---|---|
| Reads word-by-word in a monotone voice. | Reads in two or three word phrases, not adhering to punctuation, stress and intonation. | Reads with a mixture of run-ons, mid-sentence pauses for breath and some choppiness. There is reasonable stress and intonation. | Reads with good phrasing; adhering to punctuation, stress and intonation. |

**Smoothness**

| 1 | 2 | 3 | 4 |
|---|---|---|---|
| Frequently hesitates while reading, sounds out words and repeats words or phrases. The reader makes multiple attempts to read the same passage. | Reads with extended pauses or hesitations. The reader has many 'rough spots'. | Reads with occasional breaks in rhythm. The reader has difficulty with specific words and/or sentence structures. | Reads smoothly with some breaks, but self-corrects with difficult words and/or sentence structures. |

**Pace**

| 1 | 2 | 3 | 4 |
|---|---|---|---|
| Reads slowly and laboriously | Reads moderately slowly | Reads fast and slow throughout reading. | Reads at a conversational pace throughout the reading. |

| **Score** | Scores of 10 or more indicate that the student is making good progress in fluency. |
|---|---|
| | Scores below 10 indicate that the student needs additional instruction in fluency. |

Fluency Rubric 1234 (n.d.) republished with permission by Tim Rasinski.

# High impact opportunities for teaching fluency

## Foundation to Year 2

**Fluency Pairs:** Daily mixed-ability pairs are an excellent way to practise oral reading at the word, sentence or text level, and also as a repeated reading approach. As the teacher, you would pair a stronger reader with a lower progress reader. Student A reads a passage to Student B for three minutes and Student B provides feedback. Then Student B reads for three minutes to Student A and Student A gives feedback. A suggestion is to use a laminated sheet of the fluency rubric for students to refer to when giving feedback. In this routine, students read to their partner with text suitable for their own fluency ability.

**Whole-Class Choral Reading – phoneme/grapheme level:** Daily opportunities for students to review previously learnt grapheme-phoneme correspondences (GPC) and read as a whole class in unison. This is an ideal approach as part of the daily review component of the literacy block to practise previously learnt code knowledge.

**Whole-Class Echo Reading:** Regular opportunities for teacher modelling of appropriate prosody – phrasing, tone, volume – is an effective approach to improving this subskill of reading fluency. Following the teacher modelling, students can echo each sentence by repeating the way you are speaking, hence reading with appropriate prosody. Providing opportunities for students to follow along with the passage visually with phrase markers and indicators (such as an arrow for question marks to indicate that we lift our voice) may also be helpful for some students.

**Word Whiz Fluency Pairs:** In pairs, students read a chart of words previously learnt based on their code knowledge in synthetic phonics. For example, if students are currently learning CCVCC words, then the Word Whiz chart would be based on review words at a lower level, such as CCVC. The key here is that these words are already accurate for students and the next step is to increase the reading rate. Using the sand timer, one student will count how many words are read correctly and record on the bar chart and then swap roles.

**Decodable Sentence Level Reading:** Depending on the synthetic phonics code sequence you are following, utilise decodable sentences, including questions with answers for fluency practice.

**Repeated Reading – by teacher:** Students read a passage of text or a series of sentences that are visible to students, as a class in unison after teacher modelling. As the teacher, you would read a section of text to students first, modelling accurate phrasing, intonation and reading rate. Students will then read that same section out loud, in unison. The teacher then gives feedback to the whole class. This approach provides frequent modelling of fluent reading and it is a low-risk activity for less capable readers, as they are reading aloud supported by more capable reading peers.

**Audio Book Assisted Reading:** Students read along with an audio book at their independent reading level, following along and pointing at the words. This approach would be repeated several times over a week until the child is able to read the text independently without the audio support. The benefit of this approach is that it is an easy approach for setting up with headphones and iPads to free teachers up to work with other students. It is also great for additional home practice and for EALD students.

**Microsoft Teams Reading Progress:** This is a fabulous online tool for students to read, be recorded and provided feedback on errors and accuracy rate. Students can listen back to their reading and set personal fluency goals.

### Years 3–6

Daily practice opportunities to revisit previously learnt components of reading and spelling development, including:

**Whole-Class Choral Reading:** Intentional opportunities to read aloud as a class daily, even in the upper primary years. Students need many opportunities of teaching modelling and reinforcing fluency at different points of instruction (Lemov, Driggs & Woolway, 2016).

**Control the Game:** Particularly useful in the middle to upper primary years during a whole-class reading of a text, the teacher will call attention to specific features including syntax, vocabulary, mood, emotion, tension and suspense, and cue students to read with appropriate prosody to match. For example, you would draw attention to a mood or event that may affect a specific character, then ask students to consider the feeling and read the sentence or passage, demonstrating that feeling or mood. For example, to draw attention to dialogue, such as, *"You are a disgrace!" Mr Samson replied with disgust*, you may ask students to read the sentence again where Mr Samson's tone reflects disgust (Lemov, Driggs & Woolway, 2016).

**Whole-Class Choral Reading – morpheme level:** As part of the daily review, it is beneficial for orthographic mapping development to revise and practise with increasing fluency, previously learnt morphemes and morpheme word families, such as disruptive, disrupting, corrupt, eruption for the root word 'rupt'.

**Repeated Reading – Whole Class:** Repeated reading of a section of text by the teacher provides the rehearsal required to build accuracy, speed and confidence. This process is repeated three or four times with feedback each time. Short passages of 50–250 words are preferred so that students can hold within their working memory the pattern of the fluent reading modelled.

**Bridging:** This is an activity where the teacher reads a short segment of text in between volunteer student readers reading aloud independently to the class. For example, students may read three sentences aloud in unison, then the teacher reads aloud for three sentences. Students then read three sentences and then the teacher reads the next. The benefit of this approach is that it creates a 'bridge' between other students, it keeps the story moving along quickly, while supporting and maximising comprehension by interspersed quality oral reading by you, the most qualified person in the room (Lemov, Driggs & Woolway, 2016).

**Readers Theatre:** A fun approach for building fluency for older students is Readers Theatre. It is important to select the roles carefully and ensure the main parts are read by more able readers in the initial stages.

## Progress monitoring

A recommended tip for monitoring student progress is to use a line graph that indicates expected student growth in ORF for each year level. Intermittent recording of individual ORF scores can then be tracked against this visual (see graph opposite). Utilising this approach throughout the year provides a clear visual of student progress. A line graph can also provide information for parent-teacher communication, including information that parents often want to know about their child, including:

- *What is my child's current skill level?*
- *How different is my child's performance from the expected standard?*
- *What is the goal for my child?*
- *When do we expect to achieve this goal?*
- *Is my child making adequate progress towards the goal?*
- *What can I do to support my child in achieving this goal?*

(Good III & Kaminski et al., 2011)

## Line graph of ORF expected progress

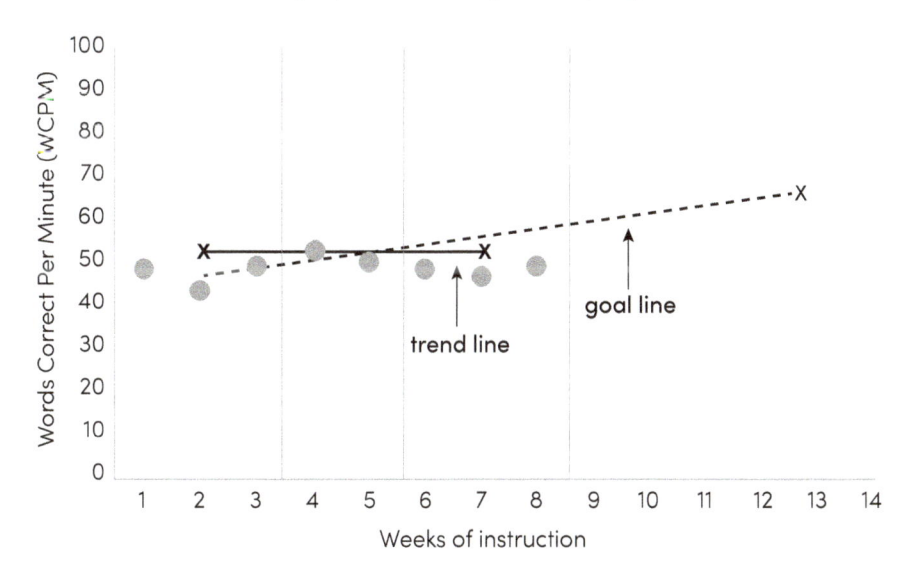

Example line graph to show the expected progress of a student against the trend line of student growth utilising Oral Reading Fluency (ORF) benchmark and progress-monitoring tools.

Recommended universal screening of a normed ORF assessment in Years 1–6 would ideally take place three times per year. Suggested times for normed assessments of reading fluency would be at the beginning, middle and end of year (Good III & Kaminski et al., 2011).

In terms of identifying which students are on track with fluency automaticity, as mentioned earlier, we are aiming for students to be achieving the 50th percentile of WCPM to be at expected standard for reading automaticity. Hasbrouck (2021) refers to three zones of reading automaticity: green, yellow and red.

Students that score 4 WCPM less than the 50th percentile mark and 10 over it are considered in the green zone. For students that score 5 WCPM less than the 50th percentile mark or 10 over it are considered in the yellow zone, and would benefit from intervention. Students scoring more than 10 below the 50th percentile are considered in the red zone. See the table on the next page for a breakdown of the zones and refer to the ORF and WCPM table for automaticity expectations fluency rates for each year level.

## Zones of fluency achievement

| Green Zone | Yellow Zone | Red Zone |
|---|---|---|
| 10+ to -4 WCPM | -5 to -10 WCPM | >10 WCPM below |

Zones of achievement based on WCPM against 50th percentile of each year level.

## Identifying and responding to fluency difficulties

When a student is identified as having difficulties with reading fluency from assessment data, it is important to consider the underlying contributing factors. Determining the underlying cause of the difficulty is essential in determining the correct course of intervention action.

Questions to consider include:

- Is the difficulty related to word level reading difficulties, such as PA, real word and/or non-word decoding or gaps in phonic knowledge?
- Is the difficulty related to language comprehension, such as vocabulary deficits, syntax, lack of background knowledge or Developmental Language Disorder?
- Is the issue related to prosody, including phrasing, tone, volume or pausing?
- Do they have poor Rapid Automised Naming?

*(Rapid Automatised Naming (RAN) is a process where students rapidly name images, colours, letters or numbers in an array for one minute. The rate at which a student can name these items is referred to as their RAN speed. Although not commonly assessed in schools, a RAN score is highly correlated with disorders of reading (commonly referred to as dyslexia), especially if there are phonological awareness deficits.)*

## Fluency intervention approaches

If a student scores in the yellow or red zone of WCPM for the year level as discussed earlier, further diagnostic assessments are recommended. This will guide decisions around next steps. For example, if decoding and phonic knowledge and/or PA is the issue, then this will need to be remediated first.

If decoding, phonic knowledge and PA skills are all secure, then it would be wise to undertake further assessments in identifying if language comprehension is the cause of the fluency deficit. Administering a listening comprehension assessment with oral retell, vocabulary and language complexity components will provide valuable information in this instance. Some specific fluency interventions are highlighted below.

## Sub-lexical interventions and high-frequency words

If a child has solid PA but is having trouble in the sub-lexical progressions of fluency such as letter sounds, then automaticity building at the letter level is warranted. Hudson et al. in Spear-Swerling (2022) state that, "If students are not automatic at naming letter sounds, meaning they cannot name at least 60 correct letter sounds per minute with two or fewer mistakes, then automaticity building at the letter level is warranted." They go on to suggest that building automaticity at the high-frequency word level may also be beneficial. This is of course once students have been explicitly taught that the high-frequency words can indeed be decoded, but they have some irregular spelling patterns that we need to attend to.

## Phrase-cued text reading intervention

If a child requires intervention to explicitly address prosody, Hudson et al. in Spear-Swerling (2022) recommend an intervention referred to as Phrase Cued Texts, which has been effective in not only improving prosody, but also comprehension. When implementing a phrase-cued intervention, the text type can be fiction or non-fiction, with a reading accuracy rate of 95% or above. The teacher explains the purpose of phrasing and models reading with and without phrasing to show how this differs. The teacher then models annotating/highlighting phrases and punctuation on the text with the student, and then supports the student to practise reading the phrase-cued text, providing immediate and explicit feedback. Using a clear sheet protector or laminating sheet to protect their books, following teacher guidance, students can also highlight the punctuation and phrase points of their texts.

## Repeated reading intervention

With an effect size of 0.67 as recognised in research by Fisher, Frey and Hattie (2017), repeated reading has been identified as one of the most effective ways to improve reading fluency in students. However, it is imperative that before repeated reading intervention has been implemented, any underlying PA, decoding and/or language difficulties have been addressed. This approach can work particularly well with phrase-cued text intervention.

## Summary

- Fluency is defined as *reasonably accurate* reading at an *appropriate rate*, with suitable expression, that leads to accurate and *deep comprehension* and *motivation to read* (Hasbrouck & Glaser, 2019).
- Orthographic mapping is the process all successful readers use to become fluent readers.
- Typically developing readers need to be exposed to an unfamiliar word one to four times before it is permanently learnt. However, children with reading disabilities often do not 'store' a word even after 12 to 16 times (Ehri & Saltmarsh, 1995, Martens & De Jong, 2008).
- Reading fluency rate is generally measured by WCPM in ORF. Using ORF as an assessment tool is like a thermometer check of reading proficiency (Hasbrouck, 2021).
- When students are reading texts independently, provide texts that are read with 95% accuracy, and 97–98% accuracy for emerging or beginning readers. A good way to determine if a text is suitable for independent reading is through a simple 100 word check.
- If a student scores 5 or more WCPM below the 50th percentile for their year level, it is important to undertake further diagnostic assessments to identify the underlying subskill deficits, which will guide appropriate intervention.
- Intervention approaches that specifically target fluency include repeated reading, phrase-cued text reading and sub-lexical fluency practice.

## Professional discussion

- How effectively is student progress and achievement progress monitored, and is this used as a guide to determine underlying literacy difficulties and appropriate intervention?
- How can your parent body be engaged to support their child/children in fluency development?
- What whole-school understandings, assessments and approaches are evident across the school in terms of fluency?

**Chapter 11**

# LANGUAGE COMPREHENSION FOR READING (AND WRITING)

"Reading comprehension is not a single entity that can be explained by a unified cognitive model. Instead, it is the orchestrated product of a set of linguistic and cognitive processes operating on text and interacting with background knowledge, features of the text, and the purpose and goals of the reading situation"

~ Castles, Rastle and Nation, p28, in Hennessy (2021)

## Chapter overview

- Anticipation Guide
- Language comprehension and its role in reading comprehension
- Reading comprehension – complex and often misunderstood
- Establishing a situation model in reading comprehension
- Background knowledge
- Syntax
- Cohesive devices
- Inference
- Comprehension monitoring
- Story structure
- Getting the gist
- Vocabulary and comprehension

- Questioning the Author
- Close reading
- Read-Think-Write-Discuss
- Moving away from guided reading and silent reading
- Putting it all together in a weekly overview
- Assessment and intervention
- Summary
- Professional discussion
- Anticipation Guide answers
- Example of rich knowledge units: Year overview planner
- Example of rich knowledge units: Term overview planner
- Questioning the author planner
- Questioning the author plan

## Anticipation Guide

Teachers require expertise in the many language systems of English, which are the foundation of skilled reading. Quiz your current background knowledge on these systems terms, matching each to its definition (Cambridge Dictionary).

| Language system of English | Definition |
| --- | --- |
| Phonology | the study of the form of words and phrases |
| Morphology | the study of meaning in language |
| Semantics | the study of how language is affected by the situation in which it is used, of how language is used to get things or perform actions, and of how words can express things that are different from what they appear to mean |
| Syntax | the accepted way of spelling and writing words |
| Pragmatics | the rules by which words can be combined into sentences |
| Discourse | the study of sounds in a particular language |
| Orthography | the use of language to communicate in speech or writing |

## Language comprehension and its role in reading comprehension

Language comprehension sometimes takes a backseat to the word level skills of PA, phonic knowledge and decoding. However, it is an essential component of skilled reading. If we look back to Gough and Tunmer's (1986) Simple View of Reading and Hollis Scarborough's Reading Rope (2001), students need to be proficient in both the word recognition strand *and also* the language comprehension strand. Efficient reading cannot be achieved without both. As such, it is recommended that in addition to the daily PA/phonics lesson, students require explicit teaching of the subskills of language comprehension.

One simple, yet effective, medium for teaching the subskills of language comprehension is through daily teacher read-alouds and novel studies. The key here is for teachers to be selecting a range of high-quality fiction and non-fiction texts that are read to the whole class. Using teacher read-alouds as the basis – combined with careful planning and explicit teaching – students can be taught Tier 2 and Tier 3 vocabulary, language structures, syntax and critical background knowledge.

Instructional routines and approaches for developing language and reading comprehension include:

- Content level instruction in unit blocks to build background knowledge
- Explicit teaching of time connectives to improve language complexity
- Explicit teaching of anaphoric reference to improve sentence-level comprehension
- Explicit teaching of a small and brief amount of comprehension strategies, including inference, comprehension monitoring, question generation, summarisation and genre structure. These should *not* be in stand-alone units of skill development
- Questioning the author approach
- Close reading
- Read-Think-Write-Discuss approach

## Reading comprehension – complex and often misunderstood

Although proficient reading comprehension is what we seek in teaching children to read, it remains largely misunderstood. This may be because for many years, comprehension has been viewed and taught as a 'skill' rather than as an orchestration of skilled processes and strategies (Castles, Rastle & Nation, p28, in Hennessy, 2021).

In addition to this view of comprehension as a 'skill', over recent years, there has been an overabundance of teaching reading comprehension strategies (RCS). Many schools adopt whole-school reading programs, where each week students are taught a certain RCS, such as finding the main idea, inference, summarisation, etc, which is largely a redundant use of instructional time. This is because in this approach there is an assumption that these 'skills' are transferrable to other contexts, when after minimal instruction it yields no higher effect (Willingham & Lovette, 2014).

Catts (2021) uses a swimming analogy to explain that "If we teach someone to swim, they can soon transfer that skill to any body of water, whether it be a pool, lake or ocean. But reading comprehension is not a skill someone learns and can then apply in different reading contexts." It is important for educators to be aware that strategy instruction is useful in a small amount, but once taught, is not something that is transferrable to new contexts.

What is far more beneficial is for students to be taught sequenced units of content knowledge (Smith, Serry, Snow & Hammond, 2021), as well as a small handful of strategies where the instruction is explicit and brief. Willingham and Lovette (2014) cites RCS as "a bag of tricks that are useful and worth teaching, but that they are quickly learned and require minimal practice".

Rather than teaching a RCS each week, it is a far more effective use of instructional time to focus on the other aspects suggested in this chapter. Strategy instruction should be taught as and when needed, during teacher read-alouds, during whole-class close reading lessons with the focus on the content of the text and not the strategy itself. The chosen strategies for instruction should be few and those identified as evidence based. These include inference, comprehension monitoring, story structure (Oakhill & Cain, 2012) and question generation (National Reading Panel, 2000).

While it may come as a surprise, any more than 10 sessions of RCS instruction yields the same benefit as 50 sessions (Willingham & Lovette, 2014). With that in mind, with such a cramped curriculum, strategy instruction is a likely candidate to be significantly reduced from the teaching and learning repertoire.

| National Reading Panel (2000) | • comprehension monitoring |
|---|---|
| ~ report listed eight comprehension strategies that had a firm scientific basis for concluding that they improve comprehension | • summarisation<br>• question generation<br>• question answering<br>• story structure<br>• cooperative learning<br>• graphic and semantic organisers<br>• multiple strategy teaching<br><br>*The empirical evidence reviewed favours the conclusion that teaching a variety of RCS leads to increased learning of the strategies, to specific transfer of learning, to increased retention and understanding of new passages and, in some cases, to general improvements in comprehension.* |
| Oakhill & Cain (2012) | • inference |
| ~ longitudinal study identified these distinct strategies as predictors of reading comprehension in Year 6 | • comprehension monitoring<br>• story structure |

## Establishing a situation model in reading comprehension

As we read or listen to texts read, skilled readers create a 'situation model' or 'mental model'. There are three levels of understanding to develop a coherent representation of texts read (Hennessy, 2021). The first is at the *surface code level*, where students understand the words and phrases of the text. The next level is referred to as the *text base*, which involves sentence level comprehension, including being able to navigate a range of complex sentences and anaphoric reference.

The third level is the *situation* or *mental model* of the text. In this third and crucial level, students draw on background knowledge, make local and global inferences from the text, while engaging in comprehension monitoring to ensure the text is making sense. These levels of processing are also influenced by executive functioning skills, including working memory, planning, organisation and cognitive flexibility (Cartwright, 2019, in Hennessy, 2021). In addition, background knowledge helps students build a more accurate situation model and can decrease the demands on working memory (Compton et al., 2014, in Kilpatrick, 2015).

It is important to distinguish between a student who can accurately comprehend what they are being read *to*, from a child that has trouble with comprehension when reading themselves. Seidenberg states that such children have difficulty due to "inadequate instruction or a learning impairment. Such children may indeed be poor at parsing sentences, understanding the situation being described, or drawing linking inferences because they cannot read the words well enough to get that far, not because they lack an appropriate 'text comprehension model'" (2017, p273).

For the rest of this chapter, I will outline factors involved in language and reading comprehension and implications for classroom instruction.

## Background knowledge

When I was a teacher in the classroom, I thought I did an OK job at activating prior knowledge at the start of a lesson or unit of study, but then it dawned on me...

What if there is *no* student knowledge to activate in the first place? Always a learner, I have discovered a lot since then about the importance of not just 'activating' prior knowledge, but explicitly teaching it in units of study. In recent research by Smith, Serry, Snow and Hammond (2021), they state that, "Explicitly teaching background knowledge should be considered foundational to increasing competency in reading."

Background knowledge consists of either *general background knowledge* or *specific topical knowledge*. An example of general background knowledge that students may have is in relation to a traditional children's birthday party – that it will usually involve an invitation, bringing a present, a celebration and a cake. Specific topical knowledge, however, relates to a reader's content knowledge, such as knowledge about the life cycle of a butterfly or the cultural traditions of the ancient Egyptians.

Studies on the impact of background knowledge has identified that "Specific topical background knowledge is so important that poor word readers outperform good readers when they happen to know more about the specific topic than the good word readers" (Kahmi, 2009, 2012, in Kilpatrick, 2015). With this in mind, reading comprehension assessments must take into account a child's level of background knowledge that they bring to the task.

Background knowledge can be developed by:

- Teaching a "knowledge rich curriculum" (Hirsch, 2019, in Smith, Serry, Snow & Hammond, 2021).
- Implementing a whole-school scope and sequence in domain knowledge related to cross-curricular subjects.
- During pre- and post-reading discussions and writing tasks and by linking to other curriculum areas.
- Teaching in knowledge-rich content units and incorporating a range of fiction and non-fiction texts to read aloud to students. This is not to be confused with doing 'themes'; as it is a specific focus of content knowledge building.
- Incorporating graphic organisers into lessons before, during and after reading to activate prior knowledge, connect to previous knowledge and reflect on new knowledge acquired. Anticipation Guides and KWLs are great for pre, during and post reading. The instructional strategy of 321 RIQ is a good option for upper primary students in a post-reading context.
- Engaging parents in this important discussion. There is so much we can be sharing with parents that they can do, such as sharing child-friendly podcasts, documentaries, virtual or in-person museum visits, etc.

### Example of a 321 RIQ graphic organiser

| 3 Recalls | 2 Insights | 1 Question |
| --- | --- | --- |
|  |  |  |

## Developing rich knowledge units

A few steps for developing rich knowledge units from Foundation to Year 6 includes the following:

1. Start by mapping out, in year levels, key units in your national or state curriculum in cross-curricular areas that lend themselves to teaching in rich knowledge blocks, for example, life cycles in science, Australia and its neighbours in Year 3 HASS.

2. Map out special weeks in the year that can be incorporated into knowledge units such as Science Week, NAIDOC Week, ANZAC Day, Book Week.
3. Identify key knowledge units you will teach each term for each year level. Core Knowledge has some excellent recommendations and resources for teachers.
4. Break your term knowledge units into blocks of time and plan your intended knowledge goals, rich texts, vocabulary and syntax you will teach. At the end of this chapter you will find example term and year overview planners for blocking out rich knowledge units.

## Syntax

Syntax is the grammatical and structural basis of our written language; the way words and sentences are put together (Hennessy, 2021). Although traditionally described as a complete thought, or in plural, the 'worker bees of text' (Scott, 2004, p340, in Hennessy, 2021, p89) sentences are defined as a group of words, usually containing a verb that expresses a thought in the form of a statement, question, instruction or exclamation, and starts with a capital letter when written (Cambridge Dictionary).

To create a mental model of a text, readers are required to first make meaning at the word (surface) level and sentence (text base) level. However, sentences can be long and dense, and don't always convey their meaning easily. When reading to students, they will often understand part of an idea but miss others or grasp a portion of a sentence, but not a subsequent aspect that contradicts its meaning (Lemov, Driggs & Woolway, 2016). This is particularly true of expository and information texts.

An example of how you might support students to comprehend the following passage at the sentence and paragraph level (in Year 5 or 6) is within this excerpt from *The Goat Who Sailed the World*:

> *"Rio was noisy. The Goat hated the noise, and the disturbance to her routine. Even worse, the crew and the captain were upset too – the Portuguese governor refused to believe they were on a scientific expedition, and it took days of arguing for Cook to get the supplies of food and water – and fresh grass for The Goat – that they badly needed for the next leg of their journey"*
>
> ~ French (2006, p63)

In this passage, there are only three sentences, yet a large amount of information that could cause comprehension obstacles. Students will need to understand the following:

1. Rio is a place that they have docked into.
2. If ships were on a scientific expedition, they were granted supplies such as food and water from other countries they are travelling through.
3. The meaning of the clause: 'even worse' at the start of a sentence.
4. Anaphoric reference of Cook being referred to as captain two lines previously.
5. Vocabulary knowledge of disturbance, governor, refused, expedition, 'leg' as in a journey and not an appendage.

In this case, you may ask students the following open and targeted questions:

- *What is going on here?*
- *What was Goat unhappy about?*
- *Who were more upset than Goat? Why were they upset? What words tell you this?*
- *In the text it said, "it took days of arguing for Cook to get the supplies...", what took so long?*
- *What does it mean by the 'next leg of the journey'?*

Through rich texts in the literacy block as well as across content areas, explicit instruction of syntax includes supporting students to comprehend challenging sentences as well as teaching students the fundamentals of these building blocks of text, including:

- The components of a sentence (subject and predicate)
- Identifying clauses and phrases
- Types of sentences (statement, question, exclamation, command)
- Complexity of sentences (simple, compound and complex)
- How to navigate anaphora and connectives

## Cohesive devices

There are several devices that ensure a text is cohesive and coherent. These include connectives, conjunctions and anaphoric reference. These cohesive devices play a role in reading comprehension as they support readers to 'track' how the meaning is being developed.

## Connectives

Sometimes referred to as marker words or signal words, connectives are cohesive devices to improve the flow of writing. Connectives bridge ideas within and between sentences. They provide the reader with signposts to link stretches of text and indicate that something is coming up ahead. Below is a table providing some examples of the range of connectives including those that indicate time, cause and result, and clarification.

| Indicating time | Showing cause/result | Clarifying |
| --- | --- | --- |
| until then | therefore | to illustrate |
| then | then | in other words |
| next | consequently | to put it this way |
| afterwards | as a consequence | as a matter of fact |
| at the same time | in that case | in fact |
| before that | because of this | in particular |
| earlier | accordingly | to be precise |
| in the end | for that reason | for example |
| finally | as a result | for instance |
| after a while | | firstly |
| at this point | | secondly |
| meanwhile | | next |
| later | | |

## Conjunctions

### Latin origin: jungere = to join, con = together

The word 'conjunction' is of Latin origin and quite literally means to join together (Van Cleave, 2012). Often confused with connectives, conjunctions only operate within sentences and join two clauses. There are three kinds of conjunctions, coordinating – joining two words or groups of words (FANBOYS: for, and, nor, but, or, yet, so), subordinating – only used to join a dependent clause to an independent one (if, since, after, when, although, while, until, because, unless, before) or correlative – paired conjunctions that join two words or groups of words of equal standing.

| Coordinating conjunctions | Subordinating conjunctions | Correlative conjunctions |
|---|---|---|
| *joins two words or groups of words, for example, FANBOYS* | *used to join a dependent clause to an independent one* | *paired conjunctions that join two words or groups of words of equal standing* |
| for | if | both... and |
| and | since | not... but |
| nor | when | either... or |
| but | until | neither... nor |
| or | while | not only... but also |
| yet | because | whether... or |
| so | unless | |
| | before | |
| | even though | |
| | as | |
| | as if | |
| | after | |
| | whereas | |
| | although | |
| | only if | |

(Van Cleave, 2012)

To comprehend a range of texts, students need to know the function of common conjunctions and how this affects sentence meaning. One way to teach students this is to explicitly teach the meanings of common conjunctions, as follows:

- *and* – used to join words and sentences that have similar ideas
- *because* – explains why something is true
- *but* – indicates a change of direction
- *so* – tells us something has happened because of something else
- *although* – joins words and ideas that contrast or contradict
- *when* – joins words and sentences to show something is happening at that time

## Anaphora

Anaphora – also referred to as anaphoric reference or referring words – is a form of cohesive tie that sets up links in a text to refer back to something that has already been mentioned. To demonstrate anaphora, consider this passage on armadillos and notice how the pronouns refer back to the armadillo and the identical babies.

> *"Each time a nine-banded armadillo gives birth, she has four identical babies. They are either all female or all male. This is because a single egg inside the mother splits into four, and all four parts begin to grow – into identical quadruplets!"*
>
> ~ Wood (2011)

In this passage, to avoid repetition, the author has used pronoun references (she, they) to reference previously mentioned subjects, as I have illustrated below. The subjects are underlined, and the **circled** items and arrows indicate the anaphoric reference.

> Each time a <u>nine-banded armadillo</u> gives birth, **she** has four identical <u>babies</u>. **They** are either all female or all male.

## Inference

"Inferences are necessary in constructing the text base (at both the micro and macro levels), and they play a crucial role in forming a coherent situation model. Texts are almost never fully explicit, so there are always gaps left to be filled in by the reader" (Kintsch & Rawson, 2005, p219).

Inferencing is the ability to connect ideas between and within sentences and integrate text level information with background knowledge. Consider the inferencing required in this passage:

> *"The sea was calm again next morning. You'd never have known the sea could lash and rage, thought Isaac, as he undid his trousers and climbed out on the 'seat of ease'. The other sailors had laughed at him when he'd used the smelly bucket below a day after they'd left port. Finally, one of them had taken him up onto the deck and pointed out the seat, perched way above the waves, and the frayed rope that dangled in the water"*
>
> ~ French (2006, p33)

In this passage, Isaac hasn't understood that going to the toilet at sea happens on the 'seat of ease' on the deck. In this case, you may ask students the following open and targeted questions to support their inference development:

- *What is going on here?*
- *What words or phrases in the passage provide clues about what is happening?*
- *What does it mean by the 'sea could lash and rage'?*
- *What have you learnt from this passage about how toileting happened on board the ship back in the 1890s?*
- *What was the significance of the rope dangling in the water? What is the equivalent of this in the modern age?*

## Comprehension monitoring

Comprehension monitoring is an essential skill of proficient reading that develops in tandem with reading comprehension. It is the process of a reader self-evaluating their understanding of a text while reading. There is a strong link between students with poor reading comprehension and the ability to evaluate and regulate inconsistencies or misunderstandings while reading.

Although comprehension monitoring is a strong predictor of comprehension, researchers Oakhill, Hartt and Samol (2005) cite, "our own experience has shown that teachers are notoriously poor at identifying children who have comprehension monitoring difficulties, and if asked to select such children, tend to do so on the basis of word reading, rather than comprehension ability". One way we can support students to develop comprehension monitoring is through modelling a think aloud with metacognitive questioning, such as:

- *Does that make sense?*
- *Do I need to read that part again?*
- *What does that mean to me?*
- *What can I infer about this?*

## Story structure

Explicitly teaching story structure of fiction texts has been identified as having a positive effect on reading comprehension (NICHD, 2000).

Story structure instruction involves the teacher providing explicit instruction in the story grammar elements during and after a read-aloud.

Starting with our youngest students – including pre-readers – this approach has also been proven to increase listening comprehension. Stevens, Van Meter and Warcholak (2010) found that during and after teacher read-alouds of fiction texts to five- and six-year-old students, children who had learned story structures recalled more ideas from new stories and answered more questions about structural elements of those stories.

## Getting the gist

Getting the gist is a structured literacy intervention, which is a precursor to summarisation and a useful approach for students with reading difficulties (Stevens & Austin in Spear-Swerling, 2015). The text is read to/with students and the following steps include:

- **Step 1:** Who or what is the section about?
- **Step 2:** What is the most important thing/s about the 'who' or 'what'?
- **Step 3:** Combine the details from steps 1 and 2 to write your gist statement.

Students complete a Get the Gist Tracker as follows:

| Step 1 | Step 2 | Step 3 |
| --- | --- | --- |
| Who or what is the section about? | What is the most important thing/s about the 'who' or 'what'? | Combine the details from steps 1 and 2 to write your gist statement. |
|  |  |  |

Get the Gist Tracker adapted from The University of Texas at Austin/The Meadows Centre for Preventing Educational Risk from Spear-Swerling, 2015, p173.

## Vocabulary and comprehension

When planning a unit of work using texts, consider the vocabulary and its possible impact on language or reading comprehension:

- What words will the students need to know?
- What words are worth knowing?
- What words have a double meaning that may confuse students?

- What Tier 2 and Tier 3 words will you intentionally target and teach? What aspects of morphology and etymology can be taught with these words?
- Are there linking or marker words that may create confusion, for example, 'however', 'nevertheless'?
- How will you explicitly teach conjunctions to ensure that students comprehend these in texts?

## Questioning the Author

Questioning the Author (QtA), developed by Beck, McKeown and Sandora (2021), is a powerful approach to building reading comprehension. QtA has the capacity to not only build the much-needed knowledge base required for successful reading comprehension, but also explicitly teaches students to be reflective and critical readers. QtA has a demonstrated evidence base with one study demonstrating an effect size of 1.02 for passage comprehension and 0.98 reading comprehension, in a study of Year 8 students (Sencibaugh & Sencibaugh, 2014).

### The QtA process

QtA utilises quality fiction and non-fiction texts that teachers read aloud to students. Prior to the read-aloud, teachers pre-read the text twice to get a gist for the text and then identify key events, or key understandings, in narrative and information texts respectively. From there, teachers also identify potential obstacles that students may experience, including Tier 2 and Tier 3 vocabulary.

Next, teachers segment the text into interspersed discussion points while reading aloud to students, posing 'queries' to students to check for understanding, make connections to prior understandings and other parts of the text. These queries are designed to check in while reading, monitor understanding and engage in short discussions throughout.

This contrasts with many other approaches while reading aloud to students. For example, traditional read-aloud sessions often incorporate a prediction question before or during the text, followed by questioning after the read-aloud. This approach is futile for some students, as for many, the meaning has already been lost somewhere along the way. You will find a QtA planner and Year 5 novel study example at the end of this chapter.

## Close reading

Close reading is a teacher-led approach for developing reading comprehension for middle to upper primary students. In this approach, the teacher methodically breaks down the complex language and structures within a passage to establish and analyse its meaning. It teaches students how to 'solve' the most challenging lines of text.

Close reading can take place as a lesson or a short burst, either planned or unplanned. For a planned close reading lesson, you would use a full 30–45 minutes to study a speech, persuasive text or short story that you have selected as part of your rich knowledge unit. Alternately, in a short burst close read, when reading along with students, if you arrive at a dense or complex passage, you might pause and say, "Hang on a minute, let's unpack that!" thus modelling the critical skill of comprehension monitoring (Lemov, Driggs & Woolway, 2016, p61).

### The close reading process

During close reading, all students follow along with a specific text while the teacher draws attention to specific lines or sentences. It requires careful planning of two types of questions: 1) those to establish meaning, and 2) questions to analyse meaning. This approach is usually finished with a short writing task where students write a sentence or paragraph about a particular part of the text or the content, to record their understandings. This approach of brief writing after reading has positive gains as opposed to students that do not complete the written component (Hochman & Wexler, 2017).

When planning units of work for close reading, you may consider the following:

- What parts of this text might we do as a 'close read'?
- What aspects might be an obstacle to comprehension?
- Are there any long complex sentences that may be a barrier to syntax comprehension?
- What vocabulary will we need to teach?
- Are there any inferences or metaphors that we will need to unpack?
- What questions will I ask to establish meaning?
- What questions will I ask to analyse meaning?

## Read-Think-Write-Discuss

Providing frequent opportunities for students to write about what they are reading has been shown to be an effective approach to improving students' reading. Graham & Hebert (2010) cites: "Students' comprehension of science, social studies, and language arts texts is improved when they write about what they read." Their research identified the following to be beneficial for improving reading:

- Writing a personal reaction to a text
- Analysing and interpreting a text
- Writing summaries of a text
- Writing notes about a text
- Answering questions about a text in writing
- Creating and answering written questions about a text

(Graham & Hebert, 2010)

A suggested routine for classroom response writing is the Read-Think-Write-Discuss cycle (adapted from Lemov, Driggs & Woolway, 2016).

1. **Read:** During teacher read-aloud or class choral reading, stop at a predetermined point to pose a query, reflection or open response.
2. **Think:** Provide time for students to process the question and generate their response; 30 seconds may be sufficient.
3. **Write:** Students are given a few minutes to write their response while the teacher is circulating to check for understanding or misconceptions. This writing time provides students with the opportunity to develop and refine their ideas before sharing with the rest of the class.
4. **Discuss:** Students share their responses with the class or mixed-ability pair.

## Moving away from guided reading and silent reading

Two approaches I strongly recommend moving away from are traditional guided reading and silent reading, both which are not aligned with the reading science.

Guided reading is associated with the debunked whole language or balanced literacy approaches with the use of levelled texts that are not aligned to the phonic code that students are learning. Students typically read in a round-robin style in ability grouping, with approximately five students. In this scenario, students are given a fifth of the airtime to read aloud in their group and four-fifths of the time listening to other readers at their reading level, which, depending on where they are at, could be potentially quite low.

If you count the minutes per week that students are reading aloud orally in this way, across a week as opposed to whole-class choral reading, echo reading or close reading approaches, there is no comparison. Additionally, ability grouping creates a Matthew's effect where the strongest readers get stronger and the weaker students get weaker. It provides no opportunity for the least able readers to catch up to their peers. It is far better to support students in differentiation via support and outcome rather than content for the majority of the time.

Unsustained silent reading – otherwise referred to as silent reading – is another common approach in schools with limited impact. If this is an approach you currently employ, I recommend making a small tweak to this by replacing silent reading with paired partner reading. Every day, for 10 minutes, in mixed-ability pairs, one child reads aloud to the other and the other gives feedback, then they swap over.

## Putting it all together in a weekly overview

Opposite is an example of how the language comprehension components can link in together over a week.

## Assessment and intervention

When it comes to intervention, sometimes a student's struggles stem from language comprehension, rather than word recognition subskills; although many students that have reading difficulties experience both. The challenge for us is to ensure our intervention addresses the appropriate sides of the Reading Rope – or both if this is the case.

As part of a preventative, systemic RTI framework in schools, it is recommended that students engage in universal screening three times per year in language and reading comprehension from Foundation to Year 3.

I recommend the CUBED NLM listening comprehension tool for Kindergarten (five-year-olds) to Year 3. For students identified at risk, I would recommend a referral for a full assessment with a speech and language pathologist who specialises in language and language difficulties.

Recommended tools for Years 1–6 include the DIBELS® 8th or Acadience. These assessments both have a maze component, which assesses comprehension linked to the one-minute ORF passages students read as part of their reading fluency automaticity screening.

# Weekly overview – language comprehension for reading and writing (30–40 minutes)

| Monday | Tuesday | Wednesday | Thursday | Friday |
|---|---|---|---|---|
| **BACKGROUND KNOWLEDGE:** Activate, review and build knowledge related to the knowledge unit. In addition to class discussions, this may incorporate KWL, T charts, Anticipation Guides **(5 mins)** | | | | |
| **TEACHER READ-ALOUD:** Text/novel read-aloud by teacher **(10 mins)** with open-ended planned QtA queries while reading **(10 mins)** | | | | |
| **CHORAL READING:** Whole class reads in unison with a specific focus. It may follow teacher modelling and then feedback **(2 mins)** | | | | |
| **ORAL DISCUSSION** Class discussion on main events or understandings  May include hot seating (student-led question generation)  **VOCABULARY** Introduce up to 10 Tier 2 and Tier 3 words from the text explicitly taught across the week  **FORMATIVE ASSESSMENT** Vocabulary Knowledge Scale, T chart/ KWL | **READ-THINK-WRITE-DISCUSS** For example, discuss characterisation of the chapter/story, summarise main facts in a non-fiction text, answer or create written questions about the text  *Read-Think-Write-Discuss in Response Journals* | **VOCABULARY** Review vocab words on slides  Word associations of vocabulary words  Unpack the morphology through Word Sums | **READ-THINK-WRITE-DISCUSS** For example, write a response to the text read, generate questions to the author, note-take key understandings, analyse and interpret the text  *Read-Think-Write-Discuss in Response Journals* | **VOCABULARY** Review vocab words on slides  Word relationships of vocabulary words  Develop interesting sentences for the target vocabulary words either orally or in written form |
| | **VOCABULARY** Review vocab words on slides  Discuss examples and non-examples | **SYNTAX** Apply target vocabulary using syntax level work  For example, adding appositives to sentences containing the target vocabulary | **VOCABULARY** Review vocab words on slides  Apply the morphology of targeted vocab words through Word Webs or Word Matrices  (following schoolwide syntax and grammar scope and sequence) | **SYNTAX** Apply vocab using syntax level work, such as by finishing the sentence stems with *because, but, so*  (following schoolwide syntax and grammar scope and sequence) |

## A word of caution

Assessing comprehension is complex and should be viewed with caution, as it is so dependent on background knowledge and vocabulary competency.

Research on 995 students found that the likelihood of the same student being identified with a reading deficit on two different reading comprehension tests were less than half. This inconsistency was also found in the highest bands of reading achievement. A more effective and reliable measure of reading comprehension is to teach children using an integrated literacy and content-rich curriculum, and to test their ability to comprehend passages covered in that curriculum. This approach offers a better match between instruction and assessment, as teachers would not just be testing the skills and strategies, but also the content-area topics that have been taught. Linking teaching and assessment in this way would be fairer and more equitable for all (Catts, 2021).

## Summary

- It is recommended that in addition to the daily PA/phonics lesson, students require explicit teaching of the subskills of language comprehension, through rich texts and novel studies.
- There is an overabundance of reading comprehension strategy instruction in schools, however, these strategies are "a bag of tricks that are useful and worth teaching but are quickly learned and require minimal practice" (Willingham & Lovette, 2014).
- There are three levels of understanding to develop a coherent representation of texts read: surface code level, text base level and situation level (Hennessy, 2021, p33).
- Cohesive devices such as connectives, conjunctions and anaphora play a role in reading comprehension, as they support readers to 'track' how the meaning is being developed.
- Inference is necessary in constructing the text base (at both the micro and macro levels), and in forming a coherent situation model (Kintsch & Rawson, 2005, p219).
- Specific comprehension difficulties are associated with comprehension monitoring problems (Oakhill & Cain, 2012).
- Explicit teaching of story structure through rich texts has been proven to have a positive effect on listening comprehension and reading comprehension.

- Explicit teaching of sequenced knowledge-rich units should be the foundation of increasing reading competency.
- Guided reading and silent reading are not supported by reading science.
- Assessing comprehension is complex, as it is so dependent and skewed by background knowledge and vocabulary.

## Professional discussion

- To what extent do you teach the subskills of language comprehension in your context?
- How might you incorporate the QtA approach and/or close reading approach into your teaching and learning?
- What assessments do you currently use to assess language comprehension and reading comprehension? Are they providing valid assessment data based on the content covered in this chapter?

## Anticipation Guide answers

| Language system of English | Definition |
| --- | --- |
| Phonology | the study of sounds in a particular language |
| Morphology | the study of the form of words and phrases |
| Semantics | the study of meaning in language |
| Syntax | the rules by which words can be combined into sentences |
| Pragmatics | the study of how language is affected by the situation in which it is used, of how language is used to get things or perform actions, and of how words can express things that are different from what they appear to mean |
| Discourse | the use of language to communicate in speech or writing |
| Orthography | the accepted way of spelling and writing words |

## Example of rich knowledge units: Year overview planner

The aim of the yearly planner is to be able to see at a glance where cross-curriculum events can be built into knowledge units. Special weeks and days can also be included here to aid in planning possible events/days, for example, NAIDOC, Science Week, Book Week, ANZAC Day. This will also lead to possible incursion or excursion planning, which also aids in knowledge building. In addition, these units will be broken into term overviews where teachers can plan literature nonfiction texts and associated Tier 2 and Tier 3 vocabulary to be explicitly taught.

Year level:

| Weeks | Term 1 | Term 2 | Term 3 | Term 4 |
|---|---|---|---|---|
| 1 & 2 | Topic:<br><br>Possible texts: | | | |
| 3 & 4 | | | | |
| 5 & 6 | | | | |
| 7 & 8 | | | | |
| 9 & 10 | | | | |

# Example of rich knowledge units: Term overview planner

Each term is broken into between two- and five-week content units incorporating a range of high-quality rich texts that may include short stories, picture books, autobiographies, information texts and poetry. Great starting points for choosing texts include: DSFs fantastic Australian Reading Spinc, Core Knowledge Foundation and Ochre Education's knowledge rich units – all which are freely available online for schools.

**Term: 3**    **Year level: 3**

| Weeks | Topic | Possible texts | Explicit vocabulary focus | Word, sentence, text level focus |
|---|---|---|---|---|
| 1–5 | Australia and its neighbours (HASS) | *Hello, Australia!* Megan McKean <br><br> *Hello, New Zealand!* Megan McKean <br><br> *Are we there yet?* Alison Lester <br><br> *Sophie Scott goes South* Alison Lester | | |
| 6–10 | Fiction | *The Tale of Despereaux* Kate DiCamillo | | |

# Questioning the author planner

Text title:  Genre:

| Major themes/ events/ understandings: | | |
|---|---|---|
| Key vocabulary (up to 10 words per week): | | |
| Segment 1 query: | | |
| Segment 2 query: | | |
| Segment 3 query: | | |
| Segment 4 query: | | |
| Follow-up activities: | | |

# Questioning the author plan

**Text title:** *The Goat that sailed the world* – Jackie French
**Genre:** Historical Fiction                                    **Year:** 5

| Major themes/ events/ understandings: | Prologue – Story starts from the point of view of Goat. It begins on board the *Dolphin* ship with Captain Wallis en route to Tahiti to find gold and spices. The goat is treasured on board as she provides fresh milk to the captain. |||
| :--- | :--- | :--- | :--- |
| | Chapter 1 – Goat is brought aboard sailing the *Endeavour* with Captain Cook who is searching for the Great South Land. |||
| **Key vocabulary (10 per week):** **Recommendation: pre-teach some of the technical boating Tier 3 vocabulary** | **Tier 2:** disapproval pen (Goat's area) privileged lowly monotonous entire trinkets barren vary clambered buttocks | | **Tier 3:** quarterdeck master's mate cannon seaman Great South Land Tahiti lieutenant tethered |

**Summary:**

*Dolphin* is a ship from Europe, and they have just found Tahiti. The goat is very special on the boat and provides fresh milk for Captain Wallis in the first part of the story. They are en route to the Great South Land to find gold and spices as no one had found it yet. Tasman had already found New Zealand. Australia hadn't yet been discovered.

**Potential obstacles:**

Quarterdeck of the *Dolphin* (top part of the ship. *Dolphin* is a ship – show visual). Teach 'quarterdeck'.

She didn't think much of them (Goat doesn't like the new people they have spotted on land wearing no clothes).

| Prologue: The Goat, 1767 p1–5 | Query | Follow-up query |
| :--- | :--- | :--- |
| Segment 1 query: (line 4) | What do you think it means by 'she didn't think much of them'? | |
| Segment 2 query: (line 7) | What does Goat think of Tahiti? How do you know? | What do you know about Tahiti from what goat is thinking? |

| Prologue: The Goat, 1767 p1–5 | Query | Follow-up query |
|---|---|---|
| Segment 3 query: (line 14) | 'The goat stamped with growing anger.' What does the author want us to think here? (Goat doesn't like what she sees. She likes green fields, grass, routine, being milked regularly.) | |
| Segment 4 query: (page 2) | After the first paragraph, read through, then ask about the line: 'the goat took her privileged position for granted'.<br><br>What do you think the author wants us to think of the goat? (She is spoilt, has the best spot on the ship, she is much better looked after than the other animals.) | If they struggle to answer, ask:<br>What do you think Goat thinks of herself? What in the story tells you this?<br><br>She is snobby, she says "they were lowly animals and deserved nothing more". |
| Segment 5: query (page 3, line 3) | Why do you think the sailors are crowding the deck, peering out into the fog?<br><br>What does it mean by 'maybe today'? (They are hoping they have found the Great South Land.) | |
| Segment 6: query (page 3, line 19) | What's happening here?<br>"We'll see if they've a mind to trade?"<br><br>(They've seen canoes near the island, 100 men and they're all naked as they are First Nations people. They want to see if they will 'trade'.)<br><br>Vocab: trinkets, trade | What do you think "We'll see if they've a mind to trade" means?<br><br>Trading means to swap; they have some trinkets (special items) that they would give away if the people that are naked will trade with them. |
| Follow-up activities: | **Hot seating:** One student sits in the hot seat of Goat, then Captain Wallis.<br><br>**Oral retelling** of the events of the first chapter (prologue).<br><br>**Vocab slides** – introduce first 10 words on slides. | |

## Chapter 12

# IMPLEMENTING A STRUCTURED LITERACY BLOCK

"We know that when we teach in an evidence aligned way, addressing all aspects of the science of reading, with preventative and responsive approaches with high expectations for every student, then 95% of students can read by the end of first grade"

~ Moats (2010)

## Chapter overview

- Self-reflection
- How do I fit it all in the literacy block?
- What is included in a structured literacy block?
- Five key points to consider when implementing structured literacy blocks
- Rethinking differentiation in the literacy block
- Planning rich knowledge units
- Advice for leading change
- Summary
- Professional discussion

## Self-reflection

| Self-reflection | Give yourself a rating out of 5 |
|---|---|
| **To what extent do you:** | |
| • Provide equal instructional time to the word recognition strand and language comprehension stand of the Reading Rope? | |
| • Aim to differentiate by support and outcome rather than content? | |
| • Explicitly teach PA with graphemes? | |
| • Align assessments with reading science: alphabetic code knowledge, decoding, fluency and language comprehension? | |
| • Feel confident in analysing assessments to identify risk and inform your planning and Tier 2 intervention? | |
| • Incorporate oral language into your daily routines and as a precursor to writing? | |
| • Provide guidance for parents on how to support their children with reading at home? | |

## How do I fit it all in the literacy block?

With such a cramped curriculum, this question is asked often. The first thing I would say is ensure you have a solid understanding of both parts of the Simple View of Reading and the subskills of Scarborough's Reading Rope. From there, choose one or two routines of the literacy block and set yourself a goal to implement those – preferably with a colleague – and do them well, over several weeks. Get some confidence and success happening, then layer on the next routine. Suggested starting points that are low risk and high impact (with minimal organisation) might be daily teacher read-alouds of high-quality fiction and non-fiction texts (including novels in Years 3–6), daily whole-class choral reading and fluency pairs.

Once you have implemented these routines for a few weeks and developed some consistency, then systematise the process. For example, if you decide to introduce daily review as the starting point, trial it with a year level colleague, planning the first week collaboratively and then develop a template for the following week so all that needs to be updated is the learning content.

The next thing (or even the first) is to audit what you already do in your literacy block and identify what aspects are not aligned with evidence-based research and de-implement those. It is so crucial that we do this, because once we are aware of what has the greatest impact on student learning in terms of explicit teaching of structured literacy, it is a case of ensuring that we always teach in this way.

## What is included in a structured literacy block?

### Daily review (10 minutes)

Start your literacy block with a daily review to review previously learnt content and build automaticity of concepts and skills. Refer to Chapter 2 for guidance here.

### PA, phonics and spelling (25–30 minutes)

This aspect of the literacy block teaches the subskills of the word recognition strand of the Reading Rope. It involves explicit teaching of grapheme-phoneme correspondences, teaching blending, segmenting and manipulation of phonemes in the context of graphemes taught. It is important to follow your synthetic phonics code with fidelity. It is not necessary to teach phonemic awareness in addition to the phonics session if taught in a structured synthetic phonics approach.

In this session, recommended routines to explicitly teach students may include:

- **Word construction** – explicitly teaching and modelling building words from graphemes through segmenting and blending; and then encoding (spelling). It is important to ensure that students are also provided with many opportunities to understand the meaning of each word being demonstrated. In this approach, students are taught the connection between phonology, orthography and meaning of each word taught.
- **Sound switching** – phoneme manipulation using graphemes to encode words, changing one phoneme each time. This is ideally done using mini whiteboards where the teacher is saying one word or pseudo based on the code knowledge being taught and then saying a new word where students are just changing one phoneme each time, for example, flip- flap- lap- lip- tip- trip-.

- **Morphology and spelling generalisations taught alongside the phonics code** – explicitly teaching students how multisyllabic words can be segmented into meaningful parts (morphemes) and their meanings and demonstrating this through a range of instructional approaches including Word Webs, Word Sums and Word Matrices.
- **Dictation** – applying code knowledge in meaningful phrases or sentences to build transcription skills; I recommend twice weekly. This routine involves the teacher reading the sentences aloud to students and the students transcribing these into their own written sentences. Please note, this is not a copying exercise!
- **Phoneme-grapheme mapping** – for spelling practice in the early years where students sound each phoneme out loud and encode them into individual boxes.
- **Decoding practice** – of graphemes, words, sentences and connected text initially with decodable text, aligned with the alphabetic code knowledge students have been taught. Once students are secure in the alphabetic principle, they can read any text.
- **High-frequency words** – these are taught alongside the phonics code knowledge and these irregular words are taught in the context of a sentence. Depending on the code you are following, are usually only one or two per week. Students are taught that like regular words, they can be decoded but they include a tricky spelling.

In Years 3-6, spelling extends to a greater focus on vocabulary, morphology and etymology. Routines may include:

- Word Webs, Word Matrices and Word Sums.
- Word associations and Word relationships, examples and non-examples.
- Applying new vocabulary into sentence level work such as *because, but, so*.
- Explicitly teaching multisyllabic words from syllable to word, and morphograph to word, with guided practice.
- Reminding students when segmenting multisyllabic words to spell, to say each morpheme or syllable precisely to avoid errors with schwas.

### Fluency (10 minutes)

Proficient fluency depends on being skilled in reading with accuracy and automaticity at the sub-lexical, lexical (word), sentence and connected text level. As such, students need frequent opportunities to build these fluency progressions. The following routines are recommended:

- Daily mixed-ability fluency pairs – students read a text at their instructional level to their partner for three minutes each. Student A reads to Student B and Student B provides feedback. Students swap. The use of a fluency rubric is helpful here as it acts as a success criterion for fluent reading when providing feedback to a partner.
- Intermittent phrase-cued reading – to improve prosody at the whole-class, small-group or partner level. This routine involves the teacher modelling highlighting of punctuation markers and when to pause in reading longer sentences.
- The paired partner reading time each day is an ideal time for you to take a small group in a pull-aside group for support or extension at the point of need, rather than 'ability level' per se. This time can also be used to listen to students reading in their pairs and provide additional feedback.

### Language comprehension for reading and writing composition (30–40 minutes)

This aspect of the literacy block teaches the subskills of the language comprehension strand of the Reading Rope to build background knowledge, vocabulary, syntax and story structure awareness. Ideally, this is taught through rich texts (fiction and non-fiction) in rich knowledge units of five weeks. Recommended routines include:

- Teacher read-aloud of high-quality texts with students following along
- Choral reading – whole-class reading in unison
- Explicit teaching of Tier 2 and Tier 3 words within the texts being read
- Explicit teaching of the macrostructure (story structure) of texts as well as the microstructure (syntax, conjunctions, connectives, vocabulary and anaphora)
- Close reading – explicit instruction in how to 'solve' challenging parts of text
- Questioning the Author – high-impact approach for reading aloud through posing 'queries' while reading
- Comprehension strategy instruction – explicit teaching of a handful of strategies particularly comprehension monitoring, inference and story structure

In Years 3–6, it would include class novels that students follow along with while the teacher is reading aloud. The Read-Think-Write-Discuss routine is also recommended. Throughout the week, after reading a section of text with students, pose questions, provide valuable thinking time, followed by a short time to write a response in a response journal and then discuss responses as a class.

## Writing (30–40 minutes)

Explicit teaching of sentence level writing, building up to paragraph level, linked to rich knowledge topics. Oral language opportunities should precede all writing tasks.

- Use high-quality model texts to demonstrate the genre being taught. This should be focused on oral only in the Foundation year. Students are taught a systematic approach to genre writing by modelling the breakdown of the text macrostructure. For example, in the case of teaching narrative, after writing a draft or plan, one day would be modelling the introduction, followed by students writing this component, with feedback and support. The following day would be modelling and then writing the build-up and so on.
- Use of high-quality mentor sentences to demonstrate the syntax or grammar focus.
- Guided practice in content level sentence, paragraph and genre writing.
- Syntax instruction that includes sentence doctoring, sentence combining, adding appositives, sentence stems with conjunctions; and Single Paragraph Outlines (SPO) for paragraph instruction (as per *The Writing Revolution* – Hochman & Wexler, 2017).

## Handwriting (10 minutes, two to three times per week)

While modelling and demonstration of correct letter formation and orientation is advised in the PA and phonics aspect of the literacy block, teaching students how to form new graphemes with similar orientations (such as the anti-clockwise letters – a, c, d, g) is advisable as a brief additional handwriting practice two to three times per week, to build transcription fluency. The automaticity of handwriting frees up working memory for higher-order writing skills and creates strong grapheme-phoneme correspondences (Ray, Dally & Lane, 2022).

Promising research on explicitly teaching of handwriting is currently being trialled in two programs entitled Think-to-Write (Mathwin, 2022) and Write-Start-K (Ray, Dally & Lane, 2022) where copying or tracing handwriting is *not* best practice.

In the following pages are two suggested weekly literacy block overviews for Foundation to Year 2 and Years 3–6.

# Weekly literacy block overview F–2

| Monday to Friday *(120 minutes)* | |
|---|---|
| **10 mins** | **Daily review:**<br>Fast-paced review of:<br>• Phoneme blending and segmentation<br>• Syntax, decoding, spelling and vocabulary<br>• Choral reading for fluency<br>• High-frequency words<br>• Oral story retelling of previously taught short passage/text |
| **30 mins** | **PA and phonics:**<br>• Explicit teaching of decoding and encoding, including word construction and sound swapping<br>• Phoneme-graphene mapping<br>• Modelling of correct letter formation and orientation<br>• Dictation (twice weekly) |
| **10 mins** | **Fluency:**<br>• Mixed-ability paired reading<br>• Peer feedback – may include a fluency rubric or a Glow and Grow<br><br>*\*Teacher pull-aside group targeting specific need, for example, fluency, decoding, dictation* |
| **30 mins** | **Language comprehension for reading and writing:**<br>• Building knowledge through rich topic units of two to five weeks<br>• Teacher read-aloud with planned interspersed queries (Questioning the Author)<br>• Class discussion/oral language<br>• Oral storytelling through explicit teaching of macrostructure<br>• Explicit teaching of Tier 2 and Tier 3 vocabulary<br>• Small amount of comprehension strategy instruction<br>• Syntax and grammar – story structure, oral storytelling, anaphora, connectives, etc |
| **30 mins** | **Writing:**<br>• Explicit teaching of sentence-level writing, building up to paragraph level linked to rich knowledge unit topic<br>• Oral language opportunities prior to all writing, including oral storytelling |
| **10 mins** | **Handwriting:**<br>Explicit teaching and modelling of letter formation and orientation |

# Weekly literacy block overview Years 3–6

| | Monday to Friday<br>*(120 minutes)* |
|---|---|
| 10 mins | **Daily review:**<br>Fast-paced review of:<br>• Syntax, spelling, morphographs and their meanings<br>• Vocabulary<br>• Choral reading of previously covered texts and standardised 'year level' texts<br>• Grammar and punctuation |
| 20 mins | **Spelling:**<br>• Explicit teaching of words with routines such as phoneme to syllable to word, syllable to word and morphograph to word<br>• Spelling of increasingly complex letter combinations in words<br>• Dictation<br>• Morphology and etymology: prefixes, suffixes, base words |
| 10 mins | **Fluency:**<br>• Mixed-ability paired reading<br>• Repeated reading approach<br>• Peer feedback – may include a fluency rubric<br>*Teacher pull-aside group targeting specific need, for example, fluency, decoding, dictation* |
| 30 mins | **Language comprehension for reading and writing:**<br>• Teacher read-aloud/novel with interspersed queries (Questioning the Author)<br>• Building knowledge through rich topic units of two to five weeks<br>• Class discussion/oral language<br>• Explicit teaching of Tier 2 and Tier 3 vocabulary<br>• Specific comprehension strategy instruction in the context of texts read: comprehension monitoring, summarising, inference, story structure, question generation and question answering<br>• Syntax and grammar<br>• Close reading lesson or bursts<br>• Brief response writing linked to teacher read-aloud text, for example, *Read-Think-Write-Discuss* cycle |
| 40 mins | **Writing:**<br>• Focus on paragraph and text level writing with planning, reviewing, writing and editing using self-regulatory frameworks<br>*Oral language opportunities prior to all writing* |

| 10 mins | Handwriting:<br>• Cursive writing practice, to develop handwriting fluency<br>*May consist of copying a spelling-based dictation* |
| --- | --- |

## Five key points to consider when implementing structured literacy blocks

As highlighted earlier in this book, structured literacy is an instructional approach that is characterised by the provision of systematic, explicit instruction that is based on the science of how children best learn to read, spell and write. It is teacher-led instruction that enables educators to provide prompt, targeted feedback in response to student error (Spear-Swerling, 2019). It is taught explicitly, meaning that teachers clearly explain and model key skills through gradual release of responsibility instruction.

There are five key considerations in planning and implementing structured literacy blocks:

1. **Content** – Is the content we are teaching aligned with how the brain best learns to read (aka the science of reading)? Are we teaching both key components of the Simple View of Reading (decoding and language comprehension) concurrently with equal weight and significance?
2. **Process** – Are each of the literacy skills taught in a structured, systematic and sequential approach, utilising explicit instruction, modelling, worked examples and feedback? The best content could be covered in a lesson, but if it is not taught in a structured literacy approach, this will not support all learners.
3. **Data** – What data is informing our teaching and learning and are the assessments we are utilising providing information about how to move our students forward? How is formative assessment applied and used? What does our data tell us about what our children can and can't do, where their gaps are and how to move them forward?
4. **Response and prevention** – How do our lessons respond quickly to student difficulties and, more importantly, prevent reading difficulties from occurring in the first place? We know that by the end of first grade, 95% of children can learn to read proficiently with effective instruction (Moats, 2010). What percentage of our students are making expected progress to this goal and beyond?

5.  **Impact** – What is the impact of our teaching? This is a greater focus than 'this is the curriculum I need to teach'. This subtle shift in mindset can make all the difference in literacy outcomes for every student.

## Rethinking differentiation in the literacy block

In terms of differentiation, there can be a huge gap between our strongest and weakest students in any one class and it can be difficult to know how to address all of their needs.

One thing I find, though, is that we either do too much differentiation, or not at all. The key is to strike the balance of high responsiveness but 'low' differentiation. A longitudinal study known as 'The Opportunity Myth' is a great starting point for unpacking this concept. The US study found that teachers were differentiating the curriculum so much that they had inadvertently lowered their expectations, creating a situation where the majority of students had no way of meeting end-of-year expectations.

To achieve 'low differentiation', a couple of considerations include:

- What requires differentiation and what requires targeted intervention? They are two distinctly different things. Differentiation provides equal access to the curriculum and intervention aims to close gaps, which, in the interest of social equity, must be in addition to the literacy block.
- What quality data do you have? Are you able to make informed decisions about student needs, gaps, extension required based on the types of assessment you use? Or are your assessments providing you with a level or reading/spelling age that make it very difficult to plan accordingly?
- Are you crystal clear on what your students need to be able to achieve by the end of the year? Are you providing ample opportunities for students to be able to get there?

A few recommendations for striking the right balance of differentiation include:

- Differentiate by **outcome** and **support** rather than by content, where possible. There are, however, times when students require differentiated content, for example, in a small pull-aside group, fluency pairs or for independent home reading. In these situations, students may require a decodable text based on their decoding ability or higher. This is when differentiation by content is necessary.

- Move away from literacy rotations. There is no research that demonstrates a positive impact in differentiation or literacy achievement through literacy rotations.
- Focus on amplifying your whole-class instruction. Pitch your content to year level curriculum ability *every day* so that even your weakest students in reading, spelling and writing are getting access to year level curriculum. Then differentiate your modelling of worked examples, questioning, outcome and support accordingly.
- Focus on building knowledge in literacy, through cross-curricular knowledge units. This is essential for reading comprehension but provides many opportunities for extending our most able students. Map out your cross-curricular unit topics and identify what specific knowledge you want your students to know, then link this to your literacy block in five-week units. Building this up to a schoolwide scope and sequence of knowledge units is key here.
- Provide daily opportunities for oral language before all writing tasks. This is essential for students who take a little longer to process their ideas or thoughts. Always provide model or mentor texts for writing.
- Provide opportunities for students to access graphic organisers for all writing tasks. Providing a visual scaffold to show the structure of a paragraph or genre is a high impact approach for reading comprehension but is also supportive in reducing cognitive load.
- Provide tactile lined paper for students experiencing difficulties with handwriting sizing. The raised lines can be a supportive aid in students learning how to write within the lines.
- Use of success criterion for fluency and writing tasks provides a GPS for students in terms of where we want them to be and is also helpful for differentiation by outcome.

It is essential that all students experience whole-class instruction based on year level expectations rather than just 'at their level'. Otherwise, this creates an equity issue and the gap will only widen between our strongest and weakest students. If we always meet students where they are at, we will not provide them the opportunity to catch up. Yes, differentiate by support and outcome, but always provide opportunities for year level instruction.

## Planning rich knowledge units

If planning a five-week rich knowledge unit seems too daunting at this stage, start by planning in two-week units and build up to five weeks. On the following pages is an example of a two-week block for Year 1 linked to science.

## Example of rich knowledge unit planning overview – two-week block, Year 1

| Topic | Science link | | Syntax |
|---|---|---|---|
| **Texts** | *The Way Back Home* – Oliver Jeffers<br><br>*I wonder why stars twinkle and other questions about space* – Carole Stott | ***Learning intention*** | I can say/write interesting sentences using *and, but, because*<br><br>I can say sentences beginning with *once, then, unfortunately, suddenly, finally*<br><br>I can use *but, because, so* to orally complete sentences with the vocabulary words for this week<br><br>I can identify the difference between fragments and sentences |
| **Cross-curricular links** | Science<br>Knowledge building | ***Sentence examples linked to texts and key vocabulary to be taught*** | Once there was a boy, and one day as he was putting his things back in the cupboard, he...<br><br>Both the boy and the Martian could hear... (noises in the dark and both feared the worst)<br><br>The plane lifted off the ground but...<br>The plane lifted off the ground because...<br>The plane lifted off the ground so...<br><br>When I was in a dark cave, I feared...<br><br>The Martian and the boy feared...<br><br>The truck spluttered when...<br><br>I might use a spanner to... |

| Knowledge building | 1. The world and everything in it, including the planets and stars is called the universe.<br><br>2. We live on planet Earth.<br><br>3. A person that studies space is called an astronomer. 'Astro' means relating to stars.<br><br>4. We live in a galaxy called the Milky Way.<br><br>5. The sun is a huge ball of superhot gas.<br><br>6. There are eight main planets in our solar system.<br><br>7. Moons are rocky bodies that orbit the planets.<br><br>8. Astronauts need to wear space suits to protect them.<br><br>9. A constellation is a group of stars that forms a pattern.<br><br>10. The Earth moves around the sun, which takes a year. | *Oral language and text level work* | |
|---|---|---|---|
| | | *Learning intentions* | I can orally retell the story using a visual story mountain, for example...<br><br>**One day/Once**... there was a boy who found an aeroplane in his cupboard so he decided he would take it out for a go right away.<br><br>**Then**... the plane <u>spluttered</u>... it had run out of petrol. What was he to do?<br><br>While he was stuck on the moon, he met a Martian. His spaceship had a broken engine and crash landed on the moon.<br><br>**Unfortunately**... the boy and the Martian couldn't think of what they could do.<br><br>They were all alone in the dark and feared the worst.<br><br>**Suddenly**... the boy had a plan, he would fly down in a parachute and swim home and get the things they would need.<br><br>**Finally**... The boy got the things they needed and the Martian helped him get back onto the moon. The boy had petrol for his plane and the Martian was able to fix his engine. They said goodbye and wondered if they would ever see each other again.<br><br>**Or modified option**: *I can identify the events of the beginning, middle and end of the story (oral/graphic organisers)*<br><br>**Beginning:** Boy finds an aeroplane; boy flies plane to moon.<br><br>**Middle:** Suddenly it splutters... as it has run out of petrol!<br><br>Meets Martian who is also stuck. They think of what they can do to get back home. Boy has an idea and goes home to get the things he will need.<br><br>**End:** Boy gets back to the moon with Martian's help. They help each other to fix their problems – the boy fixed the Martian's spaceship with the right spanner and the Martian filled the boy's petrol tank. They say goodbye and go home, wondering if they will ever meet again.<br><br>**Hot seating:** I can hotseat and be the Martian/boy in the story. |

**Week 1: – Text: *The Way Back Home* (Jeffers) – fiction**

| Vocabulary | Monday | Tuesday | Wednesday | Thursday | Friday |
|---|---|---|---|---|---|
| finally<br>spluttered<br>realised<br>feared<br>Earth | Build the field: What do you know about the Earth, moon and stars?<br><br>Class discussion. Use a world globe to represent the Earth<br><br>Read aloud – Once there was a boy with QtA approach<br><br>Introduce five vocab words (PowerPoint)<br><br>Hot seating: one student is chosen to sit in the hot seat and be the boy or the Martian. Students generate questions for the person in the hot seat | Read aloud – Once there was a boy<br><br>Oral discussion about student responses to the text<br><br>Map the beginning, middle and end of story (story structure) using a Story Map<br><br>Review vocab words<br><br>Using a graphic organiser students can write a sentence about the beginning, middle and end of story<br><br>*\*Use the oral storytelling end-of-year expectations (see page 107) (Spencer & Pierce, 2022) as a guide for differentiation and extension* | Read aloud – Once there was a boy<br><br>Review vocabulary and elaborate:<br><br>For example, Sentence stems (3–5) – finish the sentence with target vocabulary word (in PowerPoint) – mixed-ability pairs<br><br>Story Mountain – mapping out the events on butchers' paper – model and retell the story orally. May use props. Model use of time connective language<br><br>**Earth** travels around the sun **and** it is where we all call home.<br><br>The boy and the Martian **feared** the worst. | Read aloud – Once there was a boy<br><br>Choral read a small portion of the text on IWB<br><br>Students may orally retell the story to a partner with puppets/pictures of key aspects of text or use the story mountain as a scaffold<br><br>Review vocabulary<br><br>Syntax – based on vocabulary from the story including the words 'Earth' and 'feared' | Choral read a small portion of the text on IWB with teacher echo reading first<br><br>Innovate on the story by including a different character and transport, for example: The girl... took her helicopter and landed on the moon.<br><br>Children change a part of the story and orally tell it to a mixed-ability peer<br><br>Review vocabulary<br><br>Syntax: and, but, because<br><br>The plane **spluttered and...**<br><br>The plane **spluttered but...**<br><br>The plane **spluttered because...**<br><br>The boy jumped down to **Earth and...**<br><br>The boy jumped down to **Earth but...**<br><br>The boy jumped down to **Earth because...** |

| Vocabulary | Monday | Tuesday | Wednesday | Thursday | Friday |
|---|---|---|---|---|---|
| orbit<br>moon<br>constellations<br>Milky Way<br>universe | | | | | |
| | **Week 2 – Text: I wonder why stars twinkle and other questions about space (Stott) – nonfiction** | | | | |
| | Build the field.<br>Class discussion<br>What do you know about the Earth, moon and stars?<br>KWL: What do you know about the Earth, moon and stars?<br>Show a snippet of a video of the universe to set the scene<br>Discuss what they saw in the video<br>Teacher read-aloud nonfiction Text pages 1–4: I wonder why stars twinkle and other questions about space (Carole Stott) using the QtA approach (with planned queries)<br>Vocabulary – introduce four new Tier 2 and Tier 3 words from the text: moon, constellation, Milky Way, universe | Non-fiction text<br>Introduce new word: orbit<br>How many planets are there?<br>Why is Earth so special? (pages 13–16)<br>Read aloud<br>Choral reading<br>Class discussion<br>What are the key facts we have learnt from this text?<br>Model writing them in the KWL chart<br>Think, Pair, Share<br>Review vocab words (PowerPoint) | Non-fiction passage reading teacher read aloud:<br>Why does the sun go out at night? (pages 16–17)<br>Review vocabulary words, plus elaborate:<br>For example, sentence stems (3–5) – finish the sentence with target vocabulary word (in PowerPoint) – mixed-ability pairs | Non-fiction passage reading teacher read-aloud:<br>What is it like on our moon? (pages 23–26)<br>Model reading a paragraph and ask students to echo after you in a choral read<br>Review vocabulary words<br>Syntax – Are these fragments or sentences?<br>*The moon is (F)*<br>*It takes 27.3 days for the moon to travel all the way around the Earth (S)*<br>*Is a lot smaller than the sun (F)*<br>*The daily disappearance of the sun below the horizon is known as sunset (S)*<br>*Appears to rise above the horizon (F)* | Non-fiction passage reading teacher read-aloud:<br>Why do astronauts wear space suits? (pages 27–28)<br>Review vocabulary words<br>Syntax: because, but, so<br>*Some days the sun rises earlier because...*<br>*Some days the sun rises earlier but...*<br>*Some days the sun rises earlier so...*<br>Formative assessment – what have we learnt about Earth, the moon and stars?<br>Complete KWL from the start of the week |

## Advice for leading change

Depending on where your school is at in your journey, you may consider these initial four steps when implementing structured literacy across the school. (Adapted from Kotter's change model, 1996).

1. Create the urgency for change – based on the literacy evidence and student data, build on what is already having a significant impact on student progress and achievement, and acknowledge and document the areas for growth. An excellent starting point would be ACER's National School Improvement Tool (Masters, 2016) and a school-based literacy survey to ascertain staff confidence in teaching the elements of structured literacy.
2. Build an inspiring, powerful team – find your champions and develop a diverse literacy team; along with schoolwide professional learning communities (PLC teams) for collaboration and distributive leadership. This may initially start with a literacy team, then branch out into each team member having a specific sub-leadership role in focusing on one aspect of structured literacy and assessment to be the 'expert'.
3. Create a vision for change with your literacy team. It is essential to know your 'why' behind structured literacy. Consider where you want your school to be three years from now. One year from now. What are your goals for this term, semester, next year? What simple tweaks can deliver low-risk, high-yield results for students? Use your staff literacy survey to gain insight into a starting point for a small but high impact change. Many of my schools start with daily fluency pairs. This is a low risk, small change that can build early success and get you on your way.
4. Communicate the vision for change with the staff and begin building staff capacity. Ensure that the preconditions for complex change are established in the school including an orderly learning environment and high expectations for students (Macklin & Zbar, 2020). Starting a change journey without these in place is like building a house without a solid foundation, which will inevitably lead to issues later on. Map out a professional learning plan, evidence-based assessment schedule, dates for data analysis and starting points for universal screening.

5.  Develop peer coaching teams to ensure that professional learning transfers into high impact instructional practice in the classroom. Joyce and Showers (1980, 2002) identified that there is a 95% transference into the classroom when training is done this way as opposed to only a 5% transfer rate into the classroom when it's a standalone professional learning.

See the table below for a breakdown of impact of each area:

### Models of professional development, Joyce and Showers (1980, 2002)

| Professional development offered | Impact on knowledge | Impact on skill | Impact on practice |
|---|---|---|---|
| Theory | 10% | 5% | 0% |
| Theory + Modelling | 30% | 20% | 0% |
| Theory + Modelling + Practice | 60% | 60% | 5% |
| Theory + Modelling + Practice + Coaching | 95% | 95% | 95% |

6.  Develop scope and sequences and rich knowledge units to ensure consistency from class to class and year to year that are aligned with the national curriculum. Develop a schoolwide instructional guide with checklists and the why, what and how of each subcomponent of literacy to ensure consistency across the school.
7.  Embed a RTI model with universal screening, tiered instruction and rigorous progress monitoring. Tier 1 instruction must be gold standard here or we will always have a leaky bucket with students slipping through the cracks
8.  Be sure to celebrate small wins along the way, in terms of your own professional growth and also your students! Spend a few minutes at the start of staff meetings to share these anecdotes. This is the emotional fuel that spurs on the momentum for change!

## Summary

- Before developing structured literacy blocks, ensure you have a solid understanding of the Simple View of Reading and the subskills of Scarborough's Reading Rope.
- There are five key factors to consider in planning and implementing literacy blocks: content, process, data, response and prevention, and impact.
- Differentiate by outcome and support rather than by content, where possible.
- Advice for leading whole-school change includes: 1) create the urgency for change, 2) build inspiring, powerful teams, 3) create a vision for change with your literacy team, 4) communicate the vision for change with the staff and build staff capacity, 5) develop peer coaching teams to ensure that PL transfers into the classroom, 6) develop scope and sequences, 7) embed a RTI framework, and 8) celebrate small wins along the way.

## Professional discussion

- Considering the positive impact of low-variance curriculums across schools, how might you implement consistent structured literacy blocks and instructional models from Foundation to Year 6 in your school?
- How can we get 95% of our students to be confident, proficient readers by the end of Year 1 in our context? What are the barriers to achieving this? How will we overcome these barriers?

# CONCLUSION

For those of us in the business of teaching, we know it is one of the hardest, yet most rewarding professions around, as we have the privilege of working with one of the most precious members of society: children. And when it comes to teaching reading – a skill that humans are not born to do – daily in the early years of schooling, teachers are quite literally rewiring the brains of children and building neural pathways for skilled reading. So, among a huge list of other hats we wear, teachers are quite literally learning engineers.

With regard to building skilled readers through structured literacy, just as there are many components to high-quality reading instruction, this complexity also applies to the planning that goes into lessons and units of work. Not only is it essential that both elements of the Simple View of Reading are taught, but within these two constructs are the many subcomponents of the Reading Rope, that in combination, with increasing complexity and automaticity over time, lead to skilled reading.

On top of the knowledge required in teaching reading, there is the application of this knowledge into the pedagogy of structured literacy. Teachers need to be highly skilled in teaching in a high-rigour, responsive, explicit approach and this cannot be achieved without the *knowledge of* reading science and the *know-how* of structured literacy pedagogy.

However, if you have been reading this book and feeling regret or remorse about your current practices, please don't despair, as most of us have been there! It is now a case of when we know better, we do better; and when we know what the science tells us, then it is a case of following it to make the greatest impact in literacy achievement for every student. This is expected in the medical world and, in my opinion, there should be no difference with education, which in terms of future life outcomes is arguably as important as our physical and emotional wellbeing.

So, in conclusion, I hope this book brings you closer to literacy success for EVERY student. Just like a drop of water can create a domino effect with a concentric ripple effect outwards, so too does early literacy success impact upon later life. When children leave school as confident readers and writers, we are setting students up for a future of choice and fulfilling, successful pathways. I thank you for choosing to read my book and in joining me in my quest in gifting this ripple effect to every student.

Access resources and templates from the book here:

# ACKNOWLEDGEMENTS

I would firstly like to acknowledge my publisher, Alicia Cohen, for reaching out to me to write for Amba Press. It most certainly was a bucket list moment and it has been an absolute delight to work with you, Alicia, and I am so thankful for the opportunity. I would also like to thank my wonderful editor, Rica Dearman, for your keen eye and guidance, and graphic designer, Tess McCabe, for the fantastic cover design. I would also like to thank my wonderful friends and colleagues for reviewing my manuscript and providing such invaluable feedback: Zoe Sharman, Diane Pursell, Tamara Johansen, Donna Reeves, Sally Roberts and Maura Killalea.

I would like to thank the principals, literacy leaders, teachers and education assistants I currently support Australia-wide. I am in awe of what you do day in, day out, for your students and never forget what it is like to be in the classroom. I feel privileged to walk beside you in your school improvement journeys.

I would also like to thank some special people throughout my teaching career who have moulded me into the educator I am today. Zoe Sharman, my Headteacher in London, but also my confidante and friend. I am so thankful to you for taking this supply teacher from Australia into your school and the leadership opportunity you afforded me. Thank you to the Fogarty Foundation for my post-graduate scholarship in learning difficulties and thank you to Dr Lorraine Hammond for teaching me so much in that space.

Tracy Ilich, my wonderful undergrad (and lifetime) university friend, for suggesting I move into the Online Learning and Learning Difficulties teams, which were part of the Centre for Inclusive Schooling (now SSEND) when I came back from London in 2007. I am forever thankful for that career move. To Penny Curtis and Margie Backhouse, my wonderful team leaders at CIS – thank you for sharing with me RTI, the Rowe Report, Rose Review and the NITL back in 2008 and for all the learning, the laughs, lifetime friendship and mentorship. I will always cherish the years we were in the 'print cell' with our fabulous team of evidence-based practitioners.

I would like to thank some inspiring principals whom I have had the pleasure of working with: Carlyn Dyer – who gave me my first deputy principal position; David Womersley, Paul Andrijich and Andrew Britton. Thank you to the fabulous Kerry Hill – the year with you and Andrew was brilliant.

Thank you also to my Learning Difficulties Australia family, which I am so delighted to be a part of. Thank you to Donna Reeves, Principal of Tumut Public School, for taking a chance on me when I launched Leading Literacy Impact in 2021. Thank you to my incredible Literacy Impact behind-the-scenes team: Business Coach Lydia Lee and Virtual Assistant Melissa Strange. Your support and guidance allow me to get on with what I love to do, and that is work with schools and teachers to make a difference for students.

I sincerely thank my ever-supportive sisters, Kelly, Wendy and Michelle and their beautiful families; Dad and CJ, my heavenly mum, my Nana, Cos and Maria, extended family and my beautiful friends – in particular, Sally and Shana for your love and support. To my wonderful husband, Damian, and my mini-me's, Ava and Lucas – thank you for being so understanding of every time I was working or writing in the past year. You mean everything to me.

Finally, my thanks go to you, the reader. Whether you are a teacher, principal or parent, my guess is that you dream of the same thing as me – a society where:

- *Every child has access to exemplary literacy practices that enable every child to be a successful reader, writer and speller;*
- *Undergraduate degrees provide evidence-based instruction for beginning teachers; and*
- *Education departments support, follow and mandate the implementation of the reading science and structured literacy.*

Together, we need to advocate for this (and speak up with conviction when it is not in place) – and we can turn this dream into reality.

# ABOUT THE AUTHOR

Julie is a passionate educator, consultant and learning difficulties specialist. As a former deputy principal leading whole-school improvement, she has a deep understanding of the pressures principals and teachers face, as well as the varied needs of students.

As the founder of Literacy Impact, her mission is to help teachers, school leaders and changemakers bridge the gap between evidence-based research and literacy success for every student.

Julie currently works with approximately 50 schools Australia-wide, supporting them to embed high impact educational frameworks and approaches with the goal of every student leaving primary school as an effective reader, speller and writer.

For many years, Julie was a deputy principal, leading change management in the science of reading and writing, RTI and data-informed practice. Earlier in her career, she spent five years in the UK, with four years as a special needs coordinator (SENCO) in a South East London school, leading inclusive practices schoolwide.

As a Fogarty Scholar and award-winner of the Graduate Certificate in Education: Learning Difficulties, she was also a Learning Difficulties and Online Learning Support Teacher at the Centre for Inclusive Schooling (SSEND), providing state-wide school support and professional learning in metropolitan and rural schools.

Julie is highly trained in evidence-based literacy pedagogy and aims to inspire educators to get the best out of every student, every day. Her work has been published in *Education Review*, *The Reading Teacher*, Learning Difficulties Australia *Bulletin*, Dyslexia SPELD *Bulletin* and *Class Ideas K-3*.

Julie is also a Council member of Learning Difficulties Australia (LDA) and the editor of the LDA *Bulletin*. She lives in Perth on Whadjuk Noongar country with her husband, two children and fur baby, Marty.

# REFERENCES

AISNSW (2017). 'Bridging the Research to Practice Gap: Data informed practice.' *The Link*. Retrieved November 2021, from www.aisnsw.edu.au/Resources/WAL%204%20%5BOpen%20Access%5D/Data%20Informed%20Practice.pdf

American Psychiatric Association (2013). *Diagnostic and statistical manual of mental disorders* (Fifth Edition). https://doi.org/10.1176/appi.books.9780890425596

Amirjalili, F, & Jabbari, AA (2018). 'The impact of morphological instruction on morphological awareness and reading comprehension of EFL learners.' Retrieved 5 August 2021, from www.researchgate.net/publication/327778417_The_impact_of_morphological_instruction_on_morphological_awareness_and_reading_comprehension_of_EFL_learners

Archer, AL, & Hughes, CA (2011). *Explicit instruction: Effective and Efficient Teaching*. Guilford Press: New York

Auspeld (n.d.). 'Selecting a successful intervention program.' www.uldforparents.com/contents/selecting-a-successful-intervention-program

Australian institute for Teaching Standards and School Leadership (AITSL) (2017). 'Australian Professional Standards for Teachers.' AITSL: Melbourne

Beck, IL, & Beck, ME (2013). *Making Sense of Phonics* (Second Edition). Guilford Press: New York

Beck, IL, McKeown, MG, & Kucan, L (2013). *Bringing Words to Life: Robust Vocabulary Instruction*. Guilford Press: New York

Beck, IL, McKeown, MG, & Sandora, CA (2021). *Robust Comprehension Instruction with Questioning the Author 15 Years Smarter*. Guilford Press: New York

Bowen, C, & Snow, P (2017). *Making Sense of Interventions for Children with Developmental Disorders: A Guide for Parents and Professionals*. J&R Press: United Kingdom

Bowers, PN, Kirky, JR, & Hélène Deacon, S (2010). 'The Effects of Morphological Instruction on Literacy Skills.' *Review of Educational Research*. 80, 144. Retrieved from DOI:10.3102/0034654309359353

Brown, K (2022). Podcast: 'Reviewing Kindergarten Phonological Awareness Materials.' *Teaching Literacy Podcast*. Episode 35. Retrieved 31 August 2022, from www.teachingliteracypodcast.com/e35-reviewing-kindergarten-phonological-awareness-materials-with-dr-kathleen-brown/

Brown, KJ, Patrick, KC, Fields, MK, & Craig, GT (2021). 'Phonological Awareness Materials in Utah Kindergartens: A Case Study in the Science of Reading.' *Reading Research Quarterly*, 56(S1), S249–S272

Cambridge University Press and Assessment, (2023). *Cambridge Dictionary Online.* United Kingdom

Case, S, Philpot, D, & Walker, J (2006). *Sounds-Write: A linguistic phonic programme.* Sounds-Write Ltd: United Kingdom

Catts, HW (2021–22). 'Rethinking How to Promote Reading Comprehension.' *American Educator.* Winter 2021–2022. Retrieved 4 January 2022, from www.aft.org/ae/winter2021-2022/catts

Centre for Education Statistics and Evaluation (CESE) (2017). *Cognitive Load Theory: Research that teachers really need to understand.* NSW Department of Education: New South Wales

Centre for Education Statistics and Evaluation (CESE) (2020). *Supporting high academic expectations – Every student is known, valued and cared for in our schools.* NSW Department of Education: New South Wales

Chapman, J, & Tunmer, W (2019). 'Dyslexia and Equity: A more inclusive approach to reading difficulties.' *Learning Difficulties Australia Bulletin,* 51(2 & 3), 28–32

Clark, RE, Kirschner, PA, & Sweller, J (2012). 'Putting Students on the Path to Learning: The Case for Fully Guided Instruction.' *American Educator,* 36(1), 6–11. Retrieved 25 September 2022, from https://files.eric.ed.gov/fulltext/EJ971752.pdf

Coalla, PS, Ramos, S, Álvarez-Cañizo, M, & Cuetos, F (2014). 'Orthographic learning in dyslexic Spanish children.' *Annals of Dyslexia,* 64(2), 166–181

Corbett, P (2003). *How to teach writing at Key Stage 1.* Routledge: United Kingdom

Corbett, P (2015–16). *Pie Corbett's Talk for Writing teaching guide for progression in writing year by year.* Retrieved February 2019, from www.talk4writing.com/wp-content/uploads/2015/09/Progression-Updated-2015.pdf

Corbett, P & Strong, J (2015). *Jumpstart! Grammar: Games and activities for ages 6–14* (Second Edition). Routledge: Maidenhead, United Kingdom

Corbett, P, & Strong, J (2020). *Talk for Writing in the Early Years: How to teach story and rhyme, involving families 2–5 years* (Revised Edition). 128–129. Open University Press: Maidenhead, United Kingdom

Dale, E (1965). 'Vocabulary Measurement: Techniques and Major Findings.' 42(8). 895–901, 948. National Council of Teachers of English. Urbana, IL

De Bruin, K (2021). 'Response to Intervention (RTI) and MultiTiered Systems of Support (MTSS): An Introduction.' *Learning Difficulties Australia Bulletin,* 53(3), 15–18

Dehaene, S (2010). *Reading in the Brain: The New Science of How We Read.* Penguin Books: New York

Department for Education (2021). *The Reading framework: Teaching the foundations of literacy.* Retrieved 10 July 2022, from https://assets.publishing.service.gov.uk/government/uploads/system/uploads/attachment_data/file/1000986/Reading_framework_Teaching_the_foundations_of_literacy_-_July-2021.pdf

Derewianka, B (2011). *A new grammar companion for teachers.* PETA: Australia

DiCamillo, K (2003). *The Tale of Despereaux.* Candlewick Press: Massachusetts

Downs, J (Host). September 2022. Teacher Content Knowledge and Early Literacy Instruction with Dr Shayne Piasta and Dr Alida Hudson, Episode 37 [Audio podcast episode], *Teaching Literacy podcast,* Jake Downs and Patrick Wells. https://podcasts.apple.com/au/podcast/e37-teacher-content-knowledge-and-early-literacy/id1482475731?i=1000581064353

Dyslexia-SPELD Foundation (DSF) (n.d.). 'Examples of High Quality, Evidence-Based Phonics Programs and Resources.' DSF: Perth

Dyslexia-SPELD Foundation (DSF) (n.d.). 'Structured Synthetic Phonics: A Guide for Teachers and Parents.' DSF: Perth

Dyslexia-SPELD Foundation (DSF) (2014). *Understanding Learning Difficulties: A practical guide.* DSF: South Perth

Ehri, LC (2014). 'Orthographic mapping in the acquisition of sight word reading, spelling memory, and vocabulary learning.' Scientific Studies of Reading, 18(1), 5–21

Ehri, LC (2022). 'Learning to read and write words.' [Paper presentation] Learning Difficulties Australia conference: Melbourne

Ehri, LC, & Saltmarsh, J (1995). 'Beginning readers outperform older disabled readers in learning to read words by sight.' *Reading and Writing: An Interdisciplinary Journal*, 7(3), 295–326

Etymonline (2023). www.etymonline.com

Fisher, D, Frey, N, & Hattie, J (2017). *Teaching Literacy in the Visible Learning Classroom.* Corwin: California

Five from Five, Auspeld & Learning Difficulties Australia (2020). *Primary Reading Pledge: A plan to have all students reading by the end of primary school.* MultiLit: NSW. Retrieved 25 September 2022, from www.fivefromfive.com.au/primary-reading-pledge

Flouri, E, & Buchanan, A (2004). 'Early father's and mother's involvement and child's later educational outcomes.' *British Journal of Educational Psychology*, 74(2), 141–153

French, J (2006) *The Goat Who Sailed the World.* Harper Collins Publishers: Sydney

Fuchs, LS, Fuchs, D, Hosp, MK, & Jenkins, JR (2001). 'Oral reading fluency as an indicator of reading competence: A theoretical, empirical, and historical analysis.' *Scientific Studies of Reading*, 5, 239–256

Glisson, L, Leitao, S, & Claessen, M (2022). *The Oral Narrative Intervention Programme.* Retrieved September 2022, from www.trackstoliteracy.com

Goldenberg, C (2022). 'Literacy Development for ELLS.' *DSF Language, Literacy and Learning Virtual Conference.* Perth (online)

Good, RH, III, Kaminski, RA, Cummings, K, Dufour-Martel, C, Petersen, K, Powell-Smith, K, Stollar, S, & Wallin, J (2011). *Acadience Reading Assessment Manual.* Dynamic Measurement Group

Goodwin, AP, & Ahn, SA (2010). 'A meta-analysis of morphological interventions: effects on literacy achievement of children with literacy difficulties.' *Ann Dyslexia*, 60(2), 183–208

Gough, PB, & Tunmer, WE (1986). 'Decoding, Reading, and Reading Disability.' *Remedial and Special Education*, 7, 6–10

Graham, S, & Hebert, MA (2010). *Writing to read: Evidence for How Writing Can Improve Reading.* A Carnegie Corporation Time to Act Report. Washington, DC: Alliance for Excellent Education

Hanford, E (2019). *At a loss for words: How a flawed idea is teaching millions of kids to be poor readers.* APM Reports: United States

Hanford, E (Host). 10 November 2022. Episode 6: The Company, with Dr Matthew Burns. [Audio podcast episode]. *Sold a Story.* APM Reports https://open.spotify.com/show/0tcUMXBFMGMo8w79MM5QCI

Hart, B, & Risley, TR (1995). *Meaningful Differences in the Everyday Experience of Young American Children.* Paul H. Brookes Publishing Company: Baltimore, MD

Hasbrouck, J (2020). 'Understanding Reading Fluency.' *Learning Difficulties Australia Bulletin*, 52(1) 9–12

Hasbrouck, J (2021). *Reading Fluency: What have we learned since 2000.* Retrieved from www.youtube.com/watch?v=CGzQ97hh3lU

Hasbrouck, J, & Glaser, D (2019). *Reading Fluency: Understand – Assess – Teach.* Benchmark Education Company

Hasbrouck, J, & Tindal, G (2017). 'An Update to Compiled ORF Norms.' [Technical Report No. 1702] Eugene, OR: Behavioral Research and Teaching, University of Oregon

Hattie, J (2003). 'Teachers Make a Difference: What is the research evidence?' Paper presented at the ACER Research conference 'Building Teacher Quality: What does the research tell us?' Melbourne, Australia. Retrieved from http://research.acer.edu.au/research_conference_2003/4/

Hattie, J, (2012). *Visible Learning for Teachers: Maximizing Impact on Learning.* Routledge: London and New York

Hattie, J, & Zierer, K (2018). *10 Mindframes for Visible Learning.* Routledge: Oxon

Hennessy, N (2021). *The Reading Comprehension Blueprint.* Brookes Publishing Co: Baltimore, Maryland

Henry, MK (2010). *Unlocking Literacy: Effective Decoding and Spelling Instruction.* Brookes Publishing Co: United States

Hochman, JC, & Wexler, N (2017). *The Writing Revolution: A Guide to Advancing Thinking Through Writing in All Subjects and Grades.* Jossey-Bass: San Francisco

Hudson, RF, Pullen, PC, Lane, HB, & Torgesen, JK (2009). 'The complex nature of reading fluency: A multidimensional view.' *Reading & Writing Quarterly: Overcoming Learning Difficulties,* 25(1), 4–32

International Literacy Association (2018). *Reading Fluently Does Not Mean Reading Fast* [Literacy leadership brief]. Newark, DE: Author

Jake (Host). 18 June 2022. 'Reviewing Kindergarten Phonological Awareness Materials with Dr Kathleen Brown.' E35 [Audio podcast episode], Teaching Literacy Podcast. https://content.blubrry.com/teachlingliteracypodcast/TLP_Kathleen_Brown.mp3

Jeffers, O (2007). *The Way Back Home.* HarperCollins Publishers: United Kingdom

Johnston, R, & Watson, J (2005). *The effects of synthetic phonics teaching on reading and spelling attainment.* Retrieved 25 August 2021, from www.webarchive.org.uk/wayback/archive/20150221021304mp_/http://www.gov.scot/Resource/Doc/36496/0023582.pdf

Johnston, R, & Watson, J (2007). *Teaching Synthetic Phonics.* Learning Matters Ltd: Exeter

Joyce, B, & Showers, B (1980). 'Improving Inservice Training: The Messages of Research.' *Educational Leadership,* 37, 379–385

Joyce, B, & Showers, B (2002). *Student Achievement Through Staff Development* (Third Edition). Alexandria, VA: Association for Supervision & Curriculum Deve (ASCD)

Kilpatrick, D (2015). *Essentials of Assessing, Preventing, and Overcoming Reading Difficulties.* John Wiley & Sons, Inc: Hoboken, New Jersey

Kintsch, W, & Rawson, KA (2005). Comprehension chapter in *The Science of Reading: A handbook.* 209–226

Kohnen, S, Colenbrander, D, Caruana, N, Barisic, K, Badcock, E, & Banales, E (2021). 'The Diagnostic Spelling Test – Morphology (DiSTm).' Available from www.motif.org.au

Kohnen, S, Colenbrander, D, Krajenbrink, T, & Nickels, L (2013). 'Diagnostic Spelling Test – nonwords with normative data.' Available from www.motif.org.au

Konza, D (2011). *Oral Language. Research into practice.* DECS: South Australia. Retrieved 30 August 2021, from www.ecu.edu.au/__data/assets/pdf_file/0010/663697/SA-DECS-Oral-lang-doc.pdf

Konza, D (2014). 'Why the "Fab 5" should be the "Big 6".' *Australian Journal of Teacher Education,* 39(12), 10

Kotter, JP (1996). *Leading Change.* Boston: Harvard Business School Press

Kuhn, M, & Stahl, SA (2000). *Fluency: A review of developmental and remedial practices.* Ann Arbour, MI: Center for the Improvement of Early Reading Achievement

Lambert, S (Host) (n.d.). 'Deconstructing the Rope: Background knowledge with Susan Neuman.' Season 3, Episode 6 [Audio podcast episode], *Science of Reading: The Podcast,* Amplify. https://podcasts.apple.com/ru/podcast/s3-06-deconstructing-rope-background-knowledge-susan/id1483513974?i=1000514180455=en

Lambert, S (Host). 5 February 2020. 'The cognitive science behind how students learn to read with Carolyn Strom.' Season 1, Episode 9 [Audio podcast episode], *Science of Reading: The Podcast*, Amplify. https://podcasts.apple.com/us/podcast/s1-09-the-cognitive-science-behind-how-students-learn/id1483513974?i=1000464749829

Lemov, D, Driggs, C, & Woolway, E (2016). *Reading Reconsidered: A practical guide to rigorous literacy instruction*. Jossey-Bass: San Francisco

Lemov, D, Hernandez, J, & Kim, J (2016). *Teach Like a Champion Field Guide*. Jossey Bass: Hoboken, NJ

Lester, A (2004). *Are we there yet?* Penguin Group: Australia

Lester, A (2012). *Sophie Scott Goes South*. Penguin Random House Australia: Australia

Logan, JAR, Justice, LM, Yumu M, Chaparro-Moreno, LJ (2019). 'When Children Are Not Read to at Home: The Million Word Gap.' *Journal of Developmental & Behavioural Pediatrics*, 40(5) 383–386

Macklin, P, & Zbar, V (2020). *Driving School Improvement: Practical Strategies and Tools* (Second Edition). ACER Press: Camberwell

Macquarie University (2023). *Language Lift*. MultiLit Pty Ltd. Macquarie Park, New South Wales

McCandliss, B, Beck, IL, Sandak, R, & Perfetti, C (2003). 'Focusing attention on decoding for children with poor reading skills: Design and preliminary tests of the word building intervention.' *Scientific Studies of Reading*, 7(1), 75–104

McKean, M (2018). *Hello, Australia!* Thames & Hudson: Australia

McKean, M (2023). *Hello, New Zealand!* Thames & Hudson: Australia

Martens, VEG, & De Jong, PF (2008). 'Effects of repeated reading on the length effect in word and pseudoword reading.' *Journal of Research in Reading*, 31(1), 40–54

Marzano (2004). *Building Academic Background Knowledge. Association for Supervision and Curriculum Development*. Alexandria: Virginia USA

Masters, GN (2016). *National School Improvement Tool*. Australian Council for Educational Research: Australia

Mathwin, K (2022). 'Developing orthographic knowledge to help challenged early learners master writing alphabet letters.' *Learning Difficulties Australia Bulletin*, 54(3), 28–31

Mellor, A (2020). *The Grandest Bookshop in the World*. Affirm Press: South Melbourne

Mind Tools (n.d.). 'The Forgetting Curve.' Retrieved 15 August 2021, from www.mindtools.com/pages/article/forgetting-curve.htm

Moats, L (2007). *Whole-Language High Jinks*. Retrieved 25 August 2021, from www.thereadingleague.org/wp-content/uploads/2018/09/Whole-Language-High-Jinks-Moats.pdf

Moats, LC (2010). *Speech to Print: Language Essentials for Teachers* (Second edition). Baltimore: Brookes Publishing

Montgomery, P, Ilk, M, & Moats, LC (2012). *A Principal's Primer for Raising Reading Achievement*. Longmont, CO: Sopris Learning

Murre, JM, Dros, J (2015). 'Replication and Analysis of Ebbinghaus' Forgetting Curve.' PLoS One, 6 July; 10(7)

National Joint Committee on Learning Difficulties (2005). 'Responsiveness to Intervention and Learning Disabilities.' WETA: Washington, Retrieved 10 November 2021, from www.ldonline.org/ld-topics/special-education/responsiveness-intervention-and-learning-disabilities?theme=print

National Reading Panel (US) & National Institute of Child Health and Human Development (NICHD) (2000). 'Report of the National Reading Panel: Teaching Children to Read: An Evidence-Based Assessment of the Scientific Research Literature on Reading and its Implications for Reading Instruction.' U.S. Department of Health and Human Services, Public Health Service, National Institutes of Health, National Institute of Child Health and Human Development

Neilson, R (2014). *Astronaut Invented Spelling Test - 2 (AIST-2).* Australian Council for Educational Research: Melbourne

Neuman, S, & Dickinson, D (Eds). *Handbook of Early Literacy Research,* 97–110. Guilford Press: NY

Oakhill, J, & Cain, K (2012). 'The Precursors of Reading Ability in Young Readers: Evidence From a Four-Year Longitudinal Study.' *Scientific Studies of Reading,* 16(2), 91–121

Oakhill, J, Hartt, J, & Samols, D (2005). 'Levels of Comprehension Monitoring and Working Memory in Good and Poor Comprehenders.' *Reading and Writing,* 18(7–9)

Pace, A, Alper, R, Burchinal, MR, Golinkoff, RM, & Hirsh-Pasek, K (2019). 'Measuring success: Within and cross-domain predictors of academic and social trajectories in elementary school.' *Early Childhood Research Quarterly,* 46(1), 112–125

Parker, S (2021). 'The Simple View of Reading: Still Conclusive After 36 Years.' Retrieved 31 August 2021, from www.pamelasnow.blogspot.com/2019/02/the-simple-view-of-reading-still.html

Petersen, DB, & Spencer, TD (2016). *CUBED.* Language Dynamics Group, LLC

Phonic Books (n.d.). 'Phonic Books: Diagnostic Assessment Sheet.' Phonics Books: UK. www.phonicbooks.co.uk/content/uploads/2016/05/diagnostic-assessment-and-recommendation-nov-20.pdf

Quaglia, R (2015). *Importance of Student Voice.* Retrieved 25 May 2022, from www.youtube.com/watch?v=GnKg2F5ySrI

Quaglia, R (2016). *School Voice Report 2016.* Developed by the Quaglia Institute for School Voice and Aspirations. In partnership with the Quaglia Institute for Student Aspirations, Teacher Voice and Aspirations International Center, and Corwin Press. Retrieved from https://quagliainstitute.org/dmsView/School_Voice_Report_2016

Rasinski, T (2005). *Fluency Rubric 1234.* Retrieved 2 February 2023, from www.timrasinski.com/presentations/multidimensional_fluency_rubric_4_factors.pdf

Rasinski, T, & Padak, N (2005). *3-Minute Reading Assessments.* Scholastic Inc: New York, NY

Ray, K, Dally, K, & Lane, A (2022). *Learning to Read the Write Way: A policy brief. Learning Difficulties Australia Bulletin,* 54(3) 21–27

Reading Rockets (2004). 'Phonemic Awareness Assessment.' Retrieved May 2022, from www.readingrockets.org/article/phonemic-awareness-assessment

Rose, J (2006). *Independent review of the teaching of early reading: Final report.* Department of Education & Skills. https://dera.ioe.ac.uk/5551/2/report.pdf

Rosenshine, B (2012). 'Principles of Instruction: Research-Based Strategies That All Teachers Should Know.' *American Educator,* 36(1), 12–19. Retrieved 15 August 2021, from www.aft.org/sites/default/files/periodicals/Rosenshine.pdf

Rowe, K, & National Inquiry into the Teaching of Literacy (NITL, Australia) (2005). *Teaching Reading: Report and Recommendations.* Department of Education, Science and Training: Australia

RTI Action Network (n.d.). 'What is RTI?' Retrieved 20 April 2021, from www.rtinetwork.org/learn/what/whatisrti

Schuele, CM, & Boudreau, D (2008). 'Phonological awareness intervention: beyond the basics.' Lang *Speech Hear Serv Sch,* 39(1), 3–20

Seidenberg, M (2017). *Language at the Speed of Sight: How we read, why so many can't, and what can be done about it.* Basic Books: New York

Sencibaugh, JM, & Sencibaugh, AM (2014). *The effects of questioning the author on the reading comprehension of middle school students.* The Free Library. Retrieved 6 January 2023, from www. thefreelibrary.com/The+effects+of+questioning+the+author+on+the+reading+ comprehension+of...-a0429498167

Shanahan, T (2005). *The National Reading Panel Report: Practical Advice for Teachers.* Retrieved April 2022, from https://files.eric.ed.gov/fulltext/ED489535.pdf

Shanahan, T (2011). *Rejecting Instructional Level theory.* Retrieved 25 November 2022, from https://shanahanonliteracy.com/blog/rejecting-instructional-level-theory#sthash.1DqAcT9N.dpbs

Shanahan, T (2018). 'What Should Morphology Instruction Look Like?' Reading Rockets. Retrieved 5 August 2021, from www.readingrockets.org/blogs/shanahan-literacy/what-should-morphology-instruction-look

Sleeman, M (2021). *The identification and classification of reading disorders based on the simple view of reading.* Retrieved 25 September 2022, from https://ir.canterbury.ac.nz/bitstream/handle/10092/103018/Sleeman%2c%20Michael_Final%20PhD%20Thesis.pdf?sequence=1&isAllowed=y

Smith, R, Serry, T, Snow, P, & Hammond, L (2021). 'The Role of Background Knowledge in Reading Comprehension: A Critical Review.' *Reading Psychology*, 42(3), 214–240

Snow, P (2017). *Phonics Check Self-Assessment: The Sequel.* Retrieved 2 December 2022, from http://pamelasnow.blogspot.com/2017/07/

Snow, P, & Ashman, G (2019). 'Oral Language Competence: How it Relates to Classroom Behaviour.' *American Educator*, Summer 37–41

Snow, PC, Powell, MB, Sanger, DD (2012). 'Oral language competence, young speakers, and the law.' *Lang Speech Hear Serv Sch*, 43(4), 496–506

Snowling, MJ, & Hulme, C (Eds) (2005). 'The science of reading: A handbook.' Blackwell Publishing Ltd: Oxford

Sounds-Write (2020). *Teaching vocabulary in Years 3-6* [Training Manual]. Author: United Kingdom

Spear-Swerling, L (2015). *The Power of RTI and Reading Profiles: A Blueprint for Solving Reading Problems.* Paul H. Brookes Publishing: Baltimore, MD

Spear-Swerling, L (2019). 'Here's Why Schools Should Use Structured Literacy.' International Dyslexia Association. 8(2). Retrieved from https://dyslexiaida.org/heres-why-schools-should-use-structured-literacy/#:~:text=What%20Is%20Structured%20Literacy%3F,reading%20comprehension%2C%20written%20expression

Spear-Swerling, L (2022) *Structured Literacy Interventions: Teaching Students with Reading Difficulties, Grades K-6.* Guilford Press: New York

Spencer, TD, & Peterson, DB (2016, 2018). 'Story Champs: A Multi-Tiered Language Curriculum.' Language Dynamics Group, LLC: US

Spencer, TD, & Pierce, C (2022). 'Classroom-based oral storytelling: Reading, Writing, and Social Benefits.' *The Reading Teacher*, 76(5), 525–534

Stevens, RJ, Van Meter, P, & Warcholak, ND (2010). 'The Effects of Explicitly Teaching Story Structure to Primary Grade Children.' *Journal of Literacy Research*, (42) 159–198

Stott, C (2003). *I wonder why stars twinkle and other questions about the universe.* Kingfisher Publications PLC: London

Sweller, J (2016). 'Story of a Research Program.' *Education Review*, (23) 1–18

Sweller, J (2021). *Why Inquiry Based Approaches Harm Students' Learning.* The Centre for Independent Studies, 24, 1–11

The DLD Project (2023), 'Developmental Language Disorder (DLD) Information.' https://thedldproject.com/developmental-language-disorder-dld/

The Education Hub, NZ (2018). *How to develop high expectation teaching.* Retrieved January 2022, from https://theeducationhub.org.nz/wp-content/uploads/2018/06/How-to-develop-high-expectations-teaching.pdf

The New Teacher Project (TNTP) (2018). *The Opportunity Myth: What Students Can Show Us About How School Is Letting Them Down—and How to Fix It.* Retrieved January 2022, from https://tntp.org/assets/documents/TNTP_The-Opportunity-Myth_Web.pdf

The New Teacher Project (TNTP) (2022). *Unlocking Acceleration: How Below Grade-Level Work is Holding Students Back in Literacy.* Retrieved 18 April 2023, from https://tntp.org/assets/documents/Unlocking_Acceleration_8.16.22.pdf

The Reading League (2021). 'What is the science of reading? A defining guide.' The Reading League. Retrieved 25 August 2021, from www.thereadingleague.org/what-is-the-science-of-reading

Torgesen, JK (2004). 'Avoiding the Devastating Downward Spiral: The Evidence That Early Intervention Prevents Reading Failure.' *American Educator*. American Federation of Teachers: US

Torgesen, JK (2004). 'Learning Disabilities: An Historical and Conceptual Overview.' In B. Y. L. Wong (Ed), *Learning about learning disabilities* (3–40). San Diego, CA: Academic Press

Torgesen, JK, Wagner, RK, & Rashotte, CA (2012). *Test of Word Reading Efficiency (TOWRE-2)*. New York: Pearson

University of Oregon, Center on Teaching & Learning (2019-2020). *DIBELS® 8th Edition: Dynamic Indicators of Basic Early Literacy Skills Technical Manual Supplement*. Eugene, OR

Van Cleave, W (2012). *Writing Matters: Developing Sentence Skills in Students of All Ages* (Second Edition). WVCED: Oklahoma City

Weaver, K (2021). 'Equity in Literacy: Tackling Socio-Economic Disadvantages with the Science of Reading.' *IMSE Journal*. Retrieved 12 June 2023, from https://journal.imse.com/equity-in-literacy/#:~:text=%E2%80%9CIf%20your%20literacy%20program%20is,The%20Reding%20League%20Conference%2C%202021

Wheldall, K, Wheldall, R, & Buckingham, J (Eds) (2023). *Effective Instruction in Reading and Spelling*. MRU Press: Macquarie Park, NSW

Wheldall, K, & Wheldall, R, & Macquarie University. Macquarie University Special Education Centre. MultiLit Research Unit, sponsoring body (2013). *Reinforced reading: using pause, prompt and praise to help low-progress readers: booklet*. MultiLit Pty Ltd: Macquarie Park, New South Wales

Wigfield, A, & Guthrie, JT (1997). 'Relations of children's motivation for reading to the amount and breadth or their reading.' *Journal of Educational Psychology*, 89(3), 420

Williams, R (n.d.). 'Pygmalion and Golem Effects: How Positive Expectations for All are Critical to Building Inclusive School Communities.' Inclusive School Communities. Retrieved January 2022, from https://inclusiveschoolcommunities.org.au/resources/toolkit/pygmalion-and-golem

Willingham, D, & Lovette, G (2014). 'Can Reading Comprehension Be Taught?' *Teacher's College Record*. Retrieved 10 January 2023, from http://www.danielwillingham.com/uploads/5/0/0/7/5007325/willingham&lovette_2014_can_reading_comprehension_be_taught_.pdf

Wolf, M, & Katzir-Cohen, T (2001). 'Reading Fluency and its Interventions.' *Scientific Studies of Reading*, 5(3), 211–239

Wolter, JA, & Green, L (2013). 'Morphological Awareness Intervention in School-Age Children with Language and Literacy Deficits: A Case Study.' *Topics in Language Disorders*, 33(1), 27–41. https://doi.org/10.1097/TLD.0b013e318280f5aa

Wood, J (2011). *I Wonder Why Kangaroos Have Pouches*. Kingfisher: London

Yoon, KS, Duncan, T, Lee, SWY, Scarloss, B, & Shapley, K (2007). *Reviewing the evidence on how teacher professional development affects student achievement*. Issues and Answers Report. REL2007–No.033. Washington, DC: U.S. Department of Education, Institute of Education Sciences, National Center for Education Evaluation and Regional Assistance, Regional Educational Laboratory Southwest

Zutell, J, & Rasinski, TV (1991). 'Training Teachers to Attend to Their Students' Oral Reading Fluency.' *Theory into Practice*, (30) 211-217

Printed in the USA
CPSIA information can be obtained
at www.ICGtesting.com
LVHW011000140724
785423LV00007B/657